I Have Not Loved You With My Whole Heart

I Have Not Loved You With My Whole Heart

CRIS HARRIS

Oregon State University Press   Corvallis

The following chapters first appeared elsewhere in earlier form:
"Gaydar": *Sand Hills Literary Magazine*, April 2019
"One Two": *Cobalt Review*, Spring 2019
"IIII": *Post Road Review*, January 2018
"Pender Tales": *Nowhere Magazine*, December 2017
"Darrell": *Proximity Magazine*, August 2016
"Blind": *The Flexible Persona* (print), March 2016
"Closing Joe's Eyes": *The Flexible Persona* (website and podcast), July 2014

Library of Congress Cataloging-in-Publication Data
Names: Harris, Cris, author.
Title: I have not loved you with my whole heart / Cris Harris.
Description: Corvallis, OR : Oregon State University Press, [2021]
Identifiers: LCCN 2020057158 | ISBN 9780870711084 (trade paperback) | ISBN
    9780870711091 (ebook)
Subjects: LCSH: Children of gay parents—Northwest, Pacific. | Gay
    fathers—Northwest, Pacific—Family relationships. | Coming out (Sexual
    orientation)—Northwest, Pacific.
Classification: LCC HQ777.8 .H37 2021—for review | DDC
    306.874/208664—dc23
LC record available at https://lccn.loc.gov/2020057158

♾ This paper meets the requirements of ANSI/NISO Z39.48-1992
(Permanence of Paper).

First published in 2021 by Oregon State University Press
Printed in the United States of America

Oregon State University
OSU Press

Oregon State University Press
121 The Valley Library
Corvallis OR 97331-4501
541-737-3166 • fax 541-737-3170
www.osupress.oregonstate.edu

In Memory of Reverend Renne Lee Harris
April 26, 1941–May 20, 1995

and for Mary, who got me through to the good life

Contents

The Boat

"And now, boys," he says, "let's get the boat. Track it down and bring it home." He smiles, eyes watery and bright, feverish under the little velvet fez he has taken to wearing in this last year. He turns his head slightly to each of us in turn, still smiling. He would say more but talking is getting difficult, a serious sacrifice of breath.

My brother Joseph stares at Dad intently, nodding. Joseph's hair is his regulation Air Force high and tight flattop and is still so blonde I can see his pink scalp. We sit on opposite sides of Dad's bed, the Danish-made minimalist platform he had picked out and purchased as he lost weight, grew weaker, tolerated medication less and less. He chose the bed as the place he wanted to end up. Two summers earlier, we had painted the walls an awful dark brown that made the room a cave—his choice. He had a purple bookcase by the west wall where he'd set up a fairly decent stereo system, some framed photographs of men in leathers, flannels, or not much. He is the man in several of the photos. His little jade pipe sits next to a heavy black ashtray and a Ziploc bag stuffed with marijuana. Joseph hasn't moved, except to nod slowly. His eyes are the bluest of us all, and he stares down his nose without blinking, troubled. He clears his throat. "Sure, Dad. We'll do that." Dad closes his eyes, raises a trembling hand up to be held by each of us in turn, and then puts it back down. We understand that we should go.

The day had bled out quickly. He'd begun full of energy, demanding that notes be taken and his wishes followed. He'd insisted on settling the funeral arrangements and dispositions of possessions. The truck, his clothes, the dishes, the sofa, the library table, plants, cookware, books, chairs, rugs, bedclothes, paintings—none of it worth much in terms of money. He wanted us to ask for these things, and he wanted to know where they were going. Joseph spoke less and less as the minutes dripped by.

Dad began to fade out before we got to the most important item, the disposition of his ashes. The question furrowed his brow, made him speak haltingly with his eyes closed behind unwrinkled lids. Would he be buried in eastern Oregon, up on the hill in Heppner next to his father, or would he be interred in the columbarium of his last church, go home to the parish that had rejected him? It was entirely his decision, and he could not make it. Each time we asked, we would listen, sometimes for minutes, to the noises of the house: rain in the gutters, the chime of the clock downstairs, dishes clanking in the kitchen, his ragged breathing. And now this unexpected complication, the matter of the boat.

Downstairs, we fill coffee cups from the never empty carafe in the kitchen for the twentieth time that day and start to hunt. The boat has been lost for a dozen years or so, left behind in an apartment basement in lieu of back rent. I had last seen it when I was twelve or thirteen. The graduate student, master of paper and pens, I sketch out what we know while Joseph speaks. We grab a few of Dad's messy files from the cabinet by his desk, but as in many other searches to come, don't find anything useful. I get out the phone book and a Portland city map. We try to reconstruct the locations of the places Dad had lived in the first years after the divorce, but we have incomplete and contrary recollections. He hadn't had the boat on Multnomah, but what about Alberta? And wasn't there a place before that but after the house he shared with the other disgraced priest? When he was selling insurance, after the Quality Pie job but before the Harrington's Bar and Grill? It wasn't that long ago, I keep thinking, just a dozen years, but none of us can remember the details. I write down phone numbers of apartment complexes that might play out. None of the names or addresses seem exactly right.

The Boat! We'd spent so many hours sanding, varnishing, painting.

We'd learned to row, to sail, to navigate, to bear up during long silences while sailing with our father, to find our way out to a distant cove and then come back home to the little cabin on Pender Island with a sense of something like accomplishment. Watching Dad pack up the boat when he moved out had ached. Years later, finding out it had been left behind, jettisoned, abandoned in the dark, had stung. How perfect to bring it back home now, at the very end, to recapture a potent symbol of our childhood, tie up a loose end, save something. I fight down a rising sense of futility. I make calls and try to sound friendly.

"Hi. My name is Cris Harris. I'm trying to track down a small sailboat my father, Renne Harris, left behind. This would have been about ten years ago, I'm afraid. I hope I have the right number. If you could give me a call if you know anything about a small, blue sailboat in storage at your complex, I'd really appreciate it." I say it into the phone four times at four different numbers, one or two of which seem like real possibilities. This is the very first moment I realize that events of my life, not even ten years past, can be utterly, entirely, completely lost, not to be recovered. I repeat the phone number as clearly as possible.

It has been raining outside, but the clouds are breaking up a little now, and the sun dips low under their edge to light up the rhododendrons in the garden. I'd flown into Portland the night before, leaving behind an Iowa City where the snow was gone and early April had turned on the green in the pastures and fields like a neon sign. Joseph had already been home a day and would have to drive back to Klamath Falls in less than twenty-four hours.

He paces the floor. I place another call, leave another message, working the Alberta Street hypothesis. "Fuck this," he says. "Let's get the truck and some rope and the checkbook and drive over there. Don't you think we could find that place?"

"Maybe, if it's still there. Could be worth a shot." It's so tempting to go. In the other room we have a stack of papers to get through that kept us up very late the night before. There's a revision of the will we need to get signed and back to his lawyer who lives around the block. Dad has asked for help writing some letters to old friends, responses to their cards and calls. And upstairs, he will wake from his nap in another twenty minutes. We are here now not because he is about to die, but because he'd called and said it would be a good idea to come home while he could still talk. This visit is supposed to be our chance to say goodbye while he can hear it. I add up the minutes—twenty to get to Alberta in traffic, maybe thirty more to find the right place, if we can. Finding the right door, then a conversation with the manager, then the search for the boat, carrying it out to the truck, tying it down, driving it back. Hours at best. Forever at worst.

Thom Jones, the family friend Dad had taken in as "house manager," steps in to check on us. Eight months after being scraped off the street by the Hooper Treatment Center van, he is still thin, pale, and skittish but is regaining some of his old confidence. He's slowly taken over the kitchen, reawakening his skills as a chef and former restaurant owner. He's prepared the bills for signatures and bought the groceries, handled phone calls discreetly, and coordinated the visits of the nurses. Free room and board for a year isn't enough, actually, to pay him back.

Thom affects a pompous air that is only part pretense. Most of the nice things—antique furniture, paintings, plant stands—in the house are actually his, though we have been storing some of them for so many years it's difficult to think of them that way. He puts his hand on Joseph's shoulder, uses his Colonel Klink accent to make us smile: "You are up to somezink, I zuzpect. Vat is all this?"

We tell him. He snorts. Pushes his glasses up. Frowns. I ask him if he knows any more specifics about Dad's living arrangements back in those days and he shakes his head. I am watching Joseph, who is staring, it seems, at a spot several feet below the floor, his lips slightly parted as if to speak. A big man, thick-muscled in the shoulders and chest, Joseph's tension is visible in the strain of his shirt. And then he exhales, a long loud whoosh of breath. Lets his eyes soften.

"Cris," he says, "we have to let it go. This isn't how we should spend the time." He's right, of course, and the picture I had of the boat—restored, its dark-blue paint glossy, trim and spars newly varnished, the sheets white against the red sails as we take the high side and bounce through the waves of British Columbia as in a morning lifted right out of ten years old—that vision fades. I think instead of the boat in the way we try not to think of bodies long buried, in decay, alone in the dark. I see it in a basement, dry-rotted, cracked, long gone. "We probably couldn't find it anyway, Cris. And I don't want to miss any time with Dad."

I bite my lower lip, nod. Thom goes to make yet more coffee. I think briefly about how to tell Dad when he wakes up. Then I let the boat go. It's a kind of practice I need.

. . .

We trudge up the icy sidewalks toward the park, the sled fishtailing behind us. Every tenth step on the pavement is a slide back, but we make inexorable progress. The freezing rain has turned the snow to a glassine layer that gleams blindingly when the sun burns through the clouds momentarily. By the time we make the steps to Mount Tabor Park, we have already been out too long. Carolyn worries aloud that we'll be in trouble. Joseph swears at her, calls her chicken. I take his side, of course.

The park is deserted, just an expanse of snow over the sledding hills, broken pine and fir boughs scattered over the surface. We make one run, all three piled on the sled in order of size—Joseph on the bottom, Carolyn in her puffy jacket clinging to his neck. I have to get us started, push us into the glide that stays on top of the crunching ice and achieves escape velocity down the gentle slopes. I heave, Joseph swimming at the ground with his gloves, and then leap on, clutching Carolyn's shoulders, her blond hair whipping back into my face while we pick up speed. The hill ends in a flat field, normally littered with sledders and small kids and other obstacles to avoid, but this time all clear. We come to a crunching halt in the silence of the light snow falling.

Up the hill, where we want to go, where the big trees grow on the steep slopes, we watch as the wind breaks ice-laden branches loose. We have been warned, explicitly forbidden from coming here because of the dangers of falling limbs and ice. The way up is difficult, and soon we are panting and unzipping our jackets. Every crack of a branch or muffled thud of falling snow startles Carolyn, who commences a steady whispered stream of concerns. I am afraid to speak as we pass under the evergreen canopy. The snow is thinner here, pocked with craters. Near the top, Joseph finally proposes that he just go himself if we are all so afraid, but Carolyn gets right on. I start us again, my heart up in my throat, but as I try to leap on, I stumble, land with one knee on the ground. I hold on for a second, long enough to slew the sled sideways before I fall off the back, clanging my chin on the deck. I look up from where I've fallen and they are zipping away, Joseph trying to get them back under control. They pass close to one tree and pick up speed, then veer right suddenly and head into the trunk of a giant Douglas fir. They aren't going that fast, but when they hit, the tree gives a tremendous cracking roar and an avalanche of green and white and wood descends upon them. The noise of the falling is immense, filling the woods, and the impact shakes the ground. A rain of smaller branches falls all around me in the aftermath, where I stand, blood trickling from my chin into my mitten. I run to the tree, but Carolyn is already moving, pushing loose of the branches. The limb has missed them, but the boughs and the weight of the ice and snow has flattened them, bent the sled runners. She stands, shakily, but Joseph is groggy, blood darkening his shock-white hair. She pulls him to a sitting position, but he can't walk unaided. The wind picks up, and another branch breaks uphill. I begin to cry.

He arrives without warning, bundled in peacoat and watch cap, leather gloves. His face is a thundercloud, all rage and mustache and beard, but he says almost nothing as he gets Joseph's arm around his shoulders, walks his concussed son uphill toward the park road. Carolyn leans on me, and I drag the sled. I come to realize, as I walk, that he came straight to us, knew where we were, knew it because he had forbidden it, and we proved him and his warning right yet again. I can see him looking at his watch, getting up from his desk, knowing that both rescue and punishment are needed with his children loose in the world.

He has to drive the long way around to avoid the hill on Yamhill Street, and he berates us without interruption, without variation in his tone, without taking his eyes off the graveled slushy streets, all the long way home.

．．．

The Age of Reason

I.

He wasted away, like his lover before him and so many of our family friends. The pounds melted off, his face grew severe, then gaunt, then El Greco–like in its bony features. In 1995, dying of HIV means, for many, dying of chronic diarrhea, loss of appetite, a slow thinning out of physical strength. That year, which he determined would be his last, my father spends weeks in his deathbed, slowly losing the ability to speak. He sometimes feels the urge to tie up loose ends and dictates letters to estranged family and colleagues. In a nostalgic mood, he asks for the old photos, jumbled in cigar boxes, and I bring them to his bed. A sickbed tyrant, he suffers my clumsy efforts to prop him up with pillows while wearing a pained expression on his face. Once raised up, he asks for a cup of tea or a mug of bouillon; twenty minutes pass from his request to the actual images, the snapshots of lost times.

There are a number of photos from the mid-seventies, before one life unraveled on us and another began, from an era of full-blown alcoholism, some marijuana use, dark clericals smelling of sweet smoke and scotch. In those days, our family was "colorful," or loud, or to some just "trashy," but we could pass as something approaching normal. Too much alcohol, the kids running wild, the yard returning to a primordial wilderness, a reputation for being "earthy" or "bohemian" in ways that didn't endear us to the high society of Portland Heights, but didn't completely cut us off. In 1978, the man himself looks heavy, bloated with booze. In the photos, he gives a rakish smile from behind his thick mustache.

Usually he is in his collar, seated in a posh den or living room, the parishioner whose single-malt he's sipping near at hand. Sometimes he's in his beach outfit, breathtakingly short cutoffs and sandals, a polo shirt collar framing his chest hair, the belly a navy-blue bulge beneath.

"Oh God," he says about those photos. "Look at the fat priest. Here's another one. Jesus. Happy drunk. Look at those cheeks, the eyes. Puffy." His hands, the left wrist tethered by the IV, stop shuffling the glossies and I'm seeing the same wrist, the same hand two decades before, grasping a stein to clank it with four matching steins and hands and wrists belonging to four men, all of them with heads tilted back in howling song. He laughs. I laugh. He coughs, gestures angrily for the tray. He works a bit of something up, diligently spits it, lips trembling from effort, then leans back and draws air into his frothy lungs. Once a day, a home-health nurse checks the color of the accumulated effluvium. She will pass judgment on its volume, viscosity, tone. He hands me the photo, picks up another one. He is practicing making peace with a story that is coming to an end. I am feeling a tearing pain in my chest, remembering those confusing times, that sense that something was off, that something marked us as different, that we somehow didn't belong.

II.

There is a day that captures it for me. Midsummer 1978 in Portland, Oregon. A morning growing cloudy after a hot spell. Seven and a half years old. Up early and alone for Saturday cartoons on the black and white TV, the volume turned down low. Most of those summer days blurred together during the week, until I didn't know one from another. A whole day could pass with nothing to show but some trees climbed, stuffed animals posed, a book read, some blocks of the neighborhood walked aimlessly in search of bottles or cans to redeem for nickels and spend on candy at Strohecker's grocery. My siblings had a few friends in the neighborhood, and I spent my days tagging along or alone, dreaming away. There was an expectation to be home for lunch and dinner, but not much more. On the weekends, though, a rhythm returned: hours of cartoons on Saturday, services (with singing and other kids and reciting prayers) and the twin limbos of coffee hour and brunch on Sunday, and serious chores on Monday, Dad's day off from his duties as rector of Ascension Chapel, a very Episcopal church in the Portland Heights neighborhood. On this Saturday, clouds were forming up outside, a cool breeze replacing the hot, sunny days just passed.

This particular Saturday morning followed a rambunctious Friday party. Hot weather, a barbeque with the cooker spilling delicious smoke that wafted over the silvery keg in its tub of ice. There was grilled lamb, potato salad, pickles, beer foam, hot breezes, and the rising moon. Late in the evening, the hangers-on congregated in the harvest-gold-colored kitchen to smoke and nurse beers and talk while my mother tried to clean up. My father started slurring limericks and taught me this one:

> *There once was a lad name of Cass*
> *Who had balls made entirely of brass*
> *When they tinkled together*
> *They played "Stormy Weather"*
> *And lightning shot out of his ass.*

Though my mother scolded him, he repeated it till I had it learned. She shooed him out with a dish towel but he returned moments later, having stopped by the stereo, to the thunderous strains of ABBA. Standing in the kitchen doorway, he gyrated sensually to the disco beat. My parents and their friends loved disco in a way that made children uncomfortable. Scurrying away from the kitchen turned dance floor, I spotted a yellow jacket sipping from a puddle of spilled beer on the dining room floor. I was transfixed.

Wasps have a certain attraction I still cannot resist. Like car accidents, handguns, fires, knife blades, they are hard to look away from. Their caution-sign coloring, their pulsing, twitching, lethal calmness, their dauber waists and compound eyes hold my attention. At this point, on that Friday evening in 1978, I had an additional interest because, as my siblings liked to remind me, I had never been stung. My older brother Joseph had endured the stings of bees, wasps, hornets, ants, and even jellyfish. He'd fallen into a ground nest of paper wasps up to his thigh. He'd swum under a massive Lion's Mane jelly in British Columbia and hyperventilated while the blisters reddened streaks all over his back. He swelled, too, as if the opportunities for demonstrating his manly virtues weren't enough with him enduring simple pain. In the story we called the Trial of the Rope Swing, for instance, where he'd been stung by a wasp on the actual rope while he was suspended high above the ground, and though it stung repeatedly—"Like a needle. I could feel it jabbing three four five times!"—he held on. He'd stare at his palm while he told it. "And then the swelling. I watched it. Like a balloon." I'd look into his pale eyes below the messy blond hair bleached almost white in the sun, his crooked teeth and high cheekbones already showing through.

"Wow," I'd say. I wanted to be him. Not be like him, but be him, deep in my bones.

On that night, my parents were practicing moves that propelled them out into the dining room, singing along to the accented lyrics. One of the guests noticed me, crouched and staring, and my dad discoed over, drained the cup in his hand, and covered the wasp with it, the rim sealing in the spilled beer. And there he left it, a slightly drunk *Vespula pensylvanica* in a translucent plastic cylinder, feebly approaching the curving wall with tremulous feelers then backing away. I watched it for a while, even held my hand on the plastic while the wasp crawled threateningly on the other side. Eventually, long before the laughter and yelling and singing quieted down, I was ordered off to bed.

III.

The morning, before anyone else is up, is a magic time, where anything can happen. I knew this wholly in childhood and would tumble out of bed and out the door in a moment. Waking up to an ice storm, I'd head out to break ice from the sidewalk with a ball-peen hammer. I recall standing at the scene of a car accident a few blocks from our house where Vista Avenue takes a sharp turn. Sometime around 5:00 a.m., I'd heard the squeal of tires, an odd quarter-second of quiet, and then the impact of metal on metal. I ran down the blocks in the dim light to watch the action. The elderly couple who lived above the turn with the dented guardrail was already on the scene offering advice; they knew the drill. Standing there in my pajamas, I watched the tow-truck and police-car lights strobing the world into psychedelic patterns and was even invited in for a cup of tea before they walked me home and saw me inside, my parents nowhere to be seen. Mornings could be like that. Or even without car wrecks and police cars, there were toys you wouldn't have to share, and books no one would pull your nose from, and spiders with dew on their webs in the backyard.

This particular Saturday morning in 1978 started out to be the archetypical morning experience. Though I'd been up much past any reasonable bedtime, at just before seven I swung my legs out from under the sheets and into a pair of pants. While the clouds were gathering and lighting up in the west, the sun was streaming in above the treetops. My parents' door was shut, and I tiptoed by, knowing that if I made no loud noises, it could remain shut for hours. I did not understand hangovers in any technical or personal sense, but knew they came after crazy nights with jokes and song, caused dangerously bad tempers, and could essentially remove all parental supervision for sizeable chunks of time. And since Joseph and Carolyn valued sleep more than cartoons, I could look forward to blissful, solitary oblivion six inches away from the shifting blue animation on the screen. *Land of the Lost, Johnny Quest, Scooby-Doo, Road Runner, Bugs Bunny*—the whole slew was mine. I padded carefully down the carpeted hall, pausing for a moment as I always did by the hole in the plaster and the broken stair spindle. These were both scars on the house, reminders of what could go wrong. The hole was from my father pounding my brother's head into the wall when Joseph tried to run away. The spindle from where Joseph put his own head, arm, and shoulder through in a futile attempt to escape while Dad hauled him up the stairs to his room. I used to lie down and fit my head into the hole from time to time. The edges of plaster were rough against my temples.

When I got downstairs, I saw the plastic cup lying on its side out of place on the hardwood floor of the dining room, white against the finish shining like honey in the morning light. I was still remembering why there would be an empty cup in the middle of the floor when I felt a sharp pain in the arch of my right foot and stepped back to see the wasp, still jabbing its rear up into the air. My first reaction was, of course, just pain, throbbing or burning or needling, some species of pain hard to ignore, the sobbing inhalation of surprise. Second was the realization of cause and effect, the cup, the wasp, my foot, "Oh!" Something like that.

And third was joy. I had been stung and would live to tell about it. A smile of pride actually broke across my face. The pain increasing, I hobbled around and put the cup back on the wasp, who seemed disinclined to go anywhere. If I could have done it without fear of punishment, I would have whooped for my brother to come downstairs and see.

But the pain grew, in the way a wasp sting does, going from a sharp burning to a deep ache, a spasmic clench of muscle. I know now, like any adult, that the discomfort has an end, really only twenty minutes or so before welts and itching replace it. But as a child, I did not know how long pain would last, how much worse it would get. As with so many pains of childhood, I could not see the end, and I began to think about my options with lonely desperation. I limped into the kitchen, where the sink and countertops were piled with dishes and overflowing ashtrays, and sat on a stool for a minute to think. Dad was the stinger remover, baking soda plasterer, and I would have to risk waking him up. I started up the stairs to get my father's doctoring in a growing sense of disquiet. My chin wobbled, and I feared I would bray and bawl, but somehow I kept to some quiet sobbing. Out in the hall, I stood beside the closed door of my parents' bedroom, leaking tears, for as long as I could stand it. Then I pushed open the door to the darkened space behind it, whispered "Dad?" into the musty air, and waited. Soon I could make him out, one arm out flung, the other across his eyes, a look of anguish seizing his jaw and mouth. My mother had her back to the door and lay still. I waited, smelling what I think of now as a funky mixture of alcohol, tobacco, sex, and sweat, and after a few moments, he breathed a sigh.

"What is it?"

"I got a sting. A bee sting. A wasp sting, really."

"What?" he asked again, a note of complaint rising in his voice. He was always after me to annunciate, to use proper diction, to project. It took several tries to make him understand. At last, he put a hand to his forehead, clasping the temples with thumb and index finger, and told me to go back downstairs. He'd be there shortly. Downstairs I set myself up before the TV with a couple of chairs, one to prop the foot on, and turned on the set. I listened for the loony music, watched for the abstract landscape to form. But on the screen, on every channel, was coverage of a mob outside what the announcer said was the Vatican. Somber commentary punctuated by church bells and echoing loudspeaker intonations in a foreign tongue. Old tape of a dim figure in white raising his hand. Close-up shots of weeping Catholics in their European wrinkles and dark complexions. It didn't end. My father came into the kitchen to mix up baking soda and water. He walked carefully, as if his feet were made of brittle ice, to the bathroom for tweezers. He sighed with every movement. As he knelt to examine my foot, he cast an ashen, unshaven frown at the TV.

"What's this?"

"I don't know. I think the Pope died."

Dad sat down heavily, stared at the screen while the announcer ran through it all again. He switched channels, working through the four we received, still holding baking soda paste and a pair of tweezers in his free hand. "I don't think there are any cartoons," I explained, commiserating. When he turned away from the television to pull the stinger from my foot, I saw he was weeping silently, a sheet of wetness coating his cheeks. He plastered my sole with cold goop. I kept quiet. He went to the kitchen to make coffee, and I sat still as he commanded me. He returned as if to watch, but sat down in the chair next to me, leaned forward, and covered his eyes. He sat there a long time, hunched over the steaming mug of coffee while the camera panned back and forth over the masses all united in grief. My foot ached, and I did not feel any wiser, any closer to understanding, any less alone.

IV.

Later in the day, my brother and I were banished from the house for loudly complaining that the Pope coverage was interrupting our previously scheduled programming. The door slammed behind us, and we were sick at heart out in the grey day, thinking of the shows we should be watching in the brightly lit TV room off the kitchen with its round yellow table. Maybe it wasn't the Pope, maybe it was the hangover. Or maybe they were fighting again. The Pope thing didn't make sense, we agreed, because we weren't Catholics, as we had learned to explain quickly when we told folks our father was a priest, Father Harris. On the other hand, didn't we pray for the Pope and his Holy Catholic Church every Sunday in the prayers of the people? Should we be feeling something, I wanted to know? My brother soon tired of my questions and took to mocking me for limping, calling me a sissy and a pussy alternatively. The sting still hurt on the arch of my foot with every step.

We ended up knocking on Pierro Grassio's door. Pierro lived three houses down Vista and had, just the day before, mentioned his eagerness to show us his latest acquisition of *Star Wars* paraphernalia. We were eager to see and hear whatever he might share about the film, which incredibly, our parents had still not taken us to see, though its initial theatrical release had been over a year earlier. Everyone our age and older seemed to have already seen it multiple times, knew lines and tropes and jokes from it, and we had to fake it. At Pierro's house the TV was up loud and his father was talking on the phone. They didn't want company in this difficult time, they told us, but Pierro could come outside. We waited for him on the lawn, and he didn't disappoint. Out there on the dew-wet grass under the leaden clouds that had steadily covered the sky, he showed us, and generously allowed us to handle, his "action figures"—which it seemed impolite to criticize, though they were in fact dolls for boys. He also allowed us to inspect the Galactic Trash Compactor Set, a sort of brown plastic vice with a clear window on one side and assorted plastic space junk. You put the action figures in among the space junk, he explained, and then in a miniature reenactment of this exciting moment in the film, you could turn the crank on the side of the box and squish everything together. A handy escape hatch was provided to enable the intrepid Han Solo and Luke Skywalker to escape at the last moment. Pierro kept an eye on me while I turned the crank and my brother quizzed him backward and forward on the plot. Through Pierro's hazy explanations we tried to understand Tatooine, hyperspace, light sabers, the Force, droids, and an ominous figure in black robes and mask who seemed to make you choke or, Pierro theorized, perhaps he made you choke yourself, as all the victims had clutched their own throats as they expired. Pierro strangled himself and made expiring noises while we nodded, terribly confused. This was the stuff we *had* to know, just had to, and we listened carefully as a fine mist began to fall and dampen our hair and clothes.

"You know why it's raining?" Pierro asked solemnly and gazed up at the vapor that silvered his dark eyelashes. "It's God. He's crying for the Pope." We were silent about this, and I reached to give the trash another turn. We stayed out in the rain as long as we dared, knowing if we came home too early, we'd be in trouble, and if we came home too drenched, we'd also be in trouble. Pierro said his goodbyes and went back to his family in their mourning. We trudged our way back home, too, me limping and Joseph cursing. We didn't know it, but it was our last summer in that fine house with those upper-crust neighbors, with the veneer of acceptability on us wearing thin but still present. Almost home, I remembered the limerick! I stopped him, cleared my throat theatrically and recited it with my hands clasped behind my back. At "lightning shot out of his ass," Joseph laughed and laughed, his eyes wild and his crooked teeth crazy in his mouth.

"Say it again," he said.

Black Widow

We were walking the dirt road behind Nanny and Granddad's house, following its ruts up around the hillside. The late summer morning felt like fall to us, just on the verge of a frost, as it gets sometimes when it's clear out in Oregon's high desert. To me it felt wondrously strange to be so chilled, armored in coat and sweatshirt and shoes, when later in the day I would be swimming in cold creeks to wash the dust and sweat off, or at least looking for shade to get away from the heat. We were due back for breakfast soon, after which we would pack up suitcases and move a couple miles down the road to our Grandma Saling's house, a prospect we didn't relish. Nanny, our great-grandmother, lived at the edge of town, on the border of unfenced and uncountable acres dotted with abandoned shacks and sagebrush, country crossed by the occasional rider impossibly tall against the sky who would call down over the wind to ask where you were from before warning you of rattlers and riding off unconcerned. But Grandma lived right in town, in a small house most prominently inhabited by her second husband Mike and their two daughters. Properly, he would be Grandfather Saling, and the girls our Aunts Pattie and Michelle, but he wasn't our father's father, they weren't our real family, we'd been told, and they seemed to know it.

Down in the yellow house, some assemblage of Harris relatives would be brewing coffee and frying ham steaks, and making oatmeal, biscuits, and eggs, but we knew that with the good food would come the interrogations of our Great-Aunt Julia, whose eyes seemed altogether too close together behind her glasses, and Nanny herself would be muttering from time to time how it was silly of us to move down the road for our last night in Heppner when she had plenty of room. My father would take some of these remarks as insults against his mother, and his voice would be raised. I had to get much older to fully understand that Nanny, my father's paternal grandmother, had never really gotten her mind happily around our grandmother's remarrying, and that the constant tug of war between Nanny's house and Grandma's drew from that unplumbable well of a mother-in-law's disdain for her boy's widow. As we climbed steadily upward away from that inevitable scene, we curved into the shade of the hill and found it even colder, the dust settled by dew. We'd been talking about school coming, each of us with more than a little glumness. The truth was that while Joseph found school a prison, Carolyn and I were probably ready to go back to it, were tired of disappointments like this one where our vacationing family was supposed to have some idyllic experience but instead just fought the same fights in different locations. Still, we would miss exploring, our favorite way to have adventures either together or alone.

Wildness has its innocent side, I think, and we knew it well in that age. We were the kind of kids who, finding a barn door open slightly, would soon enough find ourselves wrestling in the hayloft. We knew every backyard of every neighbor and were often on good terms with their dogs. Left unattended at a funeral or wedding, we found office doors ajar, and keys in desks, and never-ending series of new doors to open. Clearly, Joseph was our leader, but we all enjoyed this pastime and could walk out into the world looking for trouble together even though we couldn't manage to watch television in the same room without violence. Summer was the time for exploring, and with the edge of premature fall in the air, we were eager for new territory as we untangled the chain across the sheet metal gate that kept us out of the junkyard on the hill. The KEEP OUT sign had a lot of bullet holes in it, but so did every sign we saw outside of town.

The place held the air of stillness that only a disused trash collection can. No one had been dropping off discarded automobiles, refrigerators, or small appliances for a long time. We saw little plastic, just rust and peeling paint, and towers of tires and buckets lining a weedy road that ran through from front to back. We didn't see an office shack of any kind, and I speculated that the place was probably not a real junkyard, but a hiding place for an army of robots that would emerge at night to overtake the town, enslaving all the inhabitants and forcing them into robot-making work camps. Somewhere high above us a hawk screeched, and the idea seemed a bit out of place. My sister chuckled at me. We were turning to go when we saw an old lawn mower tilted back on its handle, its motor in pieces that hung from the torn metal housing. The deck shone with a dewy, spindly web, but as we approached, we could see the web's inhabitant was a shiny black spider, her abdomen an almost perfect sphere. Crouching down to see, the marking was unmistakable. She was perfect, her black a shiny perfect gloss, her red hourglass exactly as you see her in pictures. In the bottom corner of the web, the little cotton ball of her egg sac hung expectantly. She moved sluggishly in the cold and hadn't dealt with the small yellow moth waiting in another sector of her domain.

If a film crew from the *ABC Afterschool Specials* people could have swept in, they would have somehow got the lens of the camera right about where the mower blades were, back behind the web. Then they could have shot us, all squeezing together to look, our faces split with grins of wonder and fear, the wreckage in the background giving way to sunlit hills in the distance. I think we'd have made good *Afterschool Special* characters. Joseph and I both had long unruly bowl cuts, mine disarranged brownly, his towheaded mess like poorly stacked, bleached straw. We were sunburned and freckled across our noses, and my glasses were broken again and taped at the temples. Carolyn's hair parted down the middle and hung down to her shoulders lankly. She hadn't gotten her glasses yet, and so squinted at the world with an expression like surprised interest. She gripped Joseph's shoulder as he leaned close, but not in a frightened girl sort of way; she wasn't in the least bit squeamish and would lick banana slugs for the way they made her tongue go numb. Shorten up the depth of field and there the widow hangs, helpless in her lethality, doomed to our intentions. Our new pet.

These things never work out the way the kids plan. You'd think we would have learned by now, one sick bird, one garter snake, one gallon jar of tent caterpillars, one dug-up anthill, one newt, one scorpion, one found kitten at a time. Repeatedly, we'd seen our efforts at adoption of the wild, or just the feral, turn sour. Experience failed to discourage us. The scorpion should have been our most pointed lesson, as I'd found it a few years earlier not a mile from this junkyard, down near the railroad tracks where we'd been climbing in and out of boxcars. Having spent a lot of my previous summers playing with shore crabs, I knew to avoid the thing's pincers and to subdue it by holding one claw in each of my hands, but the pointy stingerish thing it kept waving over its head, or alternately, swinging under its body, was new. I judged it unpleasant, and so twisted the scorpion's claws in time to its efforts to stick me, keeping it just clear of my fingers. I think I was six. I walked with care not to drop this interesting new desert crab back to Nanny's house. My arrival in the kitchen stunned the seated ladies there into silence. Around the kitchen table, aunts, grandmother, and Nanny gripped cups of afternoon coffee and held cigarettes still while their smoke went straight up in curling streams. I knew I had done something terribly wrong, worse than streaking across the front lawn with my cousin. Nanny took control, calling for my brother in her steely voice, asking him to bring an empty yellow margarine container from the pantry, and after I'd dropped my new friend to scurry around his little home, she commanded that he "take that damn thing and flush it down the toilet." I cried, bewildered, while my mother sobbed and looked over my hands, asking again and again if it had stung me anywhere. Nanny got to her feet and made me a tuna sandwich to shut me up, as she knew I was a sucker for the sweet pickles she served alongside. Down the hall, the toilet flushed.

So we should have known how it would all play out, and I think at some level we did know, even as we found an unbroken mason jar and a makeshift lid to hold over the top, and scooped the spider and her egg sac out of the nest in two separate maneuvers. She was so cold, she dropped out of her web into the glass with an audible plunk and lay still for a moment in the dusty jar.

Negotiations with our parents went poorly, in the end. We knew we needed forward momentum and busied ourselves back at Nanny's with the tasks of finding a clean jar, poking holes in a tight-fitting lid, creating a little habitat of sticks and leaves, all while ignoring the sharpening calls for breakfast. We left our prize specimen in the bedroom while we pushed forkfuls of everything into our mouths, Carolyn excepted—she was a picky eater for whom the chief enjoyment of a meal was avoiding any consumption of it. She was still trying to get Nanny's little terrier into position under the table when we cleared our plates and ran back to work; we had flies and moths to capture.

Figuring it would be best just to *have* the black widow without making a big fuss out of it, and then reveal to our parents that we had stepped up in our naturalist training considerably after we had hatched the wee ones, we hid the jar among our books and clothes as we packed up for the short drive to Grandma's house. Had we not been so concerned about checking on our arachnid charge, we might not have been caught red-handed with the incriminating evidence. In the same way that possession of a crack pipe can quickly lead to drug charges, three preteens with a mason jar capped by a perforated lid constitutes reasonable grounds for search and seizure. We arrived at Grandma's as we often seemed to, with my father yelling that he would be beating us with various found objects (switches, rocks, belts, tire irons) while my mother tearfully interceded and we all took to crying miserably, eliciting from my father the threat that we stop crying before we got something to cry about. If anything, Grandma was less sympathetic to our cause than anyone, asking that we drown the spider in the jar and bury it. She's had enough of those things in the basement already this year. Even Mom had to admit that it wasn't a good idea to bring the spider inside. We could play with it, in the jar, which was not to be opened, and we'd see how things went. I don't think she meant to give us hope, only shelter from Dad's wrath and some time before the inevitable conflict, but of course I took her "wait and see" remarks as a green light for my most grandiose plans.

We did have some activities that day, though I don't remember much except staring at the spider, who had finally come awake and was moving about her little diorama of a world. She didn't do much that was very interesting, but while I watched her, I dreamed about raising an army of her poisonous brood and setting them on my countless enemies. Sitting quietly under the shade of the elm tree in my grandma's front yard, I saw teachers and classroom bullies, family members, neighbors, the clerk who'd caught me shoplifting candy, all of them running before my black and crimson horde, who would return to their palatial glass cages when I blew on a whistle only they could hear. My siblings were long gone on other adventures, probably involving stealing half-smoked cigarettes and being sick after smoking them with our Aunt Michelle, who was about my brother's age.

After the final pronouncement that the spider would have to stay outside that night, I gave up my pleading and lay on the brown carpet of my grandmother's living room and watched TV. The reception was poor and the options limited to two channels, but Mike was watching some sporting event and we weren't allowed to do anything that would make noise. He occupied a recliner and spat tobacco juice into an empty beer can, often as punctuation to a stream of curses I hoped were directed at the action on screen and not me. Years later we discovered that he'd been just about stone deaf and kept everyone at a distance to cover up his inability to get close. When he got a hearing aid, he became, briefly, a whole new person, full of interest and laughter. Then his racism started cropping up more noticeably and we went back to our original relationship characterized by dedicated efforts to pretend the other didn't exist. I kept quiet and made no unnecessary movements, even when Joseph whispered to me that Mom had let him put the spider inside the car, so it might have a chance of living out the night, which promised to be cold. "Jeezus. Bullshit, is what it is," muttered Mike, and spat.

In the morning she was dead, curled up dead on her back with her legs contracted dead, the kind of dead you couldn't argue about. The hundreds of tiny yellow spiders, each a mote, a translucent iota, also seemed dead, though at some point in the night they had swarmed all over the sticks, leaves, and glass itself. You could shake them down to the bottom of the jar like pollen, but my folks were eager to get them in the trash before the sun warmed things up. My father looked pale as he examined the jar, noting audibly that the air holes in the top were much larger than the baby black widow spiders so recently hatched inside his car. I think he was freaked out enough about the prospect of the long drive back during a hot sunny day to be distracted from figuring out who to blame for the spider being in the car in the first place.

We had an awkward goodbye that morning. The aunts didn't come out to wave us away, but Grandma and Mike did, with looks of fixed politeness on their faces. Driving the twisty, windy road back toward I-84, I watched my parents slap at each itch with startling vigor until I fell asleep with the sun on my face, the car rocking beneath me like a cradle.

North

Walking across the oil slick pavement in the acetylenic, orange light, I held the black thermos tight to my chest. Dad said it had a lining of glass. Cautiously, I maneuvered inside the service station to the coffee urn, keeping my path to the center of the aisles. Tall for eleven, headed for six feet at twelve, my shadow lay in thin strips on the linoleum floor, extending from my oversized feet. While the coffee poured, my father pumped gas into the truck. The white line of a cigarette stood out against his black beard. I imagined the pump and the truck exploding. A white light erasing the nighttime, my father reduced to smoking chunks of meat, bone, hair. I made a sibilant explosion, quietly. I could see it. The coffee overflowed, burning my hand into spasm. I let go of the handle. The thermos cracked against the countertop but I seized and held it before it could topple to the floor. As I paid the attendant for the coffee from the two dollars Dad had given me, I watched the crimson blotches develop on the skin of my hands like a Polaroid. Walking back to the truck, I saw that Dad's cigarette was unlit. He sucked air through the tobacco, anticipating, I suppose. He lit it at the stop sign coming out of the station and the smoke made my eyes water. On the on-ramp he swore at the drivers who didn't accelerate.

"Goddamnit! Learn to drive, woman!" he bellowed. All bad drivers were women to him. Sometimes they were "cunts." When I got older, I would occasionally challenge him by pointing out that a given driver appeared to be male. "Well, he drives like a cunt," was his usual reply.

"I'll take some coffee," he demanded politely. I struggled with the lid, first tightening it accidentally, finally remembering the proper direction. Dad had a black mug with a faint gold outline of Canterbury Cathedral. Spots were all that remained of the text beneath the figure, as if someone had translated it into Morse code. The tracings sparkled. While I poured, I imagined the glass liner of the thermos must have broken when I dropped it, ice-thin shards floating like razors in the oily liquid. His insides would lacerate slowly, the cutting edges working their way to his heart.

He drove with his left hand, his right occupied with coffee and the cigarette smoldering in the ashtray. A drip ran through his black beard. I saw it shine under the hair. He was a little under six feet. He held perhaps thirty extra pounds on his belly, back, butt, and cheeks. His face tanned a ruddy color. He claimed his great-grandfather was half Spanish, half Irish, and had a temper. There were few stories about Great-Great-Grandfather Kelly, though one that I worried over narrated a terrible binge he went on, coming to in a bar outside of Pendleton where in his drunken stupor, he had sold his young son to a fellow reveler. In the weeks following, he could find no trace of the boy. It was a family game to speculate on this missing branch of the family, and what wonderful adventures and unspeakable horrors the boy had come to face. The story came back to me in situations like these, when I was stuck alone with Dad.

His chest was thick and hair curled from his shirts. He shaved his ears once a week. They were prominent, like mine. His cutoffs were embarrassingly short, and if he sat with his legs spread, as happened often when we were sailing, occasionally a ruddy ball would slip out one leg. He didn't usually bother tucking it back in. He wore crude sandals of thick leather and a dark blue polo-shirt. His gaze across the landscape hinted at disapproval, especially when he snapped his head to the right to catch me staring.

"Where did you get that mug?" I asked only to have something to say.

"It was a gift."

"From who?"

"From whom. Who gave it to you, from whom did you get it."

"Who gave it to you?"

"That's right. It's time you learned some grammar. And better diction too. You need to enunciate." Words came from his mouth as if he were forming them from iron, hard edged, hammered by tongue and teeth. He never muttered.

"But, who gave it to you?"

"Your mother."

"Oh. When?"

He sipped from his coffee, pulled hard on his cigarette. "Just after we were married. We used to talk about going someday, hear the choirs and see the cathedrals. The closest we got was when your brother went. Remember those pictures he took?" This was a sore topic with me. Joseph and I had both sung briefly in the St. Mark's boys' choir, but I was too young to stick with it. That's not entirely accurate, as there were other boys younger than me, but they actually behaved, whereas I was caught several times eating the scraps of communion wafer, sheets with holes in them where the body of our Lord had been punched out by a little mechanical press. Joseph hadn't been caught, had stuck with it, and eventually, through the sponsorship of a parishioner, had flown away to England with the choir, leaving me home with just my parents and sister—one of the worst summers ever. He returned with a deck of Pan Am playing cards, a model plastic jet, and stories of finding condoms on the beach and eating liver pasties. He steadfastly refused to tell me about the ossuaries.

"Maybe you'll get to go someday," I offered. "You can take me."

Dad laughed, shook his head, scowled at the mug. "Junk like this just sticks to you as you age till there's no room for anything of value." I closed my eyes almost shut and imagined the ossuaries all around me, bones under the seat, a grinning skeleton climbing from the truck bed to scratch at my window. A shrieking skull in the glove box.

We'd been driving since three in the morning, a dark world rushing past the windows like water. We would catch a ferry in Port Angeles by seven, drive to the terminal in Victoria, and then catch another ferry to the Gulf Islands, where we would meet up with the rest of the family who had gone the day before. I don't know how I drew the unlucky straw of riding in the truck with Dad. It should have been Joseph's honor. I had the sense this was bonding time, much like the court-ordered quality time that came later, and just as forced. When Mom and Carolyn and Joseph and the dogs and the parrot pulled out in the Volkswagen Dasher, groaning under the weight of our belongings and the little sailboat Dad had built strapped to the roof, she had given me a long look. Her brow seemed furrowed with misgivings, her eyes squinted almost shut. But then she smiled and waved before shutting her door. Perhaps she was only trying to remember if she'd forgotten anything. I had been packed for several days and had been ordered to stop my hourly countdown in the strictest of terms, but once I found out I had to ride in the truck, I didn't want to see her leave, see the whole process start.

The gray interstate blurred by, all shadows and streetlights, billboards glowing dimly. "It's the water!" I read out loud as we drew near Olympia. "What's that mean? I never understood that one."

"Cheap beer. It's the piss." I laughed hard, though it wasn't very funny. I slapped my knee while I hooted.

"For Christ's sake will you stop that? Do you want me to have an accident? Do you?"

"No, sir."

"Then keep quiet." I wiped my nose on the back of my hand. Dad drove fast and unevenly. The truck's steering was loose, and he constantly had to correct, moving the wheel back and forth in a semicircle. The cab seemed to rock and sway, like a boat riding the swells of a ferry. My mother hated to drive the truck or ride in it. She said it made her sick. Dad smoked more behind its wheel than at any other time. It had transmission problems, a hole in the muffler, broken mirrors. Paint flaked off the hood. In the dash, ancient bugs, scraps of paper, and burned-out fuses rustled arcane secrets. The wing vent on the passenger side whistled a warbling tune. The heater could be turned down, but not off; it kept my toes warm, lulled me near sleep.

"We should make Victoria by eleven," Dad was saying. "There used to be some good restaurants around the waterfront. If we have time we'll go out to lunch." My stomach growled and he laughed.

"You're hungry, I hear."

"My stomach feels weird."

"That's because you're hungry. What kind of food do you want? They've got everything there."

I thought carefully.

"Kung-Pao chicken. And root beer."

He winced visibly.

"I didn't think you liked spicy food."

"Oh yeah, I love it."

"You didn't used to like it at all. Your mother stopped making chile rellenos because you hated them so much."

"I was just a kid then." He scratched his beard, almost relaxed his jaw, but couldn't manage it.

"Or we can get waffles in the Port Angeles terminal. If we have time."

"Well, I'm not really that hungry anyway. My stomach feels weird." I put my head back on the seat and closed my eyes. My thoughts twisted like dreams, flowing with the rocking of the truck, the engine noise.

"Idiot!"

"What?"

"An idiot. People just don't drive anymore. They just don't know how to drive." Alert again, I watched his face flash into view and then fall back into silhouette as we passed a streetlight. Glints of gray coils in his beard, then he became an indistinct outline shifting in the southbound headlights outside his window.

"How come?"

"How come what?"

"How come people don't know how to drive?"

"Because they're all too hesitant. They're afraid. It used to be you could get on a highway and it would be crowded, of course, just like it is these days at rush hour. But. Traffic would move at sixty miles an hour. The passing lane would be clear, slower traffic stayed right, and when you needed to take an exit you just signaled and everyone moved aside so that you could get off. There was a sort of courtesy, the rules of the road, and you learned them." I liked his rules of the road speech. It hinted that the era of laws and easy courtesy had passed. A lawless, apocalyptic era was at hand. On an overpass a reflective sign heralded a viewpoint turnoff. "Last state landmark for fifty miles. Should we take it? Do you want to?"

"Dad. It's still dark."

"Sunrise from the hilltop. Scenic view. You're sure."

"I'm sure."

"I think we should go," he said seriously. My heart raced. I felt a sickening anticipation, like watching a race-car accident on TV over and over again. There were hundreds of turnoffs between us and my mother. North was the only direction that made any sense. "There's no reason to make this trip some kind of forced march. Let's try and enjoy it a little."

"It's just some stupid lookout, Dad. There are probably some hills, a lake or something, the sun comes up and all the tourists get out of their RVs and take slides. Let's keep going."

"Fine. Forget it."

My chest pounded. I cracked my knuckles, leaned back. The stars faded as the sky lightened. I'd eaten a sandwich bag filled with trail mix and my mouth tasted sour, like dried dates and coconut flake. The truck rolled back and forth, my father smoked, and Olympia streaked past. Maybe I was sick. Perhaps I would die. I wiped snot on the back of my hand and then on the bottom of my seat. I kept my face turned to the window for the most part, watching lightening orchards, wondering how the back rows stayed still while the front ones wheeled by.

Over the roar of the engine and the wing vent, Dad sang. Choir boy then college tenor, smoking had lowered his range a little so he strained for the high notes, but he strained with training, with support enough that when he reached, I thought of brass, polished and warm. He sang songs without words, harmonizing with the engine. The melodies soared high and plunged into melancholy. On a sweet, low rise his throat caught and he fell silent. He asked for more coffee and I poured him some.

"Why don't you take a pill and stop that sniffling," he said as I handed him the coffee. I opened the glove box and took out the brown plastic bottle. The pills were the color of verdigris and tasted like iron in my spit. They were his prescription, but I had taken them for years. Pale disks, milk green phosphorescence in their container.

"I don't have any water."

He shook his head slightly. "Swallow it without, then."

"I can't."

"Of course you can."

"They taste terrible."

"Just swallow the thing." I stared at the circle already sucking the sweat off my palm, getting mushy just from the humidity in the cab. "Stop screwing around. Just swallow it."

"I'm trying to get spit," I said through a mouthful.

"Goddamn it. Swallow." I tried. Something in the taste of it seized my throat up. It lodged near the back of my mouth and I gagged on the bitterness. "Here. Take a sip of coffee." The mug was still hot to my fingers, hot to my lips when it met them. I remembered the glass liner, the half-melted knives that could wriggle through my veins and into my heart. I swallowed and tears leaked out the corners of my eyes. He laughed. I handed him his mug back and kept my mouth shut. I had to, to keep swallowing the saliva pouring out from under my tongue.

"That gas station coffee takes some getting used to, doesn't it?"

"Awful." I managed a weak smile.

"Make sure you drink lots of water at the next stop. Your stomach will get too acidic from those pills and that coffee. You can get ulcers that way. It's always a good idea to get some water with medication."

"What's an ulcer?"

"Your stomach gets sores on the inside. They can bleed you into the hospital."

"You're kidding."

"I'm serious. They can even turn into holes in the stomach lining. Perforated ulcers. Sometimes lethal infections develop. Your digestive tract is sort of outside you, you know. It's like a tube that runs through you. Pierce it and it's just like breaking through your skin. Worse because it's not as sensitive so you don't feel the infection until your blood goes septic. Ulcers can be deadly. Stress related, just like asthma." I sniffled and swallowed back the spit collecting in my mouth. I closed my eyes and did not throw up. He took a deep breath.

"Look, I suppose you know your mother and I have been having some problems. I just want you on your best behavior these next three weeks, because your parents need some time. OK?" I nodded. He asked me again, "You miss your Mom?"

"A little," I said. "Yeah," I whispered.

"I wish, well. I wish none of this had happened. Life hurts sometimes, but it seems like you shouldn't have to find that out until later." He had his voice pitched where he wanted it, I could tell. Low, intimate and yet formally distant, delivering philosophy to the windshield. "Years just add on without erasing each other, you know, like the way a grain of sand builds up layers of enamel, sort of, in an oyster till it's a pearl. You know what I mean." I imagined thin skins of fat wrapping around me till I became an obese wise man.

"Not really."

"What I mean is that you get older, you get tougher, you become a man, but you're a boy underneath. It never goes away, even though sometimes you want it to. You're always that boy in the heart of you." No, you're not, I thought to myself, but it worried me. I'd always imagined that all of this, all of this would blow away like ashes. After a long pause, he said quietly, "My father died when I was just a little boy, you know?"

"No, I didn't. I knew he died, but I didn't know when."

"I never told you about my dad?"

"I never heard much about him." A lie. My mother had told me a little.

"He was a logger and was killed by the kind of tree they call a widow-maker, where the top is dead, and so can fall backwards onto the saw-man as he steps out of the way." I must have looked confused because he paused briefly to steer with his knees, freeing his hands to be a tree with a break in the middle, one hand falling back atop the other. I watched with frantic intensity; the highway sawed back and forth as my father pantomimed the death of his father while working the loose steering with his knees, smoking a cigarette out of the corner of his mouth, and gripping a half-full coffee cup between his thighs. "He died instantly, of course," he said around his smoke, with finality.

I've thought of this moment often, how we knew each other so poorly, and how if we'd found the right cutoff, we could have taken a shortcut to the much later days, a decade later, when he could spend a rainy Sunday drinking coffee and telling stories about the family, like the one about his father standing at a bar eating a gross of oysters to satisfy a bet; how he would pump bucket after bucket of icy water from the well and throw it on his laughing son until he shivered bluely, still laughing; how he fired up the stove in the logging camp with kerosene on a cold morning, making a huge whoosh of heat and pinging, vent pipe crackling as he got that damn fire going, for Chrissake; how he would, for a laugh, use a bullwhip to crack a lit cigarette out of my grandmother's smiling lips from across the room. In a confessional mood, he once narrated one of his earliest memories of hiding under a table when his father came in from the field, his boots a mess of mud and manure, and how for some reason he wanted that boot on his face, wanted it to come down and press muck all over him. I never did know what to say about that one. But he didn't tell me any of those stories that day in the truck, weaving north. Instead he reminded me that when he died, leaving behind two children of six and four, his dad was only twenty-eight, my grandmother was only twenty-three.

"I remember his mother, my grandmother, your Nanny, coming out into the backyard where I was sitting under the pear tree. I thought she was coming to comfort me, but then she screamed. Just tilted back her head and screamed at God, she was so angry. She punched at the tree and screamed." He drove on for a few moments in the rattling roar of the engine, the half-light coming through the windshield. Streetlights were winking out in stretches as the day came on. I couldn't look over at him, though I watched his hand reach out and tap ash into the tray in the center of the dash. When he spoke again, he was almost whispering. "I used to imagine he'd faked it somehow. Switched places or clothes with some other fellow. That he was nearby, watching me. Which would have been an awful thing to do, of course, but that way he could return to rescue me from that house full of women. You don't know how lucky you've been."

"What do you mean?" I snorted, looked incredulous. He raised an eyebrow and continued.

"After Dad was gone my mother, my sister, and I went to live with his mother. I should say his parents, but Granddad was never there. Even when he was there, he wasn't there. We were poor, not like your mother's family. No family trips to the East Coast for us. I worked every day of my life from the moment Dad died." This part I had heard, the litany of farm work, paper routes, slash-crew, dishwashing, driving truck, and jerking soda. I rolled my eyes, but he wasn't even looking. "Grandma and my mother fought all the time about money. There was no order in that house. No sense of responsibility. They didn't stick to what they said." He shook a finger to punctuate his words. "A man doesn't take the easy way out. Even though parts of him might want to. It's important to remember that. If you take the easy way out, you're not a man." He stuck his chin out and stared at the road stretching ahead in the dawn. A cool tear escaped my eye, just one before I noticed and blinked hard while squeezing my tongue between my teeth. I'd heard this speech, too, and hated it.

Suddenly, without speaking, he merged right and pulled over into the breakdown lane. As gravel rattled through the wheel wells, I wondered if he was stopping the car for a rare father-son embrace and I began to steel myself. But instead of reaching over to me he jumped out the door without looking in the rearview mirror. A second later he was back inside, the slam of the door just covering the roar as the engine caught. His jaw worked, the muscles bulged and relaxed by his ears.

"What is it?" The back end slid in the gravel as we accelerated, the motor roaring in the darkness. I imagined fire gushing from the tailpipes. "What's wrong?"

"I left the goddamn gas cap at the station." He barked this as he pulled into the traffic, squealing the tires. As he took the next off-ramp, I could not restrain myself.

"Dad, we can buy a new one." He rolled through the stop sign at the first intersection, turned left onto the overpass. "Screw the gas cap. Don't turn around, we'll miss our ferry!"

"Shut your mouth." he said evenly, and I did. He got back on the southbound side of the highway roughly, pushing the pickup till the shimmies started. I sniffled; my stomach roiled. Dad swore as a station wagon pulled in front of us. He braked hard, moved left, downshifted, gunned the engine. When he popped it back into fourth, the shifter broke free of the column without a sound and stayed in his hand, raised in front of the windshield. His head darted birdlike between the shifter in his hand and the road in front of him. I didn't fully understand what this meant, how to interpret the relative danger of highway driving without the ability to shift gears, but I knew enough to be concerned. When he spoke, his voice was controlled and calm.

"There's a screw somewhere on the floor. Find it."

"Where?"

"Probably under the pedals." I slid awkwardly down into the space between glove box and seat, resting my elbows on the floor. The dash light filtered down through ganglia of wires. Crusts of old leaves. Pistachio shells. Cigarette butts. My father's calves loomed, hairy and flecked with moles. His feet sprouted tufts of hair between the straps of his sandals. The big toe on his right foot bore a yellow and horny nail.

"Do you see it?"

"I'm still looking." The rubber mat was burning hot and sticky in spots. Sometimes the exhaust leaked out directly under the cab and Dad would make us ride with the windows open, even in winter. Poison. I scoured every surface with my eyes, my sliding fingertips. His foot flexed and relaxed, a tendon jumping out of his heel. Sometimes he let the gas pedal rise as high as it would go and twitched his foot to hold it over the brake. "I see it."

"Where?"

"It's under the brake pedal."

"Are you sure?"

"The middle pedal?"

"That's it." It had seemed I'd been close before, but I hadn't brought my hands even over the halfway point of the cab. Now I inched closer, expecting fumes, soot, the touch of his flesh against mine. I slid my arm around behind Dad's knee. My back twanged above my kidneys and I reached, trying not to touch him. "Hold on!" He yelled, slamming the brake pedal down over my fingers, knocking my chin with his knee. My head slammed into the ashtray and then I fell on my side as we accelerated.

"Cocksucker!" he screamed. "Learn to drive!" I pictured a semi hurtling toward us, or a burning oil tanker about to detonate. My fingers closed around the screw. I climbed into the seat and fastened my lap belt.

"Here," I said. "Here's the screw." I couldn't watch the road ahead of us, or Dad's attempts to tighten the screw with a thumbnail while driving with his knees. The sun came orange over the hill, and for an instant

I could see my reflection in the glass. Snot ran down my lip to my chin; ashes clung to my cheek. My palms were stained black. We passed a dog, burst open and spreading in the shoulder of the highway. I wondered if it was a pet or a wild dog. I'd have howled if I could. Outside the window the land streaked north.

Pender Tales

Feeding the Bullfish

On the sunny afternoons when it's a little cool for swimming, I lie on the dock, the water bobbing and sloshing beneath the splintery boards of its surface, and feed the bullfish. The process is simple; I have learned it from my sister, maven of choosing the right mussel, expert at crushing it under a heel without cutting her foot, exemplar of lying still, arm floating in the cold water, palm upraised with the crushed mollusk cradled, saint of patience who waits for the pug-nosed, bigheaded, whiskery fish to dart in and tug at the floating bits, the revealed mystery of the mussel's flesh. I spread my cotton T-shirt out flat and feel the cracks between the decking against my ribs. I rest my head, Buddha-like, on one arm, while the baited arm rests in the water. I keep my hand in the shadow of the dock so that, mysteriously, I can see through the surface, can see the green glow of the sunlight beneath the shining little waves, can watch the anemones spread their tendrils, the barnacles flick a feathery tongue through the salt water, can observe all that eats and is eaten in the narrow shady realm six inches off the dock's underlying structure of cabled logs. The avowed purpose of the afternoon is to feed bullfish, a goal whose attainment is measured in the number and size of those who slick across my palm or nestle firmly in the webbing between my fingers, or succeed in pulling the mussel loose of its shell to fall, beleaguered by squadrons of fish that chase it spiraling down into the realm of the perch who shoot out from the dock's shadow and return with a flash.

I am not afraid of the spider crab—am not afraid, only startled. Others shriek and lose their bait, but I do so only out of surprise, not fear. He is smaller than he appears, shell covered in seaweed bits and spines, and whatever he can use to hide his hideous self. So he moves quickly, swinging up from the dark to clamber over mussels and barnacles and patches of bare wood to claw across my palm and take what I'm offering. I am not afraid of his spherical midsection, his three-kneed legs, his locomotion of wrongness, which is crabwise not at all, but somehow spidery. I prove my lack of fear by my very presence on the dock, where alone, unsupervised, I put my hand into his realm and watch for him to make his appearance. I am not *not* hoping he will show, not exactly.

One of my earliest memories of the ocean comes to me whenever I look down the shafts of light into the murk of green. On a cloudy summer afternoon when I was five or six, I sat in an inner tube and paddled in ineffectual circles. It seemed to me my mother was allowing me to paddle out to a great depth, much farther than I would usually swim myself. My brother poled the raft he loved, a giant log halved and the halves joined into a massive catamaran with double wedge-shaped prows. Over the years, the raft will lose buoyancy, grow waterlogged, and float along under the surface, creating the illusion that three or four laughing children are sliding along the water without support. That summer it still rode high, even with all the children we could cram onto its surface; my brother liked to poke around in the shallows, force it up the creek that empties out by the wharf. He was close, just the other side of the dock, by the tied-up logs, but I still felt very alone out in the dark water, at the mercy of the little waves and wind. I liked, however, to look through the hole in the inner tube, where the shadowed surface lost its reflective mask and the water seemed to glow. In this instance, I began to cry as quietly as possible while huge fish nibbled at my tiny wrinkled toes. They could have been salmon jacks, I suppose, but were probably just perch. It hurt when they lunged in for a taste, though they never broke the skin, but what terrified me was the realization that they were all around me in the water, unseen just a foot or two below the undulating waves. My mother called my brother over to get me and I shivered on the beach for a long time.

My face is inches from the water; when a small boat whines by, way out in the bay, the three-inch wavelet remnants of its wake wet my chin and cheek. I don't move, except to stroke the backs of the bullfish resting in my palm with my tremulous thumb, or switch the finger holding down the broken mussel, leaking its cloudy brine into the water. The sun is a hand pressing down on my back, the dock a wooden palm pushing up against my ribs. My eyes close and I listen to the water sounds, the rattle of pebbles on shore in the waves, the *lunk lunk* of the water trapped beneath the dock, the slow creaking of chains between dock floats. This isn't sleep, but something as perfect, a state of mind worn smooth as green glass, or a lozenge, translucent, unyielding, complete. My eyes snap open when I feel the crab climb into my palm, its claws gripping with surprising strength. What I see doesn't jibe with the sensation in my hand, as if I'm watching a television reenactment of the event. Having floated nearly weightlessly in cool water for forty minutes, graced only by tiny fish the size of my pinky who rest as easily as light, or tug at the mussel with comically minuscule fury, my palm feels like a wafting bit of kelp in the water. The spider crab feels massive, heavy, like something from the deep seizing my hand to pull me in. What I see is a tiny creature, really, his ball of a midsection smaller than a golf ball. His size is all the illusion of his spindly, far-flung legs. His front legs have pincers like tiny sewing shears, not the cruel pruner pincers of the shore crabs and red rock and Dungeness. I examine the object of fear coolly, without admiration or affection, but with what I can muster of detachment.

When he pinches a crease at the base of my thumb, I jerk my hand involuntarily. He tumbles loose, legs spread wide, falling in slow motion, slower than the mussel that precedes him into the dark. I am wishing a farewell to him, misunderstood, unfrightening symbol of the dragon in the water, of childhood fears, when a dark shape glides out from the dock's shadow, seizes him in its piscine jaws and turns neatly back to its domain in the dark.

Carpenter Ant

Carolyn always has earaches, the kind that makes a child moan and rock and cry. One summer they devil her, turn the sunlight pale as milk and her eyes wide. She can't sleep, even in her much-coveted real bed in the cabin's main room, where the woodstove burns down at night with its crackling and smoky smell and she can read by the light of the kerosene lantern. Her hair, never curly nor wavy, grows lank and bleaches in the sun. She isn't allowed to swim and cries on the bleached wood of the dock for hours on end. She whines that something is moving around in there, that it hurts, that she can't stand it. She wails. We ignore her as best we can, and our best is pretty good.

One night we are alone with the Bocott's youngest daughter, a big, happy girl whose accent seems even thicker than her parents' because she uses a teenage vocabulary. She sounds like a British hoodlum when she turns the light down and tells the story of the hook. We've all heard the story before, but not in Canada, and not in a cabin on an island, where the wind knocks tree branches against the roof and the night's rain taps the glass, and the kettle murmurs on the back of the stove. We've never heard it in Canadian either, where hook sounds like it has extra ooh in it, and the kids in the car are fooking as well, right on shed-ule, the whole story A to Zed in Canadian, bet yur Mum. It's creepy too, how she invents new graphic details to the story, steals cigarettes, lights them from the top of the lantern chimney, and leers over the spiraling smoke.

"So he's really banging her, you know, got her ankles behind her neck and she's screaming, eh? She's bloody loving it and begging for it up her ass next, eh?" Every sentence is a question with no safe answer. Joseph, just a few years her junior, squirms in his seat. I jump when something scrapes on the roof. It's a great relief when the girl speeds off in the car, the bloody hook dangling from the handle, though in this version the boyfriend also ends up dangling from the tree they have parked beneath. The babysitter turns toward the window and cuts her eyes at us across the table. The kettle is almost boiling for tea, or hot Ovaltine, or whatever is next. Carolyn whimpers on her bed, and the dog at her feet raises his head to look at her with concern. I hate that she gets to sleep with the dog at her feet. I hate the dog for his disloyal refusal to sleep on my cot out on the cold porch.

"Her earache, eh? Still bothering her, eh? Funny, I knew a girl who had an earache like that. No, really. And you know what? There was something in there. Something in there, eh? I'm fooking serious about this." And she seems it, not just a crafty teen putting a scare into us on a stormy night when her parents are out with our parents getting smashed on scotch at the marina bar across the bay, but a scared teenager. She pulls a hard drag on her cigarette. "Isn't that what she's saying too? Something moving in there? Jeesus."

"What was it?" asks Joseph from beside the stove, where he's adding yet more wood though it's already toasty. With the firebox door open there's a rush of ruddy light spilling out on us at the table, then he shuts the iron door and we're back in the lamplight's circle. "What was in her ear?"

"Carpenter ant, can you fooking believe it. Crawled in there, eh, and wouldn't come out."

"Jesus," he says.

"Jesus," I say, and he gives me the look that says not to copy.

"What did they do?"

"Hot oil treatment. Smothered it and then drained it out. But it was too late. She lost her hearing in that ear. And you know what else? She went mad. Totally fooking crazy, eh? Bonkers from it scratching and chewing—Oh God, did you see that!" her chair scrapes as she stands, hand halfway to her mouth already. With her other shaking finger she points to Carolyn, whose face is toward the wall, points to the visible ear.

I don't see it, I swear, couldn't have seen it, because it's a joke, a ruse, a trick to scare us, after all. But I do see it, in memory's impossible close-up, the black glossy head noselessly nosing up over the pink whorls of Carolyn's inflamed ear, its antennae tapping the faintest of tattoos before it turns and goes back inside to the tender, moist hollows where it blunders and chews. Somehow, I see it, though it can't be there. When they come home, my father singing a song and my mother shushing their way up the muddy path, they find me crying in my sleeping bag, crying for fear of madness chewing its way into us all like a whispered secret, unforgettable.

Devils on Horseback

The first oyster I ate came wrapped in bacon. It had been skewered and roasted over an open fire. I was eight. The oyster was probably three, having had the luck to be formed by freely released oyster gametes that met by chance in the shifting, cold currents of the Pacific, having swum through the hostile waters of jellyfish tentacles and filter feeding marine life as a spat for a season, having precipitated out onto a rocky outcropping a few feet below the low-tide mark and stuck fast to the bones of the earth where it grew on whatever happened by, until it measured perhaps three inches in length in the shell—just a baby really—waiting for my father to wade out into the still waters of an evening low tide and cut it loose with his knife. In the happier days of their marriage, this ritual of my parents seemed particularly sacred. Mom perched on a log, arms wrapped around her knees, a cold beer in her hand catching the light of sunset in its brown glass, Dad in his ragged cutoffs, his shirtless back and sandaled feet, up to his thighs in the calm, cold sea, filling a bucket with wild oysters he collected. Back at the cabin, as the sun got low, my brother and I would build a campfire while our parents and their friends drank scotch, shucked oysters (cutting their hands often while wrestling with the bony shells and sharp knife, swearing profusely when the salt of the oyster stung a new laceration, talking their incomprehensible adult talk so full of jokes we weren't meant to follow). My brother, always fascinated by all things incendiary, reliably created a frightening blaze that, until we were forced to let it die down, competed with the last glow in the western sky, made the dog bark at the popping wood, and wilted maple leaves from the ancient tree whose lower branches encroached on the firepit.

In summer, in British Columbia, the sun stays up late, so it must have been nine or nine-thirty when my mother handed me my first oyster. It was not quite full dark, but dim enough that it was hard to see exactly what I was pulling off the skewer. It smelled incredible, full of smoke and salt and a fishy smell I wasn't sure I would enjoy, like someone had barbequed the ocean. As I held it, the bacon was still hot and slick with rendered fat, dark from the flames. What I remember of the taste: chewy, sweet, salty, fishy, smoky, and hot. Delicious. I had six before my parents cut me off and switched me over to hot dogs and corn. Though we kids could go to the edge of the pasture where the cows watched us with incredulity, or throw oyster shells off the cliff to the water, or make the frightening trip together back to the outhouse's reek in the woods, we mostly stayed around the fire, waiting for the singing and marshmallows and the enameled kettle that produced piping hot chocolate as the evening's chill came on. We had to wait, of course, while the real oyster-eating went on. From the shell, brimming with fresh ichor, no adulteration save lemon, salt, horseradish or Tabasco. In my memory, the men were bearded, reddened, and shadowed by firelight. The oysters dripped on their chins as they slurped. Everyone seemed to smoke a pipe or a cigarette, as they exclaimed satisfaction with the cold, fresh oysters, so recently hauled up from the water. My brother, four years older and a big fan of soft-boiled eggs and other squishy things, would stand with his hands clasped behind his back—the innocent altar boy— and beg for one. He would chew his, and if no one caught him, stick out his shellfish-covered tongue at my sister and me before swallowing the grey black mess down with audible gulps. "Tastes like snot!" he would whisper sotto voce, and then beg for another.

It is with great sadness that I recount how I, like so many children, forswore my promising start as a gourmand. How I, like all the others my parents had hoped I would not become, came to despise squash, peas, spinach, artichokes, fish, cooked tomatoes, peppers, crab, the crusts of bread, garlic, uncooked tomatoes (unless sliced thick and coated with white sugar like some ultramodern vegetarian dessert) and of course, oysters. No joining in the ritual of looking for the tiny irregular pearls and saving them in a used, brown prescription bottle. No communion of raised lemon and shellfish, no chorus of gustatory sighs, no shared struggle to shuck the stubborn, stony shells apart and reveal the unlikely and mysterious goodness within. Yucky, I said, and perhaps thought. When is a child's taste real and when is it posture? From whom did I learn that I was not expected to like oysters as a child, that they were an "adult" food? How did it happen that, after a magical time filled with discoveries at table, I became a strictly traditional eater for the second half of my childhood?

It came to pass, in any case, that at eighteen, I shared a dozen oysters on the half shell with my father, at Dan and Louis' Oyster Bar just off Burnside in Portland's Oldtown. In those days, the neighborhood and the restaurant seemed dark and dingy. We met there after a long day of work for him one winter night. The room was windowless and hazy with tobacco smoke, which competed with the smell of frying batter from the kitchen. My parents had been divorced for six years. My father's health was declining. He drank nonalcoholic beer in a green bottle. The oysters were larger and looked tired, somehow seemed embarrassed to be garnished with parsley on a platter, as if the "presentation" heightened their sense of innate ugliness. I had never eaten a raw oyster, nor had a cooked one since the age of ten.

The conversation buzzed on around us. The clink of cutlery and china, the guffaws of the waitress continued in the background. My father held a burning cigarette in his right hand and said nothing, waiting to let me choose the mollusk of my choice. I raised it to my nose. Over the oyster, my father's eyes swam in their blue, sad and tired it seemed to me. I added a squirt of lemon from the slice I pulled from the tiny metal bowl. A dollop of horseradish from the frilled paper cup, keeping in mind my father's previous advice about not using the tartar sauce or the cocktail sauce—those abominations. When I ate the oyster, salty, cold, fresh, sour from the lemon and spice, with its smell of the ocean, I regretted so much all that I had missed.

Communion

Sundays back home are work days for us all. I am acolyte, or boat boy with my little cup of incense for the thurifer, or treble in the choir, or a helper in the coffee hour set-up. Joseph and Carolyn take turns as thurifers and crucifers, sing, even read a lesson once in a while. Mom plays the organ, and Dad is out of the house in the first hours of morning, returning only after the eight o'clock, the ten o'clock, coffee hour, and rounds to housebound parishioners and the sick in hospital, which sometimes takes until the early evening. The services are high church, solemn and ornamented, perfumed, vested, scripted, dressed up, formal in every sense. Participation is passive or responsive, but always comfortably social; you never say anything alone, except to whisper a prayer in the quiet of individual intercessions during the prayers of the people. You march in step.

Sundays on Pender depend on the tide, the weather, how late we were up on Saturday. Some Sundays start with buckets and shovels, out catching the low tide and digging for clams in the muck. Dad digs a hole that slowly fills with water, and you paddle around in the sand, pulling cockles and butter clams and massive geoducks from the liquefying silt that runs through your fingers. You walk handfuls down to the water's edge, wade out a few feet to rinse them in the clean salt water before putting them in the bucket. Back at the cabin, the bucket sits in the shade of the back porch, and we sprinkle the surface of the water with cornmeal, which the clams eat with their enormous rubbery feet, replacing the muck in their bellies with sweet corn.

Some Sundays we sleep late and wake to find one or another of us has gotten up early and collected twigs for the fire, or has started sourdough biscuits, or has gone for a walk to see what birds are on the quiet shore. Sometimes, I am the early one, and go to the stink of the outhouse, then wash my hands, then wake the family by pumping the water from the old well behind the kitchen, which sings a squeaky, rusty song that ends in a thick stream of cold water rushing into the buckets with a faint sulfur smell. Sometimes I am the early one, and I go looking for snakes sunning themselves or for the cows in the meadow, and hours go by before my sister comes down to the dock to tell me it's time for breakfast and I haven't pumped the water and I'm in trouble. In these ways, Sundays on Pender are like all days on Pender—quiet, unplanned, provisional, held together by the shared goals of finding good food and water and carving out time in the afternoon for a nap or a book.

But lots of Sundays have church in them, of a kind new to us. We go down to the little clearing by the cliff overlooking the harbor, all of us, and sit in the grass, which is sometimes still wet with dew, or other times is dry and hot from the late morning sun. There, in a loose circle, sharing two red, leather-bound prayer books, we go through the office, taking turns with the readings, singing hymns a cappella from the one hymnal, and are intermittently reprimanded for becoming distracted by bugs or dandelions or boats motoring across the harbor in the distance. My mother sits on her heels but the rest of us, including Dad, sprawl or hug our knees or sit however feels most comfortable. Everything about the early part of the service goes easily.

But this is not a joyous or even pleasant occasion by the end of the liturgy of the word. Dad has his bleary eyes on us, his disappointments, and he closes them in frustration when we don't know the prayers or fail to pay attention. During the readings, I usually stare into space or the grass or the woods; unless I'm reading, it's just storytime. If I'm reading, it's an agony of corrected pronunciation and frequent interruptions for definitions of words I don't know. But then the sermon comes, which isn't a sermon. It's an inquisition, an exam we are doomed to flunk.

"But what's the connection between the epistle and the parable we read?" I can feel him looking at us, but we all stare at the ground.

"Christopher Sean? What connection can you see? Were you listening to the epistle? Do you need to read it again?" He hands the good book over and I scan through the swimming lines of tiny print and numbers. Joseph groans and Dad snaps his fingers at him in warning. Having left my glasses up at the cabin, I have to hold the text right up to my nose, and then be told to speak up.

The sensation is bewildering. At church, we are the in-crowd, the ones with the answers in vacation bible school, the favored acolytes, the kids who get away with murder. Here we have to rely on delays, obstructionist attitudes, feigned disinterest, anything to play for time while we figure out the answers. He seems surprised every Sunday to find that his children know nothing about scripture and can engage in only the most limited exegetical analysis. But he is relentless, forcing us to know every word and think, think on a Sunday, about how they go together. His take on the parable of the sower is horrifying. Yes, it's about love and the good news in part, but is that all they taught you to parrot in Sunday school? Think about the seed, cast broadside by an uncareful hand, sown on rocks and among weeds and where the birds can eat it. This is the world of an inhuman generosity, a fecundity that above all emphasizes how cheap life and love is. If the sower is God, he is pouring life on all surfaces that it might die young, except for the lucky, except for the few who get a decent chance to make it to the harvest. It's a warning, and a stark reminder of the stakes. He stops, asks us to look around and think about it for a minute, and we look at all the trees, the meadow

grass being munched by the cows, the ruffled surface of the ocean holding so many hungry mouths, the rocks with their bands of mussels and
barnacles, and above that, gull-spattered stone otherwise bare.

At communion, we kneel, and Dad opens up the communion set
with its tiny silver jars for the host and the wine nestled in slots of purple velvet. He blesses us gently while he gives us bread and wine, and
we conclude the service chastened, quietly reading our prayers together.
The rest of the day spins out before us, but often we tiptoe through it,
feeling we've misunderstood something important, carrying with us
questions that linger until dinnertime, when we steam the clams and
dip them in butter, when we break open the steaming biscuits, when we
crunch through a salad of dandelion greens and lemon, when we kids
lug the bucket of shells down to the cliff, and one by one, send them
spinning off into the air to be chased by gulls and bats as they soar out
over the sunset water and fall into the waves.

. . .

Christmastime in the house on Yamhill, and the house smells of dust and paint. It is this way almost every year, but this time he has gone too far. It is one thing to rebuild the mantle or paint an upstairs room, but in the midst of the season dominated by extra services, choir recitals, arrangements for a midnight mass, the usual frenzy of gifts and cards and baking, he has stripped the hardwood floors in the living room and dining room. Sheets hang over the doorways, hazard lights glow in a haze of sawdust in the evenings. Other families, we imagine, go caroling or host beaming relatives. They wear snowflake-patterned sweaters and crowd around bright fires with mugs of hot cocoa. We are refinishing floors. One by one, we are assigned corners and a scrap of used sandpaper, folded and refolded till it becomes soft in our soft hands. One by one, we demonstrate our incompetence and are banished temporarily. My throat is tacky with dust. Dad is an infernal figure, swaddled up and masked, laboring always in a cloud of particles and work light, singing along with the whine of the sander. He takes the plate of fudge in there behind the sheets and puts it on a shelf above the shrouded piano. When he catches us taking a piece out from under the dusty plastic wrap, he orders us to drink four glasses of water and watches us do it. He has a reason for this torture, something about sugar and our kidneys. Something about training us out of fudge.

In the kitchen, my mother weeps over the stove while we try to watch television shows that have no holiday themes, like a new Twilight Zoneish series called Darkroom *where in small vignettes narrated by James Coburn, army men come to life and kill their owners, and a caretaker removes the legs of unwitting houseguests, forcing them to act the part of the murdered disabled veteran whose checks the caretaker is stealing. We are punished for this. On December twenty-second, the vacuum runs nonstop and the house fills with the fumes of the oil finish. He gives up on the dining room, realizing that with all the furniture piled up in every other large space in the house, there is no place for a Christmas tree. He rushes the job in the living room, leaving little bubbles of finish that delight me for years afterwards as I find them and crush them with a fingernail.*

Christmas eve, he goes out to the postage-stamp front yard and cuts down the pine tree he never liked at the Northeast corner, leaving a two-foot decapitated stump with branches fanning out to the tree's full diameter. He plans to clean this up later. It occurs to me for the first time how fortunate it is that none of his parishioners live on our block. In the living room, where we are given the impossible directive to avoid walking on the floor unnecessarily, we put the couch back by the fire and set up the tree all day. Dad looks longingly at the unfinished project, rattles his car keys, and runs in to the church. The dining room, behind its dusty sheets, remains quiet and veiled.

We all see each other at the evening service, where everyone plays a part. Like every Christmas, Carolyn and Joseph play thurifer and crucifer, alternating roles. I sing in the choir, treble, where more adults can keep me from trouble with gentle hands on my shoulders. We come home after midnight. Christmas day we open presents and then he goes back to the dining room, but we all have new books to read by the fire, and in the evening, we eat sprawled in its glow. Dusty, sore, exhausted, resented, Dad relaxes. Joseph and I vie with the dogs for spots in front of the fireplace, play chess in the circle of its heat, obsess over a puzzle of interlocking red and yellow plastic pieces. Mom laughs at her bloopers on the organ during the evening service, and Dad chuckles along, safely disinterested. It is, perhaps, our best Christmas ever.

. . .

I Have Not Loved You With My Whole Heart

I had childhood obsessions about the circus. During the prayers of the people, that interminable litany of sore knees and aching backs, I pressed my lips to the dark grain of the pew before me and prayed for God to take my parents and make a traveling circus adopt us. I wanted to be a tightrope walker, though my balance had not so far turned out to be performance worthy. I could have saved my pleas; my family members were already showmen, we kids parading crosses and candles and thuribles, singing in angelic voices, Mom playing the vaudeville pipe organ, some of us sneering at the rubes who paid up in the collection plate. My father the ringmaster reeled them in, told them that the Paul Masson would turn to blood in their mouths.

Not that we didn't believe. We each had moments where we felt that the Episcopal ritual was the key to the world's unfathomable justice. We intoned "ashes to ashes, dust to dust" over the graves of small animals we buried in the backyard, even if we had killed them ourselves with the wrist-rocket or the air guns or our own hands. We attended classes on Christian education, though we often spent the time playing mercy or bloody knuckles. We were just too familiar with all the workings of the parish. We split our time between home and church and treated them as identical spheres. We'd seen the holy water drawn from the tap and haphazardly blessed. We'd climbed inside the bowels of the organ. Having dared to race in the stations of the cross, tripping siblings to beat them

49

to Christ's third fall in the Lenten dark of the church, we never fully recovered our reverence.

When I was twenty-six, I visited the Trappist abbey that my father called his spiritual retreat, Our Lady of Guadalupe in Lafayette. The abbey holds hundreds of acres of Willamette Valley forest, including a swampy piece down the hill, huge stands of rotting box elders. When I visited, the boxelder bugs were swarming. At every service, from matins through compline, while I knelt in the ceremonial darkness and asked to understand the events of my life, trying to imagine my father and his devotion to these men who never uttered a word but in praise of God, I heard the steady beat of the monks stamping the beetles against the parquet floor. As kids we were heedless of etiquette, devoid of the outward show of respect demanded, nearly as comfortable in pews as in our own beds. Both milieus came with their risks of judgment, punishment, salvation. We were happy to help my mother place cremation urns in narthex vaults. We were equally happy to pour the excess ashes, chalky and filled with flakes of bone, behind the azaleas. We prayed as fervently kneeling around Joseph's bed when our grandmother died as we did around the body of a roadkill cat we were interring ceremoniously behind the rosebushes. I can't say what the others prayed for. Perhaps their eyes were open even more than mine, perhaps they pointed at me while I pleaded with God to strike my father down, but I don't think so. Fearing God was easy for us. We lived with one of his terrifying emissaries, had heard his voice evicting us from the bathroom, putting us to bed, had seen his hand slap the TV to off.

We imagined that we knew the trials of asceticism. Episcopal priests don't make much money, we were often told. When our father was transferred from toney Ascension Chapel to the working-class Anglo Catholic parish of Saints Peter and Paul, which had a small population of "recovering Catholics" and a large group of very high church Anglicans, we moved across Portland to Mount Tabor, to a modest house on Yamhill Street. It was the first and only house my parents actually owned, and it needed a lot of work. We'd hear our parents argue about money every month when the mortgage came due, debate whether it was right to tithe to the church and trust that providence would provide or keep the money and avoid having the power shut off. Right about that time,

I started growing into what elderly ladies with rosaries around their wrists called "a tall drink of water." In third grade, I went from scrappy kid at the Portland Heights public elementary school to scholarship kid at Oregon Episcopal School across town in Beaverton, where my proficiency with the liturgy did not endear me to my peers. Nor did my outsize growth, nor my bookworm vocabulary, nor my incredibly shabby clothes. In fifth grade, my feet began to grow freakishly large, three sizes bigger than my father's or my brother's. My big toes wore through the canvas of my sneakers, and my other toes curled together in the front of my shoes. I burned through socks at an alarming rate, ending many days with bare toes sticking out in the rain. At school, when the subject of my shoes came up among classmates, I'd throw a punch. When it came up among adults, I stared straight ahead until someone would cough and change the subject.

Temptations of the material world loomed. We confessed to our parents that we yearned for a color TV, cold cereal with prizes in the box, frozen pizzas, and rooms of our own when we didn't have them, rooms without the six-foot-tall Mickey Mouse mural the previous owners had left on the wall of the room Joseph and I shared, which became mine off and on as we churned through the permutations of sleeping arrangements. I asked, unquietly, for clothes that were not patched, clothes no one had worn before me, ideally. Of course, my mother preemptively ironed patches on the knees of my trousers when they came home from the store to make them last longer, just as she bought them inches too long and then hemmed them up to be let out over their compressed life span as I lengthened inexorably.

Had Joseph and I not been metabolically altered monsters, maybe the household food supply wouldn't have been such an issue. When I learned, in college biology, that the locust is really just the migratory phase of a grasshopper that looks, well, like a grasshopper until a set of stress triggers changes its serotonin set point, makes it grow to enormous size and become a voracious eater, I felt like I was meeting a kindred spirit. When I learned a researcher could trigger the change in a grasshopper just by hassling it repeatedly, I felt I understood my childhood memories of eating a loaf of toast and a pound of butter in front of Saturday cartoons, my predilection for drinking a gallon of whole milk in front of *Magnum P.I.* and *Simon & Simon* when that was the Thursday lineup. Joseph started me on this practice, but it did seem convenient to drink right from the plastic jug, finish it over the course of two hours, and not have to put it back. In the same way, I learned that a blender loaded with a dozen eggs, two cups of sugar, a dash each of vanilla and nutmeg, and topped with milk made a good Sunday morning snack to tide one over until brunch, though if there were no eggs nor milk nor bread at brunch time, that meal wouldn't necessarily be forthcoming. When there was food in the house, we tended to eat it without authentic consideration of the consequences. Joseph might say to me, or I to him, "Yeah, brother, verily let us consider the consequences of our actions. If we eat this bounty of bread and dairy products, of leftover chicken or even thin soup with the abomination of overcooked zucchini, Mother will offer up lamentations and there will be nothing but dust for our next meal. Thus we should practice a modicum of restraint and self-control; it could only be meet and right so to do." After such a pronouncement, we would throw our heads back in laughter, and then gorge with even more abandonment. Somehow the food tasted even better when we had already admitted it was wrong to eat it.

One cool summer night we lay awake, sharing visions of the perfect meal. Meat played a leading role in these little imagined films. We held our bellies and moaned in agony at our own descriptions of pork chops, ice cream, hot dogs, roast beef, apple pie, and Coca-Cola. I liked to dream about massive roasts or grilled steaks. Joseph had a weakness for Chinese food, sweet and sour pork in particular. He could narrate dipping a piece of breaded pork in terms undeniably pornographic.

Joseph said the parable should be "easier for a fat man to go through the eye of a needle than to enter the kingdom of heaven." I grew so thin I often wondered if I could pass the needle test myself, could slip through the eye right into grace.

I comforted myself by scorning our more prosperous neighbors. Though unsure of my own salvation, I affected a self-righteous attitude about what I considered our poverty, convinced that all our neighbors would burn for their wealth. When pride failed me, I shoplifted candy bars from the drugstore and reveled in chocolate sin. At such moments, crouching dramatically in an alley, I dared to whisper toward heaven,

"Fuck you, God." When you know in your gut that you'll have to pay for it in the end, anything is possible in the short term, or so it seemed to me.

One July day, Joseph and I rooted through the bottles in the recycling boxes on the back porch. Dad never remembered to drive by the collection center, but insisted on saving the environment at the expense of our domestic ecology. The bottles hadn't been returned in months. Most had price tags on their lids and we began to total the expense represented by the wine jugs, the clear pint bottles of whatever scotch could be afforded, the brown and green bottles of beer. I read Joseph the numbers; he totaled them on the calculator he'd swiped from school. I don't recall the actual number now, just that it was some large fragment of what we knew to be Dad's salary, that it was much more than our car was worth, that it represented the single largest expense we'd heard about. We burst into the kitchen, shouting and waving our paper at Mom and Dad. I remember very well the tableau. They stood close together on the other side of the counter, two cups of coffee in the foreground. The lights in the kitchen were off, and the hideously decorated orange and harvest-gold room actually seemed shadowed and serene, lit by the sunlight coming through the sliding-glass doors to the porch. My mother looked at my father and bit her lip when we read the numbers from our sheet.

"Get out of here," he said softly. We must have looked puzzled because he stomped his foot and shouted it again. We ran in the direction he pointed, back outside. While I didn't understand the crime, I felt lucky that we were only banished. Mom's look, the quantity of bottles, Dad's hoarseness, the mildness of our punishment—these should have been clues. But our capacity for denial was endless. Joseph and I did not look at each other. We suspected that other priests didn't ordinarily spend Saturday nights with a bottle of scotch, the Bible, and their sermon notes. But he held the congregation's respect, heard their sins, married their children, buried their spouses and parents. Hadn't he left the altar at communion once to help the widow Burton back to her feet when she slipped on a stray bulletin? Hadn't he spent his Sunday afternoons with convicts at the jail? Didn't my father break through the hospital bureaucracy to bring communion to the governor stricken with prostate cancer? Didn't he put coins on Jerry Purnell's eyes after he slipped away? Didn't he wash the corns and calluses of every single parishioner's feet tenderly and with a smile on Maundy Thursday? Who could say he was a drunk? We ran to find Carolyn, engaged in some quiet bickering over the tire swing, and started a game of tag. I felt my mind regulating itself as if heavy steel doors were sliding smoothly across my brainpan to shut this in, keep that out, protect myself from what I could not understand.

I still don't know whether Dad's drinking fueled his anger or if his anger fueled his drinking. I suspect they fed off each other. If there was some root cause of both behaviors, I never knew it. Rubbing my bruises, I agonized over this mystery. He sure acted like a man with a secret passion. Over the subsequent years, he offered many explanations, in roughly this order: addictive personality, alcoholism, closeted homo-sexuality, Irish/Spanish ancestry, unresolved grief for his own father, bipolar disorder (which he still called manic-depressive tendencies), fundamental flaws in the Western model of human sexuality, the virus, fear of mortality. A pointed societal criticism explaining his rage as a reasonable response to a fucked-up world ran alongside these changing reasons. Perhaps he had some of the truth, but I never bought these explanations, separately or together. He raged because of who he was in the world. He pounded out deeply melancholic piano pieces of his own composing, broke into tears at the sight of American casualties on the TV set, and once sobbed when I played with army men at the dinner table. His trained voice rattled the house when he shouted for joy, which happened rarely, or when he was displeased, which happened often. In the little sailing dinghy he built from a kit with his hands and a lexicon of profanity, he laughed loudly when the wind had us going for the high side, when the chunky little boat would plane with a hum over the waves. Occasionally he embraced me roughly, upon his return from a bar, or his rounds to the hospital on a Sunday afternoon. At these moments, his stubble grinding my cheek, his eyes wet with inexplicable weeping, his breath rank with drink and ashes, I might have forgiven him. But his passions extended to his sense of justice, and I learned something of slow anger myself.

We were, he said, too much for him. He slapped us, pushed us, drummed a knuckle on the side of our heads. If the offense had been serious or the liquor powerful, he would beat us with his fists and feet, his belt swinging in one hand. We always began stoically, but since he wouldn't stop until we were crying and admitting our failures as children, we always ended up sobbing, even rolling on the floor, ruined. His voice boomed out. His face darkened to purple. He stood over us and cursed with the vilest language I have heard to this day. It wasn't the vocabulary, but the way he meant it. A smell came off him: incense, tobacco, sweat, guilt.

Once, we had taken our tongue lashing and some shoving, nothing too horrible, and been banished to the basement crying, all three of us. The offense is gone in time, as are the hands that pushed us against the wall, the voice that pelted our backs with threats as we scurried down the stairs ahead of the door's slam. This incarceration was not a hardship; we had a couch down there, and a phone, and the TV set, and a freezer that once in a while held popsicles. The floor was linoleum over concrete, but a thin, blue rug covered the corner where we spent our time. The carpet was excellent for wrestling, a sport Carolyn had given up years before, but which grew ever more interesting to me as I got bigger. It seemed like one of these years I might actually win a match.

You learn things when you have to, like how to roughhouse instead of mope, how to switch the stomach clenching of sobs into the stomach clenching of restrained giggles which, like the sobs, cannot be uttered out loud without consequences. I suspect various colleagues of mine with degrees in psychology would not see these as healthy skills, but I'm not so sure. I've relied on them to great advantage over the years and sometimes wish they were as sharp now as they were when I was twelve, or fifteen, or twenty-one. Perhaps the problem is that I no longer have a brother handy to wrestle with, to start antagonizing with faces, an "up yours" pumping of the fist, and then some whispered insults smiled across the air, like "dickbreath" and "asswipe" and "buttface," to which can only be replied "dogfuck" and "shitsuck" and "faggot." Carolyn chuckled on the couch, which just heightened the tension, because if we made her actually laugh, she'd bray and yuck till the wrath of God came leaping down the stairs in apoplectic fits. The added danger made us snort with laughter as we closed in on each other.

"Gimme a hug, Bro," he whispered with open arms.

"Oh, that's sweet, you penis-nosed fuck-wad," I replied as I held my arms wide as well. My bravado was really masochism. He was so much stronger, so much thicker in the arms and chest, so much more explosive in his movements. But I knew how to bear hug and how to tangle his legs and, to tell the truth, right up to the moment when he'd twist a joint too far or shove my face into the rug my face or otherwise cause me searing pain, I loved to wrestle with him, to be all tangled up and pushing our strength against each other. We tried to bring each other down by sheer force, then by tripping, then by switching holds. Carolyn began to yawn. I punched him in the gut. He shot right back with a blow that made me grunt. "Fucker," I panted. He did it again. I lowered my head and butted his teeth together with a clack.

We were into it now. He bruised my kidneys; I crushed his instep with my heel. He drove an elbow into my lower back and I kneed him in the crotch—not hard enough. "Stop it. Stop it, you idiots!" hissed Carolyn from the couch. Joseph and I made little sound. We clinched to strike each other's ribs. I tightened my forearm against his throat till his knees began to buckle. He rallied at the last moment, bent forward abruptly with his shoulder against my chest to get a little space, then somehow got his arm around my throat and his hip to my back. He bent me backwards, my hands scrabbling ineffectually at his grip across my throat. When he flipped me, I felt my feet leave the carpet, saw the arc my shoe made as it whipped up toward the ceiling, up over my head, up through the single bare light bulb in a burst of shinings, of glints. My head struck the floor in darkness. A second later, Joseph crouched over me with his lighter flame high. He was grinning. Carolyn's eyes shone from the corner. My father's yells shook the walls for a few minutes and then ended with the slam of a door. We sweated like dynamite.

One August Sunday I held the copper basin in one hand and poured water from the glass pitcher with the other. My father stood before me. The altar rose behind him. The organ soared on a sweet high note. I released the water in a thin stream as he cleansed himself for communion. The liquid rolled over his hands. His fingers shook, yellow from cigarettes, clenching in the cold. He began to cough. I stopped pouring. His chest heaved, tears rolled from the corners of his eyes. Unshaven bristles poked from the drawn lines of his face. When the coughing subsided, he pushed his palsied hands under the water again. Holding the chalice for Deacon Thompson, he spilled a little wine. After Deacon Thompson served him, he knelt very still for a minute, his hands still raised as if pantomiming. Dad flickered, as if for a moment he would simply become some stranger kneeling in soiled vestments by the altar. The deacon watched him intently. The moment passed. He celebrated communion and even drained the last cup, as was his duty.

Saints Peter and Paul was in some ways a good match for my father. Among the working-class, east-side parishioners, he was more at ease than back at Ascension Chapel. It was an Episcopal church, so there would still be mimosas on Easter morning after the vigil, but when they held a night of English and Irish song and dance, they also served Old English 800 in big bottles. It was ordinary to have a Saturday afternoon work session on the grounds, where families worked side by side weeding, laying down black plastic and mulch. Later, coolers of beer would open up in the parking lot. Dad would work and drink right alongside the congregants. And his interest in the mystical, in the ritual, in the theatre of "high church" fit with a parish festooned with statues of saints, where sometimes the whole congregation processed around the block singing a capella, where we performed passion plays during Holy Week, where prayers for reunion with the Roman Catholic church were regular. There was an active shrine to Our Lady of Walsingham, the Virgin always dressed in newly sewn silk robes and lit by flickering candles. The Irish ladies who made up "The Walsingham Cell" said she had a reputation for offering miracles for those who made offering. The old confessional booths were maintained with velvety cushions and a sliding screen between them, though they also had 1950s-era red lights like something you would see on a submarine above each door to indicate a booth in use. Fridays, there were always a few members of the church who dropped by in the afternoon to ask my father to hear their confessions.

My father was my confessor on the one occasion when I dared to shrive myself. I didn't know how unorthodox my request was. I didn't realize that there was anyone else in the city, or even the world, who would be a more appropriate choice. Who else could judge me? Who else could prescribe a fitting penance for a boy as rotten as me? There were never many seekers of forgiveness, so that particular Friday, I didn't have to wait more than an hour for Dad to emerge from his side of the booth. Only one hour of watching the second hand on the parish office clock. One hour of picking at scabs and straightening my hair. How much could I tell him, how badly would he hurt me, was forgiveness really so easy to gain? Everyone has such an hour in their childhood, which they face with grim resolve. I tasted bile in mine. I sweated a musky sheen over my hair. With one supplicant left, I discovered time's plasticity, its ability to stretch down to a weightless filament so thin I was sure time had broken, had snapped. I felt stuck in my moment, with the threads of before and after floating away, leaving me with only my burning bladder. The last parishioner walked away. I stood from my chair and walked toward the curtain. Its purple fabric billowed and rustled when he stepped out to make sure no one else was there.

"Dad?" His hand was reaching for a pack of cigarettes; his eyes registered only annoyance. My own hands trembled inside my pockets, where I had jammed them.

"What is it?" he asked.

"Will you hear my confession?" I could never read his expressions well. At that instant, one set of wrinkles, those around his dark eyes, relaxed, and another set above his eyebrows deepened. He took a deep breath and looked at me with his head turned slightly. He might have been suppressing a laugh, but I think now he was holding back tears. His skin seemed pale in the blue light from the stained-glass window. I would give anything now, anything at all, to know what I meant to him right then, in the moment when I surrendered myself to his mercy.

"Yes," he said. "Come on." Kneeling on the velvet, the dark and dust pressing on me, I read from the tattered confessional form. At the prescribed moment, I confessed my most notorious sins: my shoplifting, my schoolyard brawling, my lust for Miss April of '79, my false witness against my brother, my gluttony. He asked, gently through the wicker screen, if there was anything more, prompting my memory of a stolen test and cruelty to a stray cat.

"Anything else?" I thought my voice would betray me, but while I felt the hot tear run down to my chin, I managed to whisper.

"I cursed God. I cursed him as hard as I could." It was almost my greatest secret, but it did not seem to satisfy him.

"Anything else?" At last I lied.

"No, sir," I said, though my failure to honor my father burned brightest among the fires of my guilt. Prayers for his death breathed through my lips every night. I'd pretended his face was the one I spat on, the one I beat. I'd written a vow to kill him on a piece of stone, signed it with blood and thrown it into the river. Actually.

"Nothing else? You're sure?"

"That's everything."

"Well then, how will you make amends? What will you do to correct your mistakes?"

"I don't know," I stammered. I was surprised to find I had a role to play in my penance. "I could work at the drugstore for free. I could do Carolyn's chores. Or I could volunteer for litter detail at school."

"Those are good ideas, but not quite what I meant. Your sins are not really the theft or the lies, they are really failures to love."

"Sir?"

"You've got to love Christ, son. And that means loving everyone, as hard as you can. It's not easy, but if you concentrate on how good people are, how worthy they are, how God loved them so much he sacrificed his son for them, then you'll think twice about stealing, and lying and so on." Silence pervaded the air while I scanned the confessional form in the gloom. I didn't know where we were, or how to respond.

"It's the hardest, and the most important thing, son. Living with fierce love. I think it's a good sign that you cursed God. The opposite of love is apathy, not hatred."

"Sir?"

"You wouldn't argue with someone you didn't care about, would you? Why would you fight with someone unless you gave a damn about them? Oh, and don't worry about the lust. That's perfectly natural. That's just the way you're made."

Could this be my father? This gentle, understanding man? We finished the ritual and he put his arm around me as we left the booths.

"Wait a second and I'll give you a ride home," he said and went to kneel before the statue of Our Lady of Walsingham. He lit a candle with his cigarette lighter and bowed his head. My absolute shame overwhelmed me. So magnanimous had his forgiveness been, so gentle his counsel, that I knew my prayers against him were truly prayers against myself. He was a man of God and I, an ungrateful sinner, weak and cruel. He had given me no penance to say. No way to expiate my sins. When he rose, minutes later, he wiped his cheeks with a handkerchief. He didn't speak again until he yelled at me for playing with the car radio on the way home.

I've told it all wrong. Our lives were much more than I've written. I haven't told enough of the good times. As available acolytes we often missed school to work a funeral or a wedding. We stole beer from the kegs at wedding receptions. One Easter I drank champagne and necked roughly with the usher's daughter. There were midnight masses with the lights out and candles dripping wax onto the prayer books. We had water fights while we were supposed to be weeding the parish beds, and once at a clergy conference I sat next to the bishop of Oregon and he showed me how to peel oranges with a spoon. Vacation bible school, paper airplanes made out of bulletins, Lenten potlucks on Fridays where, after the interminable services, we would fill our plates exclusively from the dessert table before hosting wrestling matches in the basement. We had a radio for a while in our room, and listened to the Dr. Demento show late at night, laughing into our pillows.

And I never explain my mother well, her penchant for eating lemons with salt, for dry sherry and all things bitter or sour. She fought Dad in little ways. She burned dinner often, misplaced Dad's favorite socks, bought such cheap wine he could hardly drink it. She told us to save the heels of the bread loaves, because they were Dad's favorites, and he ate them with martyred distaste. I didn't discover the truth for years, that he hated them and ate them out of a sense of duty. She had bad eyesight and swayed her shoulders when she played the organ. She was tall but stooped. She liked mystery novels and courtroom dramas. The violence of one and the eventual punishment of the other appealed to her. We grew up singing the theme of Perry Mason and shouting that we knew the killer's identity. We were all close to her, adored her open-faced cheese sandwiches and bedtime stories. She was an abysmal housekeeper and seemed to believe the things Dad said about her, that she was an incompetent cook, a lazy gardener, and an unfit mother. This attitude contributed to the disarray of our home, the cobwebs in corners, carpets textured with balls of unvacuumed lint, colorful mold in the bread box, unweeded flower beds, and the generous freedom we enjoyed in Dad's absence.

One late summer weekend, Dad went to a conference in California. The rest of us drove to the coast early one morning and dug for clams in the green flats of low tide. That evening when we returned to the city's still heat, Joseph and I tossed a ball back and forth in a kind of labored play under the piled masses of scorching air. It was like wrestling under wool blankets. I soon tired and chose to follow intently the passage of an ant across the driveway until it disappeared into a crack in the foundation, and I stood up feeling dizzy and thirsty. Inside I found Mom standing over the stove. The drapes had been pulled all over the house to keep out the burning light. A dim redness came from the electric coil under the skillet where cockle's feet sizzled in bacon grease. She gave me one to chew on. It was sweet, fishy, and salty hot all at the same time. I asked her if what Joseph had told me the week before was true, that Dad had given up a lucrative offer to manage a pesticide plant in New Mexico in order to join the priesthood.

"Yes," she said, "That's true. And before that he gave up a position as a floor manager at a top-drawer department store in Boston, Massachusetts, to go back for his doctorate in chemistry." She turned back to the pan, and my eyes were adjusting so that I saw her half illumined by the stove light. Her hair was still dark then, with gray streaks in front, and her crooked nose softened in the shadows. I saw for the first time that the enormity of her eyes, her long neck, even the hintings of a crooked back combined into a certain honest beauty. Outside, the starlings came to roost in the walnut tree in a cloud of eerie chirping. I could not swallow.

"When we left, he bought me a very expensive dress. Your father could be so extravagant. I didn't want to leave Boston. We had a lovely apartment, and Joseph was still a babe-in-arms. Your father bought me an original. A dress made just once by a designer there at the store. A burgundy color. It was just beautiful." She sighed then, and chuckled. She extended another cockle's foot on the end of a wooden spoon. Even in my sadness I opened my mouth to consume it.

"What happened to it?" I asked through my teeth.

"Oh, gosh, that was so long ago. I lent it to your aunt for a party and she spilled food on it. But she didn't want to take it to the cleaners for some reason, and when she tried to wash it herself it was ruined." These words pierced me, a stake driven neatly into my guts and I began to weep, sobbing through a mouth filled with shellfish. "Oh hey, it was just a dress. That was so long ago." She wiped at my nose with the corner of her apron. "It's alright, it's alright." I would not be consoled. Someone had to weep.

The first time I tried to write about this chunk of time in my adolescence when my status of preacher's kid and roughed-up son of an alcoholic seemed to ball up together in some unavoidable way, I was in college, and I wrote it as a story for a fiction class. I edited out my sister and added twin younger brothers. I took on a gloomy, artificially weighty tone, and I wrote an ending. An ending, I've been taught, and in turn taught my students, often tells us what the story is about as it resolves or fails to resolve the causative situation at the heart of the narrative. And how is a family a narrative? What is at its heart? I wanted a shocker of a story, so I played up my father's heavy hand, composed a climactic scene where Dad goes too far and knocks one of the twins out cold. Then I step up and beat him to the ground with a crowbar. At the hospital, there's a scene between him and my mother where she forces him to get his story straight and stop crazy-talking about leaving us. I have him walk off stage when no one's home, and then provide "the occasion for the story" by giving a bleak account of his funeral. I never explain "the knot inside him that could not be cut" and in this, and this alone, the story's ending rings true. The rest, I came to realize, was eluding me.

It is true that in the fall of 1981 my mother got him drunk and we drove him to Raleigh Hills Treatment Center, located just a golf-course's length from the private school we all went to that year, Oregon Episcopal School. He was singing to himself in the passenger seat and paddling his fingers at the hair at her neck. It is also true that after five days of aversion therapy, where they closed off the bottom valve of his stomach and let him drink from their extremely well-stocked bar, we were to go see him after school, and we ran across the golf course's wet grass, each of us drawing water up our pants legs as we cut across the greens and avoided the shouting men in electric carts, out there in the misting rain. It seems odd now, but it was arranged that we go there without our mother, who would have been teaching piano on campus after school. Somehow, we got into Dad's room, where he looked yellowish and deathly. The whole place, not just his room but the attached bathroom, the hallway, the stairwells, all stank sourly of vomit. Dad's eyes were shot with blood, and his voice hoarse from weeping. The room was dim, but I wished it were dimmer. He sat up in the bed a little, pulled a pillow behind him and beckoned us into his arms. His whole body shook as he embraced us one by one. Then he explained everything.

In his confession, he admitted to things he had done and things he had left undone. Thoughts were off the table for the moment, but words and deeds, his strictness, his heavy hand, the awful things he had said to our mother, his generalized failures that remained unnamed but which I thought had to do probably with financial matters, he laid these offenses down on the coverlet of his bed like invisible cards. These problems stemmed, it turned out, from his alcoholism. "My alcoholism is a disease that has hurt me and my family," he said with a glassy robotic gaze and atonal speech. Okay, I'm making that up, but the speech was practiced, formal, and somehow forced. More honest, or at least more genuine, was his tearful promise that everything was going to be different from here on out. When we ran back across the golf course in the failing light, we stretched out, each finding our own space to run in. I had thought I might cry and was glad for the widening gap between me and my sister, my brother a vanishing point we moved toward.

At one of the three family meetings we had to attend over the next three weeks, big affairs where all the patients' families sat with them at the cafeteria tables and ate lousy institutional food before a speaker from AA or Alanon or the treatment center's own staff labored through a horror story about the demon rum, I pushed pork and beans around on a Styrofoam plate and followed my father's example of just drinking coffee. He still exuded exhaustion, but also an old mischievous spark I'd only seen when he was in his cups, or meeting an old friend, or crying out "hard alee" as our little dinghy tacked in winds that leaned her over. A nurse with the first digital thermometer I'd ever seen was making the rounds, checking temperatures and writing them on a clipboard. She bantered with each man as she made him hold the probe in his lips. Some of the guys at our table seemed to need the joking to break the guilty, shameful silence between them and their families, the wives who clutched hands and the kids who leaned in so close. The nurse actually looked like a waitress at a diner, or even a barmaid, and had the tired hilarity of her position down pat.

My dad was never a prankster and actually hated most humor. He once told me that he resented comedic writers because he didn't like to feel manipulated into anything, even laughter. So it was a shock to see him do it so smoothly, turn his head to the man next to him right as she changed the plastic cover on the thermometer. "What did you just call her?" he asked, grinning, and while the other man denied saying anything and the nurse put her hands on her hips to feign anger, Dad smoothly tilted half a cup of steaming coffee into his mouth, swallowing it only as the repartee behind him died down. He opened his mouth and she inserted the covered tip and her machine bleeped in alarm. The nurse actually gave a little shriek as Dad rolled his eyes back and pretended to faint, then everyone was laughing. "How did I do?" he asked her coyly.

"Just a hundred eighteen," she shot back, her head wagging. She made him cool down with water, then sit for the extra minutes while his temperature came back up. He looked sheepish with the cord sticking out from under his mustache and his cigarette burning out in the ashtray, but not as sheepish as he did when we said goodbye for the evening at the door, and he leaned against the porch rail as if it were his decision to stay there. Things did seem different.

It is also true that when the drinking stopped, his pot smoking went out of control and he funked his way through many a weekend, could not be removed from the bathroom for enormous stretches. Stoned, he was less likely raise his hands against us or crash his car into the cherry tree on the parking strip, but he was no less distant from us, and still capable of stomping up from the basement in a rage and slapping us to the ground. We all went to Canada one last time that summer, and he and my mother fought. Dad kept painting and repainting the hull of the boat—something was wrong with his thinning technique and the paint blistered in the sun while it dried—and that's where he was for days at a stretch, off from the cabin, sanding, painting, smoking, sanding, painting. The whole family began to move from passively fraying to actually unbraiding the ties that bind that summer. Carolyn and Joseph were eager to return home to friends and high-school diversions. Mom was so edgy that one night, when Joseph and I wouldn't keep quiet while we read by the candlelight on the porch where we slept, she came bursting into the room stark naked and swore she'd kill us if we didn't stop "fucking around!" We blew out the candles and lay there in perfect silence. It was like Dad had become a frightening woman and Mom was somewhere else. Then one day, Dad announced that he and my siblings would be headed back to Portland a week early, while Mom and I stayed on.

Mom and I have always been good at killing time together. When I was a kid, we were remarkably similar in our preferences for passing a sunny afternoon or a rainy morning. In either case, there would be books, mystery novels or science fiction probably, to flip through. We both napped shamelessly and liked to keep a fire in the stove if it was at all cold. We both liked to wander off into the woods or along the beach by ourselves, turning over rocks to see what we could find, eels or crabs or starfish. At night, we liked to read by the kerosene lantern and tell each other ridiculous stories with tenuous relationship to the truth. She let me drink coffee with as much sugar as I wanted, guessing rightly that I would use less and less as I got older and grow to only like it black or with a little milk. It was a quiet, strange week up in the cabin together. The highlight was our one trip in the boat, when we sailed across the harbor to the marina to buy some groceries. It was a grey day and while we were setting out a little squall came up. I'd been out in the weather many times before, but never with my mother at the tiller. Fear tightened in my gut as she hesitated in choosing a tack, as her voice climbed into a nervous register and foaming waves slapped the gunnels. This was a bay I had paddled across on an air mattress, a bay ringed with shoreline cabins so close that a few minutes swimming would have me safe, but I felt on that trip that the whole place had changed, become unpredictable and hostile, a trap for the foolish and unwary. We waited out the storm at the marina before heading back.

At the end of the week when we got home, I ferreted out of my siblings that Dad had taken them to see the new Steven Spielberg movie *E.T.*, even though they had promised, had sworn to wait until we got back so we could all see it together. Going to movies was one of our few successful family outings; we all went to *The Black Hole* and *Close Encounters of the Third Kind* and *Superman* (though the last was particularly weird, because a 747 crashed out on east Burnside and we had to wait until a midnight showing so we could see the passenger list scroll across the screen on the late news to be sure no parishioners had been on board). Dad seemed sheepish, but also kind of giddy about going to see *E.T.* again. Joseph and Carolyn kept torturing me by hinting at plot developments even though I started fistfights each time they tried to spoil the movie for me. Mom and I went alone a couple days later, and though we both expected to cry, and told each other so, we ended the movie with hard lumps in our throats, and shining eyes, but no tears. A couple of toughies we'd become. How's that for an ending?

Or this: I confess that I am often more thirteen than forty-nine, that I exist in a world formed years ago, that I am tortured by the very things that can no longer touch me: my father, the church, and the God of my childhood. I try to love the world with all the passion my father did, I try to make the best of the considerable joys of my life, and for God's sake, to not live in self-pity. But I do live often in a summer evening of that year, when Dad was headed back to the church for evening prayer and stopped in the driveway next to the old Nova to give me a hug. He had thrown on a leather jacket as the evening was turning cold, and the leather creaked as he squeezed me. Oh, Dad, I am so sorry that on that summer day when you hugged me tight and flipped your Irish ears against mine, when you said you loved me and waited, when the sun grew hot on our backs and you waited, the birds flew from the trees when the wind came up and you waited for me to speak, I kept still, just because I didn't want to lie.

Physics

The asphalt shingles of the roof burned with a sticky softness under my bare feet, searing right through the calluses I'd built up over June and July. The five-gallon bucket I was lugging had lost the plastic on the handle, and the wire cut into my hand while I maneuvered up over one dormer and down the other, following my brother step by silent step. When he wasn't looking, I splashed a little of my water on my feet to cool them, but I only got about three slow steps before the moisture steamed away. My green bucket was about two thirds full, but the sun was shining through the white one Joseph carried with visible difficulty and I could see the water line was near the top. I was proud to see that he was struggling too, because it meant I wasn't doing so badly. At twelve, I was almost six feet of pure gangliness; what muscle I had jumped around under my skin. Up there, as we approached the highest peak of the north-side dormer, the midafternoon sun was brutal. We were wearing next to nothing, just shorts, and the light was like a pressure on our backs, our arms, our faces. I was more preoccupied with burning up than falling, at least until we neared the edge. My tendency was to kneel down at the edges of rooftops, but we needed to be able to keep the buckets upright, and so had to stand there where the flashing banded the barrier between solid footing and a three-and-a-half-story drop to the side yard, where our sister was sunbathing.

We had thought this whole thing through in a limited way. Among the factors we had considered, though not fully, were the perfect surprise we could expect by striking from above; the baking heat down there on the browning grass; Carolyn's untied bikini top and exposed, half-sun-burned back (we could see the shine of sweat on it from the roof); the coldness of the water to be had from the utility sink in the basement; and that our window of opportunity would pass if we didn't get up there while the thin ribbon of sun that came between the houses was still directly under the highest point of our roof. We were giggling hysterically as we lugged the buckets up through the house, trying not to spill in the foyer, up the stairs, or from the steps of the ladder as we entered the oven of the attic, where blown insulation clung to our sweaty shins and forearms. I was just about incoherent with glee and breathless with effort as I passed my bucket out the window to Joseph. Then some of the things we hadn't considered began to nag at me. The roof had quite a pitch, and we had to get up on top of the dormers, a task that always left me feeling like the next wind would tumble me to a messy death among the rhododendrons off the front porch. Holding both buckets while Joseph scrambled up, I swear I could feel the rotation of the planet trying to rock me back on my heels, just when I had no hands to hold on to anything with. The trouble really started when I had to pass the bucket up to Joseph, who was swearing in a long unbroken hiss as he pressed his bare chest to the hot shingles to reach down for his bucket, which I couldn't lift with one arm. Finally, I put mine down carefully, losing some more water in the process, while I used both hands to pass the full one up. Once I'd gained the upper roof, I moved dizzily in a realm of white light. I could just about feel my pupils shrinking to pinpricks.

Part of what we hadn't considered was our motive. Surely we were operating in the same mode that has characterized sibling cruelty through time immemorial, but specifically, why did we want to startle, soak, shock, and embarrass Carolyn into rearing up with her top untied in sudden panic? I submit that in part, our temptation to ruin her afternoon was the same one that drove us to stomp around in untrammeled snow or graffiti newly painted walls. She was a little too perfect there in her pink bikini. Carolyn was fifteen that summer and had just begun the magical transformation from greasy-haired, ungainly, weirdo girl into the stylish, attractive blonde with the Irish cheekbones she would become. These days, whenever I visit Carolyn in Sacramento, I am reminded that my awkward, messed-up sister turned into a happily married, well-educated professional with a knack for finding the right sunglasses to accentuate her pale blue eyes and upswept, thick blond hair. At fifteen she was becoming, for the first time in my consciousness, something beautiful, grown up, sexy even. I think it fair to say that that cusp of change drew us to the line of the roof in the August heat, had us teetering on the edge of the dormer with our buckets of cold water, and it was also what made us pause for a long second before mouthing a silent three two one and upending our buckets.

The way I had thought it out was that the water would splash over her back, already glowing with sun, and she would scramble up, fumbling for her top, hair drenched and tangled, voice rising in the familiar wail of curses and insults, all her serenity and beauty dashed into bedraggled chaos. She'd be reduced to the state we saw when we dumped salt on her cereal, when we called her fat in fifty different ways in about 150 seconds, the same state I knew from the inside out when they teamed up to tell me I was the mailman's child, when they sat on me and read aloud the last page of the book I was reading. We would roar with laughter and spit at her if she figured out where we were. If my brother foresaw more of what was to come, he didn't say.

The one factor we really needed to have considered was physics. I've had a lot of time since to think about it. The side yard was downhill at essentially the same grade as the basement, putting Carolyn the height of the basement, the height of the main floor, the height of the second floor, the height of the attic, and the height of this attic dormer's peaked roof below the approximately 8 gallons—17.6 kilograms or 64 pounds (pint a pound, the world around)—of water accelerating towards her at 9.8 meters per second squared. We hadn't thought about hydraulics either, how water is essentially incompressible, leading to phenomena like skipping rocks and blistering belly flops and hydraulic jacks that use water to transmit close to 100 percent of the force applied on one end to the other. We would never have just swung two five-gallon buckets of water out over our sister and dropped them three and half stories to crush her back, but we didn't hesitate to do that with their heavy, cold contents. If we had poured the water slowly it wouldn't have been such a big deal, but we upended the buckets together and could watch both the leading edge of the falling deluge and its trailing droplets strung out a few feet above. It took a long time to hit; I held my breath and felt that tingle of adrenaline you experience when you can't take a thing back. The water hit with a smacking thud, and instead of screaming or wailing, Carolyn convulsed on her blanket and curled up in a ball. The noise of the impact was so bad we didn't laugh even once. Joseph started moving right away, calling down to her was she alright? In a second he was far ahead of me, running to the front of the roof, throwing his bucket into the front yard where it landed with a clatter while he swung himself down to the window and ducked inside. He didn't wait for me, even though dropping down to the slanted roof below was always the scariest part—I felt like I would tumble backwards right after I hit.

It took me a minute or two longer to get down from the roof and attic and through the house, so I wasn't there when Joseph scooped her up into a hug from where she was still gasping, her face turning colors. He held her and told her over and over again to breathe until, eyes wide and cheeks bluish, she finally started to get air in appreciable quantity down into her lungs, from where it would return as a sobbing interrogative. She sobbed, "why?—why?—why?" over and over, trembling in his arms. He helped her get her bikini top back on and got her to her feet. Following behind, still mute, I could already see the welts forming on her back, as if four hands had slapped her as hard as possible at the same moment. The bruising didn't peak for several days, but Carolyn didn't really complain about it. What continued, continues to be the mystery, both to her and to me, is why we would hurt her so badly, come out of the sky like disaster itself and knock the wind out of her, bitch-slap her innocent, harmless afternoon into a choked struggle for breath and then the hyperventilation of pain and anger and betrayal, become for a few terrible moments the agents of a world always ready to rear up against the vulnerable and harmless without more than a second thought?

Somehow we convinced her not to tell. I have always been afraid of what we convinced her about all three of us and the way life was bound to be.

One-Two

What I didn't like about boxing was getting hit. Specifically, I didn't like getting hit in the face. Really, any blow on the head resulted not only in sharp pains, lingering headaches, the occasional migraine, but also more seriously, a sinking sensation of doom, an elevator-dropping queasiness about how things were going to be. I couldn't help it—even if I covered well enough to avoid black eyes and re-breaking my poor blood-spouting nose, a tag to the temple left me reeling. In one of the last matches between Joseph and me, a bout suggested by our mother, who was tired of hearing us call each other increasingly foul names, I took the first hit on the head, right on the cheekbone, and it made me dance with the harried feeling that it was only a matter of time. The lamps in the picture window flooded the front lawn with light. We circled on the frosty grass, careful of our footing, and I tried to go after him whenever the light was behind me, so that I could come out of darkness like an avenging angel or nightmare. When we were nine and thirteen, this might have been the advantage I needed, but now, at sixteen and twenty, we were mostly grown, both of us over six feet, both athletes, and he played college football. When I waded in for what turned out to be the last time, I came at him hard with three backhand left jabs and a right to the body, and he grunted with it, but didn't back down. A left knocked my guard hand into my own face and then I guess it was a straight right that made the world explode in light, and the feeling that something was broken behind my eyes. I came to with the cold seeping into my back, my brother grinning down out of the dark at me.

What I liked about boxing was hitting, making the tag, driving home. When we started, we had only one pair of gloves, so he took right and I took left. We held our ungloved hands behind our backs and worked exclusively from the defensive crouch, bodies turned sideways to each other. In that position, you can hide behind your glove, protecting your head, while you move into position for an uppercut or jab. You only throw a cross when your opponent is already reeling or dazed, when his guard is down; otherwise, since you have no second hand, you are terribly vulnerable to a series of fast shots. So you work on speed, on patience, on wearing the other guy down, intimidating him. With few full-power shots, no one is bleeding much, and you can while away an hour circling and circling back in the driveway, sweating despite the fall chill. We had a beat-up old radio with one speaker that we plugged into the garage outlet. While we wore each other down, we listened to classic rock. If Survivor's "Eye of the Tiger" from *Rocky III* came on, we'd go berserk, taking any amount of punishment to get in there and do some damage. We swore at each other mercilessly and I remember laughing a lot, usually right before I got knocked down. Sometimes I'd crack him up with a goofy expression and then windmill past his half-hearted defense and we'd both end up laughing about it. Once we had two full sets of gloves, my favorite moments were in the clinch, a one-armed hug that puts you inside the opponent's arm while you work the body, just hit and hit and hit and he hits and hits and hits until one of you breaks apart or you both fall down in agony. That felt like love to me.

I didn't like the fear. So many kinds of fear to deal with in the moments when we laced up. It felt a little like getting ready to die to me, and more so as I got bigger and stronger and boxed with others who weren't always kind enough to let me win once in a while. I had the distinct and entirely accurate sense as I sized up an opponent that I was about to cause him bodily harm, bruise him, knock his brain about in his skull, cut him above the eyes, bloody his lip, bloody his nose, cause his eye to swell shut, and pummel his midsection till his organs hurt underneath muscle clenched in soreness. He would hurt for days. Of course, I also had the distinct and entirely accurate sense that his tight-eyed grin was all about the same intentions.

"Gonna fuck you up so bad we'll be scooping you off the pavement with shovels by dark."

"You sure can talk."

"Don't worry, I walk too. These shoes were made for walking."

"That's a fucking Nancy Sinatra song, you feeb. For that, I'm going to have to break your jaw."

Could he actually break my jaw? I gave him my back to hide my worry, looked up at the gnarled walnut tree that hung over our backyard, dropping black-hulled fruit that stained our clothes in the late fall. My bigger fear was that I would cry, especially if boxing someone other than my brother. It had happened before, after one of those blows that knocks the breath from you—not the air in your lungs, your actual breath, your capacity to breathe, knocked out, unavailable, and the tears start welling. I wanted to be the fighter, but holding a bandana to my nose—probably broken again—I was just the child, weeping in my blood, thinking of the long ache the day would become. I was afraid of tripping—I had to box without my glasses and kept my opponent close inside the fog that blurred everything beyond five feet of distance, but I couldn't watch the pavement or grass, and sometimes fell. I'd ask for mercy, get back up feeling shameful, feign an injury if I had to, then wallop him while he was distracted.

Tell you the truth, I liked the fear. I ate it up. The fear was what made it real, made the whole exercise of gloves and footwork, the speed of attack and backpedal, something that mattered, because if I did it right, gave in to my adrenaline and quickness, my basic gut-level desire to do damage to another human being, I could watch the fear widen in my opponent's eyes. And I could fight it off myself, come through the weight of danger to act, push into the circle of his blows, take several and keep on swinging until the chance for a solid right came through and then, arms burning with fatigue, snap his head back with one sharp contact, and he would fall.

There is a species of writing, often used by applicants for schools or jobs, that always ends with what the writer has learned, and if I were in that mode, I'd talk here about what boxing taught me—the discipline, the toughness, the knowledge that I could fight on through adversity. It wouldn't be true. I was never disciplined about anything, never particularly tough. What boxing really taught me was the combination, the one-two, the basic fact that a blow can rock you back on your heels, and a second one can take you down. That tough as you are, disciplined as you are, courageous and joyously masochistic, the second one leaves you cold, spinning, worrying about what the world will hit you with next, sick with the pain of it, looking up at the stars or the cloudy sky, waiting for the rest of it to come.

IIII

In the kitchen at my father's place, where the orange Formica island formed a head, were four surprisingly distinct and parallel lines. They were grooves, blackened by age, that cut through the color to what lay beneath. They ran two inches perhaps, growing deeper as they approached the counter's edge. When I set the places at the counter for a Sunday dinner before *60 Minutes* and the Disney movie, I put his napkin on the left, folded so he could grab the far corner and unfold it in one smooth sweep of his hand, the fork just inside the ironed edge, the plate in the middle, and the knife and spoon directly on those marks. When alone in the kitchen, I sometimes fingered them, digging into the grime there with my thumbnail and no doubt making them deeper with the tip of a pocketknife. The four marks remained after he left, and marked his place so completely that no one else liked to sit there. Not my mother, or brother, or sister. Not me.

They were formed, of course, by the edge of his knife as he beat on the countertop to a roared "Enough!" or "Goddamnit!"—the former providing him one short opportunity to whack his cutlery down, the latter affording three, timed with the *g*, the double *d* and the *t*, each louder than the last, the knife finally lifted well above his head before coming down with a tremendous bang. The first time he did it, we all jumped. Formica chips ricocheted off the water glasses, the dog stopped barking, and my sister and I stopped arguing. The parrot squawked and shuffled to the other side of his cage, sending down a fine, dandery dust to settle in the silence. Dad's eyes flashed at each of us, sitting bolt upright on our stools, in turn. Carolyn, who had been crying already—as was her wont when I refuted her arguments by calling her stupid, fat, and hideously deformed—let out one of her braying sobs and broke for the stairs, *waaah*ing all the way to her bedroom. Normally, my brother and I would have begun our much-practiced impression of a fire engine siren, wailing in tones that rose and fell just slightly out of synch with each other and the keening upstairs. On rare occasions, not only would the dog howl along in reasonable harmony, but even Dad would join in the cruelty, tilting his head back and making us laugh when we stopped to try and get breath. On this occasion, all was still at the counter. We could hear Carolyn, of course, in the distance, and close by, my father's angry breathing. I kept my eyes on my plate and waited.

In 1986, when news came from Mount Hood that the initial discovery of three of the missing climbers had only been the discovery of their bodies frozen in the snow, muted crying began all over the hall. I turned my head left and right to my freshmen classmates whose shining eyes made my own start. The headmaster began to speak about prayer for our remaining friends and teachers, but Scott Klemp, friend of so many who died and so many of us left behind, lurched his bulk off the floor and strode angrily down the hall, his voice rising. He was huge and bearded at seventeen, and a kind bear of a man-to-be. We heard the crash of the locker door he hit on his way out of the building, and later we saw the metal caved in beneath the ridged air vents. He shattered something in his hand doing it. Some said it was a stupid attention grab Scott would regret as he wore that cast to all the funerals of the spring. I was proud of him somehow, and envious—what a clear sign of grief and rage.

While my father favored knife-banging at the kitchen counter, whose mid-seventies-inspired color scheme of orange, black, and gold was never really in style, he was less destructive at the dining room table, whose antique mahogany he had lovingly refinished. There he used open-handed slaps that sloshed drinks and made the china and my mother jump in unison. He also employed strangely complex maneuvers, like the one he demonstrated when he caught my brother and me watching TV on a sunny day when we were supposed to be cleaning the garage. He had already come downstairs once and unplugged it, but we had come back inside on some pretext and plugged it in again, keeping the volume low. We were, unfortunately, unaware that he had since relocated to the living room. When I heard him coming, I hunched my shoulders and squinted against what was sure to hurt, but he just stomped across the floor, pulled the plug, and wrapped the wire once around each fist. I don't know anyone with freakish enough strength to pull electrical cord apart, though I think he'd hoped for the cord to split in a fraying and awesome visual reminder of his capacity for correction through destruction. In any case, the plug did rip off. Holding the cord in one hand, he launched into a fiery sermon on obedience, the idiocy of commercial programming, and our failures as sons, but we did not hear it well, distracted as we were by a telepathic exchange occurring while we stared at the shameful little plug lying uselessly on the counter.

"My God, he's broken the TV. Our lives will be empty and cheerless."

"Alas, woe to our summer plans. But wait, I see the exposed wires."

"Yes. We are saved. Do you still have the electrical tape and pliers from our experiment with electrical detonation of homemade explosives?"

"Indeed, little brother. All will be well."

And in fact, Dad worked himself into such a state that he exited the house with the accompaniments of 1) a slamming door, 2) a slamming car door, 3) the roar of his Chevy Nova's engine, and 4) a squeal of tires as he pulled away from the curb. Mom came into the kitchen with a stunned look and questions about our latest success in driving our father to evil, but we were already at work with her good paring knife, stripping the wires a little further. That evening, when Dad stumbled in with his customary reek of beer and tobacco, the whole family was watching *The Muppet Show* while something sizzled on the stove. He never said a word about it, and I have never known if he was glad, defeated, angered, amused, or had forgotten already the impulse that had led him to reach out and break something.

The explosives did in fact exist outside of telepathic reveries. Though in today's world my brother and I would surely have drawn the attention of child welfare authorities or juvenile law enforcement for a variety of reasons, our successful creation of sophisticated bombs before either of us had completed middle school best captures our wildness. My brother gets almost all the pyrotechnical credit, but I helped with research, bought ingredients at the drugstore, and provided unskilled labor and morale-boosting chatter. We devised a method using an empty CO_2 cartridge from our parent's soda siphon. We bored out the opening and hacksawed crosshatching on the body—it looked cool, but we were also thinking of shrapnel possibilities—and pushed our homemade black powder in there carefully, along with some wadding. Our guide in this undertaking was our ever-handy copy of *The Anarchist's Cookbook*, that tome of advice for the would-be disrupter of societal institutions. The cookbook gave us the recipe for the powder, household sources for the ingredients, primers in shaping charges, etc. It also discouraged us from working with black powder, not by directly criticizing pipe bombs, but by sexing up other possibilities like plastique, homemade nerve gas, and nitroglycerine. We agreed to delay building these other, more exciting weapons of destruction until we'd mastered, perfected even, the simple task of creating a reliable, old-fashioned explosive with electronic ignition.

The real pride of the thing, the genius of it, came from a discarded toaster. We harvested the heating elements in long sections of wire, which we had discovered were able to develop explosive resistance to unchecked wall current. So, down in the basement, with the stereo blasting Journey or Def Leppard or Night Ranger, we inserted a loop of toaster wire into our prepared casing, topped off the powder and wadding, and dripped melted wax from a lit candle to seal it. The charges looked lethal, too good to be true. We buried the first one under two feet of dirt in the yard, after splicing one end of an orange extension cord to the fuse wires. The cord snaked under the side door of the garage and was plugged into a switchable receptacle there, next to the window we stood behind to watch. The window was actually plastic, a fact I mention just to point out that we were not so stupid as to set off an explosion that might shower us in shards of glass. In fact, though we doubted it would go off at all, in our wise maturity and forethought, we actually stepped aside from the window before Joseph flipped the switch.

It wasn't such a big noise, just a deep whump and a sharp crack, the former caused by the blast that blew a three-foot-wide crater in the ground, the latter by a diamond-shaped chunk of steel we found embedded in the windowsill. We figured that a similar one, or perhaps just a rock, was responsible for blowing one of the asbestos tiles off the corner of the house near the master bedroom window on the second floor. We buried later charges in concrete blocks and other muffling to contain that blast.

What were we about exactly? What were our goals? This challenge was different than our efforts to boost the transmitting power of walkie-talkies until they crackled interference on the TV set, or tap phone lines and record our parents' private conversations, or build a radio-controlled model boat, or electrify each other's doorknobs. Nor did we plan bombing campaigns or abuse of animals. We worked simultaneously to build a stronger and stronger explosive and a stronger and stronger container for the explosion. With each successful effort we were left exactly as we were that first day, listening to the debris rain down and then watching the steam rise from the damage we'd done.

I hesitate to write such a secret, but I had forgotten those four marks at my father's place until the spring of my thirty-second year, when, in a drunken rage, I yelled at my wife and beat the tabletop with my fist. I confess, this is not the first time I hit things in my adult anger, each time reinjuring an old strained knuckle on my right hand, which swells and sends purple bruising all down my pinky. I have struck out at things in rage much of my life, and I have broken things: cutting boards, tools, windows, carpentry projects whose remnants I then had to pick up and reform with shaking hands. At eleven I kicked through a door behind which my sister was calling me names. In my middle thirties, I still cleaned up scrap lumber by snapping it into smaller and smaller pieces. I have hit other people, though not in anger in many, many years, I think in part because they are not the target of my anger. I have sublimated anger into more productive venues, but never as successfully as when the real mark is on myself, when I've worked my body into a knot with lifting or backpacking or running or just pushing through too many hours without sleep.

"You're pretty hard on yourself, son," my buddy Todd used to tell me. And I know he was at least in part right. This all became clearer to me on that night I had beat the bejeezus out of my hand on the kitchen table again; while Mary cried upstairs, I picked up a steak knife and cut a series of lines into the side of my hand, as if to teach it a lesson. When I had four, I stopped.

The marks at my father's place have occupied my thoughts frequently over the years. I think of how often a dinner's hilarity or chaos culminated in such an explosion, and I marvel that there were only four lines, cleanly cut and not wide. Wouldn't you have to aim for them? Wouldn't you have to be thinking on some level that, while the room was tastelessly decorated, and the children really needed correction, you didn't want to fuck up that countertop too badly or else you'd have to replace it? Walk yourself through it: you are supremely pissed off at these bratty kids, the overall squalor of a life with too many pets, not enough money, a failing marriage, your own personal demons, including the alcoholism that makes you really want to just sweep your wife's crappy cooking off onto the floor in a glissando of crashing china and glassware and cutlery so that all that is left is a bottle and your pack of cigarettes and they would all leave you there, just you and your goodies. You're at the edge, about to yell, and when you do let out the outburst, you can't help it, you've grabbed your knife and you've raised it up and then . . . you strike it down methodically, exactly, with precision to minimize the material damage. You are out of control, in control. You are snapping, deftly. This is kicking the dog but not hurting it, picking up the ceramic figurine to smash on the floor and then remembering that it's the one your grandmother gave you, and so putting it back ungently. This is agreeing to run the errand, but not putting on your seatbelt when you pull out of the driveway, at least not until the first intersection. This is drinking too much at the funeral of a friend, but not enough to make yourself ill, as if your grief is worth a hangover but not actual vomiting. When I cut lines into my hand with a steak knife, I was not doing permanent damage, nor endangering my health in any significant way. Oh, it was crazy, about the most clearly crazy thing I'd ever done, but not life threatening. I wasn't cutting my wrist, or slashing with the thing. In fact, I cut four, careful, slow, neat lines, each time letting the serrations of the blade catch and dig in until it made my hand clench with pain. And then I stopped, and I stared at what I'd done for a long time.

. . .

Thom Jones has come for the afternoon and dinner, and the day is full of hilarity. He makes droll jokes, speaks in thirty different ridiculous accents, laughs his ruddy face ruddier. He and Mom are in cahoots in the kitchen. He and Dad are drinking cocktails well before the usual happy hour. When he finds we have no salad spinner, he asks us how we live. It's 1980 for Godssake. I mean, people. I don't know if I can work in these conditions. Then he puts the greens in a tea towel, folds the corners together and whips it round and round above his head. Drops of water spray the parrot, who squawks, the dogs, who bark, and me, who squeals. Thom Jones has come, and there is never crossness or spankings or yelling when he is here, just laughing and silliness and good food. I hang on him, call him my best friend, get in his way at every turn. Mom reminds Dad that he has an errand to run at a boat shop out by the airport, just fifteen to twenty minutes away. Maybe he should take me along and give Thom a break. Like me, Dad seems disappointed to have to leave the fun, but he downs his drink and we get into the car. When I reach for the radio, he slaps my hand. We don't speak as he heads out toward the river.

He is quick at the shop, picks up something for the boat without his usual coveting of equipment, charts, and books. Back in the car, we travel back east toward Mount Tabor and home. The afternoon sun is behind us, bright on the empty lanes of the road. Way up ahead, I see a silver sedan, or at least it seems silver in the bright reflection, heading the opposite way. It takes a long time for the distance to close. I'm staring at the other car carefully, because it seems to be in our lane. I take my eyes off to look at Dad, whose eyes are fixed forward, examining the road ahead. I look back to the windshield, and see that we are far over the yellow line, headed inexorably, without even a slight turn of the wheel, at the other car, which seems to be slowing, flashing its lights. In the last second, Dad stands on the brakes, and there is a mighty squeal of skidding tires. We hit full on, the driver's-side corners of both cars ramming together at the bumper. Glass breaks, my whole body wrenches against the seat belt, the hood crumples subtly. Dad looks out the window as if he's just woken up. He puts his forehead on the wheel for a second, makes sure I'm OK, then steps out of the car.

. . .

Gaydar

A lot of narratives about closeted gay people include heavy emphasis on why everyone should have known. Hypocrisy brings schadenfreude, it seems, and anyone with a double life is doubly interesting. I'm sure lots of other people thought my father was gay. But the idea never, ever crossed my mind until the night he came out to us around the dining room table.

Years later, walking or driving around Portland, or even just watching TV, he would pronounce that his gaydar had pinged, and he would declare a stranger's orientation with conviction. "Oh. He's gay. I mean, look at him. It's so obvious." I might turn my head to watch a man in a T-shirt and jeans, work boots, short hair, no belt, walking ahead with his back to us. Or a man in a tailored blue suit, grey at his temples, swinging an umbrella. Or a man on a motorcycle, leather jacket, handlebar mustache. What was the signal? The haircut? The gait? Were there secret codes in the colors of their socks? What? Dad couldn't explain. He was sure, completely sure, about several of my friends in high school, and I always worried what he thought about me. But as a kid, gay people to me belonged to another nation, or race, or planet. Gay men anyway—I had some ideas about lesbians, whose activity could be seen in various pornographic magazines. In those spreads, they seemed to favor soap suds, showers, bicycles, and a lot of suntan lotion. I guess my twelve-year-old ideas of lesbians were about as sophisticated as my ideas of mermaids—really sexy, but only available in mythology.

Gay men, whom we called "faggots" or "fags" or "queers," just weren't really on my radar. Now, in the twenty-first century, when gay rights and the issues of marriage and military service and bullying and hiring policy are front-page items in every newspaper, that seems bizarre. But try and think back to 1983. Gay men were mainstream comedy items, like John Ritter in *Three's Company* or Tom Hanks in *Bosom Buddies*. In both those cases, the character in question was only *pretending* to be gay, but was actually a red-blooded heterosexual American man in a strange situation. There was a guy on Dallas who was supposed to be bisexual, but I could barely follow that show anyway—it seemed like a soap opera in the evening with twang. I think the closest thing we had was Tom Sellek in *Magnum P.I.*, who had the butch mustache and simpering relationship with Higgins (who had the Dobermans mind you) and the serially pathological relationships with women. But Magnum was supposed to be straight, even if Tom Sellek played him a tad queer.

Queer, by the by, was a term I mostly heard in reference to the game Smear the Queer, which I hope has another name now, but probably still is based on the idea of tackling and crushing the one who is different. Funny, how in that game, what you wanted most of all was to be the one with the ball, to be the center of everyone's attention, to dodge and twist and stay alive until you had to pass it on to some other runner, who you then pursued with the hope of taking him down.

There was a child in my third-grade class who, in retrospect, was at least questioning the standard construction of gender. His name was Ashley, and we got along fine. Our school uniform allowed for blue, green, or white shirts—he always wore white or pale blue. He was thin and fair, with fine longish hair he parted in the middle and combed straight. He wore nail polish and loved to put on lip gloss with the girls on the playground. That year, scratch and sniff stickers were the tradable, collectible, must have items, and the kids, mostly rich kids to be frank about it, at my school competed to have full collections. I remember Ashley, standing at a railing above the stairs to the main playground and made up like a member of a glam band, tossing his collection to assembled masses of second through fifth graders, who squealed and cheered and called for more. I remember too the day he went away. He'd insisted on wearing the girl's uniform all morning, and by lunchtime recess the school had had enough. I really do remember that day especially clearly, as Ashley had been ensconced with a group of girls out on the playground and seemed really happy in his tartan jumper and white blouse, happier than any other boy or girl. He had a tin box, like a lunchbox but smaller, that he was carrying around, and he had his stickers and a deck of playing cards in there. Rumor was he had some dirty pictures too, but by third grade we all had found caches of those in a brother's or uncle's or father's or grandfather's closet. By third grade, most of us boys had perused a *Penthouse* or *Hustler* or at least a *Playboy*. Some of us had read all the articles in multiple issues of each. For the record, the pictures were always titillating and relatively harmless, but the letters and fiction were downright disturbing and kept me up at night. In any case, the PE teacher came to get Ashley during recess, took him by the arm, and dragged him across the playground to the office. Ashley wept, he sobbed, he screamed. Many of us ran alongside crying too, but we couldn't help him. We didn't even know, still don't know, what was happening. He went into the office, the bell rang, we walked silently in a single file line behind the designated line leader back to class. He was never mentioned again.

So how might I have known? What should have clued me in? I didn't really know the stereotypes, even if Dad was falling into them. Looking back now from such a distance, I guess my Dad's whole swarthy, earthy, volatile nature should have been a red flag. Add to it his bushy mustache and leather coat, his pacificism, his love of singing, his predilection for really tight jeans, and his tendency to fall for the pitch of the Greenpeace guy, the storm-window salesman, or the Encyclopedia Britannica representative (as long as they were lanky and bearded), and you could have a compelling case that he was sending a signal. But it was the late seventies and early eighties I'm talking about here. Dad didn't exactly stand out in terms of appearance or behavior a twelve-year-old would know about, at least not one as clueless as I was.

In the last years of my parent's marriage, Dad did give me a couple of heavy hints, intentionally or not. One of these worries me still, because I have no way of taking it back or making it better. The others were just "huh, don't know what to think about that" moments that I really just put aside until they made sense. For instance, I asked him what "buggery" was during the summer of 1982. It wasn't an idle question; I was reading William Golding's *Rites of Passage*, which I'd found on my parent's shelves. I'd loved *Lord of the Flies* and was hungry for anything by the same author, only to find that his other books were much more difficult. We were sailing in light wind, which is how I got away with holding the jib sheet in one hand and a paperback in the other. We were still close to shore, not even around the big rock in the middle of Browning Harbor, when I asked what I thought was an innocent question. He jumped in his seat.

Now I know that he had negotiated some freedoms of his own in that year, and was in fact engaged in several ongoing relationships with other men. He went to bars too, and picked up tricks. I've wondered if he took off his wedding ring and his clericals before he walked in and ordered his drinks, but I'll never know. Maybe he thought I was on to him, or that I'd overheard some conversation involving archaic slang. He didn't say anything for a long moment before he asked me why I wanted to know. I explained that the word kept coming up in the book I was reading, which was about a long sailing voyage to Australia where some of the characters seemed to be doing something that made everyone else mad.

"Buggery is also called sodomy, or anal sex," he explained in a tight voice.

"Oh," I said.

"It's a way that men make love, that's all," he said.

"With each other?" I asked. The wind was picking up and I would actually have to start paying attention soon. We had planned to catch the evening breeze and sail across the harbor to pick up a crab pot which, if things went well, would hold our dinner. Talking about anal sex wasn't really on my agenda, but at twelve, you can't actually admit what little you do know about sex, so there was no way out, except the one Dad gave me.

"Buggery often implies some inequality too. Is one of these men older, or in a position of power over the other man?" I paged back through my book, searching Golding's dense prose, evermore disappointed that this novel wasn't the easy read *Lord of the Flies* had been.

"I'm not actually sure. I can't tell what's going on," I admitted. He encouraged me to hold on to the book for a bit.

"It will get easier as you get older. Don't rush it," he advised. "Now, prepare to tack, we've got a bit of wind coming." I was glad to end the conversation, but it did strike me how it made him jump.

We had another, simpler interaction that summer that probably had nothing to do with being gay. Or maybe it had everything to do with it. We were in the boat again. Seems like that summer, once Dad got the boat painted, he was always wanting to go out with one of us kids. We took turns, not enthusiastically. I think we all liked to sail, but the enforced closeness with our father never felt natural. Especially when he put on his wise, pastoral voice. On this occasion we were coming home, not fifteen minutes from shore, when he began talking about his own childhood. The sails were bright red sheets of color in the setting sun, and the glassy surface of the water was ruffled by light breezes, "cat's paws," he called them. We were crawling in against the turning tide.

"You know, when I was a boy, I thought I was the dirtiest child in the world," he said. It hung there for a minute. I wasn't sure what to say. This didn't sound like an invitation for questions, or I would have said "Why? Did you rape sheep? Kill drifters? Burn stray cats?" Any positive answer here would have been welcome, but I didn't dare ask. Small waves lapped the side of the hull. I was hoping the harbor seals might make an appearance again, as they did once in a while on an evening sail. I'd settle too for an orca, or even the sea lion that liked to bump the centerboard. We had it corded down, but she would still knock it almost out of its housing if she thought we needed a nudge.

"I thought no one, no one in the whole world could be as bad as me," he said, very seriously but in a tone I'd come to associate with sermons, and thus distrust.

"Why?" I asked. I meant it too. I was bad, bad in many ways. But I was nowhere near as "dirty" as my older brother, or his friends, or even some of my friends in middle school. You'd have to be pretty bad, I think, to compete.

"I just didn't want you to feel alone," he said, with uncharacteristic gentleness. "That's all."

"OK," I said, pulling in my sheet a little. Did he know about my masturbatory sessions in the woods when I was supposed to be gathering firewood? Did he know about the time I killed the garter snake not entirely on accident? He didn't say anything else for a while, and as we approached shore, I earnestly attended to keeping my sail taught, shipping the oars, and removing the oarlocks so we didn't slash ourselves on them jumping out in the shallows. Just before we got to shore, when I would turn loose my sheet and hop over the gunnels to catch the boat before it ran aground and scratched its dark blue paint, I spoke up.

"I don't feel alone. Or dirty," I said, and he seemed surprised to hear it. Maybe a little sad too, either at my response or the way the conversation hadn't really gone anywhere. I don't feel at all bad about either of these sailboat moments. I don't think he probably remembered them much past the week or day when they happened.

But the more difficult memory, the one I have a hard time placing exactly in time, still bothers me. It must have been June, and my brother and I were looking at a copy of the *Oregonian* laid out across the dining room table. It was dark though, so if it were June, it must have been a particularly late or rainy night. Dad was in the kitchen, and I think Mom was in there too, but can't be sure. The *Oregonian* was running a photo spread on the Gay Pride parade downtown. I had never heard the phrase "Gay Pride" before, and I couldn't stop asking about it. My brother shrugged without saying much, just pointed at some of the more outrageous characters, men in drag, men dressed in rainbows, men in leather, women in drag, women in rainbows, women in leather. I think Dad had been at the stove but had stepped back from it, so that he was framed in the doorway when he asked us what we were laughing about.

"It's Gay Pride," I said, with a laugh.

"And what's funny about that?" he asked. Normally, this type of question would be entirely rhetorical, with exactly one correct answer—nothing, and I'm ready for a smack on the head with a wooden spoon. But though he did have a spoon in his hand, Dad's voice was careful in asking what was funny. His eyes were down, and he waited, as if to hear bad news. I guess I gave it to him.

"I don't see what they have to be proud about," I said. "I mean, they're *gay*. Shouldn't they be ashamed?"

Dad didn't say anything, a bad sign. I looked to my brother, but he seemed troubled. I had said something badly wrong, I could tell, failed some test. Idiot child of eleven or twelve that I was, I couldn't figure out what.

In the spring of 1983, my mother went on an unpaid lecture tour to other Episcopal churches in the Pacific Northwest with a presentation she had about symbols of the masculine and feminine in biblical literature. The presentation had grown out of a manuscript she'd been typing away at for years, but she'd attacked it with a certain urgency that winter, and the basement office was filled with onion-skin pages, carbons, hand-drawn triangles pointing up and down. Her reviews of the tour were not positive. She described showing up at what was supposed to be a friendly church, one where we had a connection and a contact and the expectation of a group of like-minded academic/spiritual scholars on similar quests. What she got was low attendance, bad coffee, and a high number of women who wanted to "get her in the sack." This idiom escaped me, and I had to beg my brother to explain, as Mom wouldn't.

While she was gone, on one truly rainy night, the kind where all over Portland, storm drains clog and streets are flooded and no one even bothers to mop up water in the basement because there will be more before it's through, Dad brought us into the dining room and sat us down for a talk. He had a manila file and a stack of books with him. The dining room had a wrought-iron chandelier with six small bulbs for a light source, and it didn't ever turn up that bright. He had to squint a bit, even with his reading glasses, to read what he had written on a yellow legal pad in his angular, spidery script. He made ample use of scripture, the Kinsey report, and his own psychological profile as compiled by his psychologist Carol Menustik, who we learned he'd been seeing regularly for several years. He had reports from his doctors at Raleigh Hills treatment center, and pastoral letters, and his own diary entries to support his argument. His thesis? That he was gay and was going to divorce our mother.

The introduction took a bit longer than I've written; he started at the beginning, way back with his own father's death, and walked us through everything from his sudden urge to marry to his sudden urge to enter the priesthood, to his alcoholism and recovery. I remember him, as he worked up to the point, saying that in the depths of a suicidal depression during his treatment for alcoholism (and he had documentation for the severity of this low point) he had come to realize the truth, the hard point that could no longer be denied.

"The truth is, I'm gay, and your mother and I are getting a divorce," he said. A significant pause ensued. After a minute, he went back to his carefully prepared case, but I don't remember it well now. Part of me was overjoyed—I'd prayed for my parent's divorce, literally. Kneeling, hands clasped, in church with Mom noodling on the organ and Dad up at the altar, I'd prayed fervently for them to call it quits. I'd included this prayer on a weekly and then a daily basis for years. Any idiot, even me, could see that people who threw plates at each other, who spent their meals in silence, forced cheeriness, or explosive accusations, were not meant to stay together. Any idiot could see the abuse, the dysfunction, the misery of pretending to be a family, and would wish for an escape. So this was answered prayer, and I imagined a quieter, freer life with my mother, Dad gone off the horizon somewhere. But the gay thing was difficult. I really couldn't think what that meant. How was that going to change things? What did it mean, exactly? This question may seem a naive one, but from a twelve-year-old boy's perspective, it could have many answers. Did this mean Dad had never loved our mother? He said that he had and always would, but that they could not live together. Did this mean he wasn't sexually attracted to our mother? We never asked about this matter, but unfortunately, both our parents volunteered that they had had an active, very active, sexual life. Did this mean that he had chosen homosexuality, or was he just of the damned and we the elect, or vice versa? And if that were so, how did we know we wouldn't discover ourselves totally queer, as in smear the queer, when we were in our early forties?

Dad presented us each with a paperback copy of a book he thought would be helpful, Don Clark's *Loving Someone Gay*, with glossy dark-brown covers and mustard-yellow title text. I read the first chapter eventually and found it the kind of smarmy pop-psychology aimed at people who stick affirmational messages in the frames of their mirrors to pep themselves up each morning and night. Like my mother did, eventually ringing the entire frame of her dresser-top mirror with note cards and paper scraps that told her she was loved, was capable, was on the right path. I hated that book, somehow took it personally, and burned it in a trash can after Dad moved out.

There were some tears that night as he went on, but not as many as you might expect. To me, the most upsetting thing was my brother, red-eyed and sniffling. Dad used the trick of those accustomed to talking through difficult subjects and just plowed through the tightness in his throat, the pain in his voice. I took the dog for a walk—which was my normal job, even in the rain, though I walked farther than usual that night. It was raining so hard that I couldn't keep my glasses from beading up with drops that reflected every streetlight dozens of times in each eye. I ended up in Mount Tabor Park, walking among the pines, soaked through my jacket and isolated by my inability to see. I tried to cry, but couldn't. Or didn't.

Back home, where I had half-hoped to reject an offer of concern over my sopping wet state, I discovered my dad and brother in a protracted discussion in the upstairs bathroom we all shared. The topic had turned from marriage to work. He told us he would be leaving the priesthood unless the bishop relented and allowed him to come out without consequence. It was a given that he would come out, if not from the pulpit, at least to the vestry. He talked about high-tech chemistry, about being a stock broker. He went on for some time that night about the salary scale for commercial pilots. He said, while brushing his teeth, that he was pretty much tired of the poverty, chastity, and obedience thing. Especially the poverty. He joked, was irreverent, asked us to imagine a whole new life. He seemed weirdly *younger*, ten years younger than the man who had assembled us downstairs and spoken to us like a jury accepting his plea. I felt myself excited by the brave prospects he described, the chances that suddenly opened up. Carolyn had gone to her bedroom to cry, I think.

When our mother returned a few days later, she found us angry that she hadn't told us what was afoot. She found herself nearly hysterical in her own anger, her voice rising through registers as she asked, incredulous, what he had told us, what he'd sprung in his cowardice. She called it that, "cowardice," a disclosure he didn't dare make while she was in the house to challenge his version of events. There were, it turned out, alternative evaluations of his psychological makeup, versions of his running away into marriage, of his capacity for falsehood. He had promised, she said, promised not to do this while she was gone, and it was just unfair to do it this way, to take this step with our lives without her. She had a point, but as I approached and passed his age in this moment, I began to think about that night when he came out to his children in the rain-darkened quiet of the dining room. What did it cost him, I wonder, to levelly expose himself as a thing we didn't understand and probably reviled? And why did he do it, when he could have just walked out the door, into any given night, and we would have locked it behind him? I imagine his heart pounding as he called us in and waited through the scraping of chairs. I imagine the pulse in his neck as he reached out with a finger to open the file folder, clear his throat, and begin all that was to come, and I wonder at how he could do it at all.

Blind

I idealized the blind characters of my youth, or they were idealized for me. I adored Marvel Comics's Daredevil, blinded by accidental exposure to a radioactive isotope that also heightened all his other sensory powers, gave him a radar sense, and apparently, set him on the course to becoming a lawyer. Laura Ingalls Wilder's sister Mary, as played by Melissa Sue Anderson, turned from slightly prissy, blonde antagonist to noble, vulnerable young woman possessed of an unbreakable strength once scarlet fever robbed her of her visual world. I'm not sure if it worked out the same way in the books, which I could not read, being a boy, but on TV the effect was clear. There were blind Chinese martial arts masters who, paradoxically, "saw" what escaped everyone else, and Ben Grimm's blind girlfriend Alicia, who not only tamed the love of the Thing but was also hot enough to be constantly preyed on by world-ending super villains who found her exotic enough to stalk.

I read biographies of Helen Keller, learned every word of every song in The Who's *Tommy*, and was obsessed by an illustrated life story of Braille, who blinded himself as a young child trying to punch a hole through a piece of leather with an awl, the leather held before his face so he could see what he was doing as he pushed the awl through from the other side. I could always vividly imagine the strain, the resistance he felt as the tip of the awl raised a little nipple in the leather before punching through and entering his eye. It stuck so deep in his optic nerve that the other eye went dead a few days later. In his preteen years, having become a devout Christian at the parochial school for the blind where he ended up, he ran his hands over the open gospel displayed in the chapel and found he could make out the illuminated letters of the text. This moment in my book was accompanied by a full-page illustration of the boy with his hand glued to the Word like someone grasping an electrical wire, his unseeing eyes wide, jaw dropped in awe, light emanating from his figure to cast the lectern and the altar behind him into sharp relief.

Even the ordinary actual blind people I knew or saw on the bus seemed to have a composure, an apartness that did not invite pity, but rather respect. They could do so much without their eyes that I had trouble doing with mine, or so it seemed anyway. They received special honors, chief among these the right to take their dogs everywhere, tap at the eminently tappable world with a white cane, and like the parishioner Ralph at church, be escorted, arm in arm, up the aisle to the communion rail, and back down to his pew, by a procession of children who competed for the honor.

I tied bandages over my eyes for hours at a time. I spent afternoons learning to navigate my house, armed with a relatively straight branch from the walnut tree. A child who could not sustain attention to the simplest drawing project, I could devote an hour to handling, blindfolded, the objects on the mantle, studying their tangible mysteries in silence and darkness, unlocking the secrets of my father's recorder, the soft silver pitcher, the glass paperweight, the surface of the blue-grey abstract painting that hung there. I left the house blindfolded sometimes and wandered through the backyard, the garage, even painstakingly finding my way up the embankment to the neighbor's fence, inching up the fence till I reached the top rail, waving around my right foot until I found the garage's gutter, and climbing on all fours, the gravel of the shingles rough under my palms, up to the peak of the garage roof, where I sat, blindfolded, not seeing the four yards around me, the waving branches of the trees, the pavement of the driveway below.

My teachers found me out in third grade. That was the year I changed schools, starting at Oregon Episcopal School with my brother, both of us on clergy scholarships. OES is a pretty progressive school now, but in those days, the elementary school culture was lifted right out of 1945. Uniforms, walking silently in lines, reciting the *Venite* in chapel, the one Jewish kid in my class left alone in the classroom with the lights out during services. There were very few children whose families were not white and wealthy, and who hadn't been there since kindergarten; I was considered "new" into eighth grade. The elementary curriculum required me to learn italic printing. I couldn't get it, and my teacher, Mrs. Nolte, would lose her coiffed, made-up calm when I turned in my page of Qs that represented my guess as to what the letter should look like. The other kids had started learning this alphabet in kindergarten, and I was embarrassed into stunned sullenness every time I failed so visibly to make progress. I was, at that time, trying to learn not to wipe my nose on my green uniform sweater cuffs, but in these moments, standing in front of her desk with my substandard letters, I'd fall back to the habit that left what looked like snail trails over my cuffs, and her cheeks would redden under the matte of her base coat. If she got really worked up, you'd see cracks appear.

"Honestly. Look at the chart! What are you thinking! I've told you before, if you don't know the letter, look it up! What's wrong with you?"

"Sorry. I keep forgetting. I'll try again." I smiled sheepishly and tried to edge away, but she wouldn't have any of it. If I could just stall a little, I could get someone to show me a good Q and I could learn to copy it. That's what I should have done from the start, but I didn't have many friends yet, nor would I for several years, as it turned out.

"Sorry won't do it. You. Right here. Now look at the capital Q on the chart and write me one right here. Let's go, mister."

I considered my options. I could disobey and push the moment to its crisis, a strategy which might result in having to copy down a dictionary page, with all entries, symbols and minutia—a task which I couldn't actually ever complete, because it had to be in italics, which I didn't know yet, and so I would have to keep at the page, copying and recopying, guessing at the letters I didn't know, until she decided I'd missed enough recesses and wanted me out of her hair. The last time, when I'd blacked the eye of Kristen Ramsey, the daughter of a prominent judge, this had taken three days. Or, I could admit that I didn't know what chart she was talking about.

I looked all around the room, but from where I was I couldn't see an alphabet chart, just a "Who Reads" poster with a perky, mortarboard-wearing cartoon owl atop a stack of books, a display of student artwork (my spaceship sketches not among the selections posted), a blurry times-table chart that came in handy for those sitting right next to it, etc. Members of the class were looking up to the front of the room, some with evident pleasure at seeing the new kid get it again. I didn't know what to say: if I pretended to see the chart, what then? "Oh, right, the chart. Don't know why I keep forgetting to look at that. Great, I'll just go back to my seat then . . ." I could see how that would play out. Asking for a clue also seemed out of the question. I stood there and snuffled, and wiped my nose, and a smile broke out across her face. It was a smile of triumph as she figured me out, and it was without kindness.

"You can't see it, can you? You're squinting and you still can't see it! Why, you need glasses!"

"Four eyes," the class clown stage-whispered, and she was off to reprimand him. Allison, who was brainy and occasionally nice to me, pointed up toward the corner where the wall met the ceiling.

"Up there. Around the room."

I put the tips of my index fingers and my thumbs together to make a small diamond shaped hole, raised it to my eye and narrowed its aperture almost to darkness—a trick I'd learned trying to read the sign announcing the hymns in church so I could mark each one with a separate ribbon in my hymnbook and be ready to sing without that tiresome shuffling and paging. If I pushed hard, I could read the numbers posted all the way across the nave. When I tried it this time, the muddy yellow banner that encircled the room right at the top of the wall resolved into an unfurled, parchment-colored strip of paper, about a foot high, striped with two solid lines and a third dotted one. Allison wasn't lying; the alphabet was printed, or at least italicized there, in delicate sepia script. Within the hour, Mrs. Nolte had me in the nurse's office, with her cruel pyramid of shrinking, stylized *N*s, *Z*s, *O*s, *C*s, *A*s, and mostly *E*s. I've hated those charts ever since.

When I got my glasses in early October 1979, the first thing I noticed was not the leaves on the trees, it was the edges of the buildings. Driving home east across the Morrison Bridge, I looked back at downtown and trembled in fear. The buildings were impossibly clear, their edges sharp and towering. How could they stand up? I looked away, afraid to see them come tumbling down, and sad already, to see the comforting cloudy figures of their former looming selves transformed into monoliths, distinct and knifelike. It was the same in my classroom. I still remember how it looked before I got my glasses: warm, fuzzy, a mix of yellows and browns and greens. When I looked around with my newly four-eyed face for the first time, my head hurt at all the specifics of posters and light switches and coats hanging on hooks, the spines of three hundred workbooks, all the writing on the board, and that damned banner encircling the whole room. It was as plain as the blackheads on the nose on my face, and it wasn't a nice creamy off-white, it was more khaki, grimy-looking somehow. How could I have missed it before? The world with glasses was harder, sharper, less forgiving, full of cruel contrasts, and I felt unready for this new way of seeing.

It wasn't long until I learned why the kids with glasses were so bad at dodge ball—which we called "bounce bombardment" or "bouncemen" for short. When the iconic red rubber ball smacks your face, it drives the glasses into your eyebrows, cheeks, and the ever more sensitive bridge of your nose. If they get you hard enough, the frames can crack, though more often they fall off and the lenses get scratched or shatter when they hit the pavement. After a few rounds, you get hesitant, fearful, and a stink of doom comes off you that every strong-armed kid with a ball can smell.

I hated my glasses, but I looked forward to blindness, imagined my deteriorating vision would somehow make me noble or enviable. Having climbed high in a tree, or wandered lonely to some corner of the playground, I stared at the sun until tears ran down my cheeks, because I heard it would blind me. I paid attention to the warning that reading under low light or sitting within inches of the television screen could rob me of the light, and so I turned down lights to read and sat so close to the screen I couldn't see what was happening at the edges. My eyes did actually grow worse and worse. I didn't tell anyone; I was saving it up, all the pity and sorrow and guilt no one seemed to be feeling on my account. Each year's eye appointment solicited sadness and worry from my mother, who could barely walk without her own thick glasses.

The first time I ever actually feared going blind should have deromanticized the whole idea for me, but the effect only lasted a few minutes. My brother and I were home alone, and up to mischief. I don't remember why we were cutting several lengths of electrical cord, but it couldn't have been for noble purposes. Perhaps we were binding something or were planning something spectacular with the neon power supply we used to burn elaborate, carbonized trails across the surfaces of doors, chests of drawers, and cherished books no one looked at very often. My glasses were broken again and wouldn't stay on my face when I tried to practice with my brother's nunchucks, or "nunchacku" as he liked to call them. It was 1982. He called me over to the lamp in the living room, where he was measuring out an old extension cord, and asked me to hold it tightly with both hands while he sawed through it. He was using a Buck lock-back with a five-inch blade that he gave me a couple years later when he'd forgotten to purchase a Christmas present. I obliged him, wrapping the ends around my fists and spreading my hands apart as hard as I could. My right I held close to my waist, and my left I extended about two feet away from me. The wire was insulated and didn't bite into my palms too badly. But even with my help he was still having trouble, and I couldn't hold the wire up when he pushed down on it. So he switched to sawing from below, so I could put my weight against his cutting force. I wanted to go get my glasses so I could see what he was doing, and after a few moments struggling and swearing, I leaned down to get the wire within my close vision. My face was probably less than a foot from the knife when it came through, too close for Joseph to stop his upward motion. The blade went in my left eye socket, hit bone inside my face, and bounced my head back.

Joseph screamed, but I was stumbling away, my head ringing like a bell, my left hand covering my eye, holding back the pulp I imagined was ready to fall out on the living room rug. I moved toward the bathroom mirror. Joseph couldn't follow. He told me later that he was almost sick right there, and he was already wailing with regret and horror and shame. I don't remember what was coming out of my mouth, but there was a lot of pain roaring in my ears, and it was hot and wet under my hand. His noise, his teary apologies receded like the sounds of the surf. I hesitated in front of the mirror, and I have the image firm in my memory, the wire still wrapped around my hand, my right eye open as wide as it could go, my face white with fear, a trickle of blood running out from underneath my left palm. I pulled it back and I could see the wound, a perfect, half-inch line on my left lower eyelid, dark blood seeping from it, already slowing. I blinked, and I could see it with both eyes. The whole left side of my head, deep in my face, ached, but I could see. That's how my brother found me, laughing as I wiped the blood away and watched the line of red slowly reform. It was like a miracle.

The blade, turned so that its flat ran parallel to the width of my eye, had punched through my eyelid but gone neatly *under* my eyeball and had hit the bone at the back of my eye socket. It's possible that it hit the orbital and never actually went in deep, but it didn't hurt there at the surface; the cut was the full width of the blade, and the bruise that came was higher up on the lid. My vision was teary and pinkish from the little bit of blood in my eye, but the tissues I dabbed with went from dark to red to pink to just damp over the course of ten minutes. I've thought about the moment the wire came into focus and the knife flashed up often. I remember a flash of red, not unlike what I saw when I took a good right jab in the eye or when I once grabbed an electric stock fence, or when I fell out of a tree and broke my left arm at six. Flashes of red, like a blinding red light masking the whole world. A red curtain swirling over everything, and the sinking feeling that if I couldn't get it to part in a second or three, or five, it would stay with me forever.

When Joseph and I talk about this particular close call, one of many, he still gets the chills. "It's just that it hit so hard," he says, and shakes his head. "I was so sure I'd killed you, just punched into your skull."

"Nope. Dodged it that time," I say, and it's not that I'm trying to be brave, it's just that when I remember this incident it's mostly with a rising giggle at my fortune. I grin as I recount with him: a half inch, a quarter inch even, and it would have been a different story altogether. As it was, we didn't even tell our parents, though for a while I could threaten him by calling, "I'll tell Mom you stabbed me in the eye!" But those threats paled away. It would have been hard to explain, and soon there was some new secret we were keeping anyway. When I was in college and we did finally tell her, she just sighed and looked lost, one more piece of evidence that her sons were doomed, claimed by a violent fate outside her control. Eventually, we stopped telling her those stories, tales that seemed to her, I think, accusations of her neglect, testimony to her failures to parent us.

In some ways, the knife in the eye just made me more aware of blindness, more curious about it. At church, I'd gotten good at making sure I was on hand to seat Ralph, to sit with him, to offer him my skinny arm when we made our way up the aisle. I'd tilt my arm up to indicate through the pressure that we were about to step up, and Ralph would raise his foot for the stair, believing me without hesitation. I led him to the communion rail, where he stared straight ahead, listening for the approaching celebrants, who placed the host on his upturned palm and sometimes said, "the blood of Christ, right in front of you, Ralph," as they held the chalice out so he could guide it to his lips, "the cup of salvation."

Ralph was in his late sixties I guessed, stout, bald, red-faced, dandruff flaking the shoulders of the tweed jacket he wore in winter. He had a seersucker suit he wore to weddings sometimes, which made him look quite dapper. He never quite looked you in the eye, but always looked in your direction and smiled. Approaching Ralph, I knew I was outside the circle of his awareness until, all at once, he recognized my voice or turned toward me and asked, "Who's that?" He'd affirm my presence with a nod, as if he'd expected me, I'd just confirmed his expectations, and he was happy about it. He smiled for every meeting and thanked everyone, and shook my hand at the passing of the peace with a palsied grip. His eyes were watery blue and crinkled at the corners in a kindly way. His watch had a brass cover that flipped open and no glass over the hands. Sitting beside him, I'd watch him recite his prayers, warble through his hymns, kneel and stand just a hair behind the crowd. Sometimes I'd shut my eyes for long periods to see the service as he did. Sometimes during the readings he'd lean down and ask me what the reader had said. If I knew, I'd whisper in his ear, and he'd nod seven or eight times to show he understood.

As I got older, I started going to the eight o'clock service once in a while, which included no music, and I could be home alone by ten instead of noon. I missed the singing but liked the monastic, spare, solemn quality of it. Even Dad's sermon seemed starker, probably because he was still hung over. Or, after he went through rehab and quit drinking, because he hadn't yet toked himself into a rapturous daze at eight in the morning, though he would be feeling no pain and vacuously grinning by ten. Sometimes Ralph showed up at eight o'clock service too, and I would escort him as usual. It was at one of these quieter, more restrained, and poorly attended masses that I realized Ralph didn't actually know all the prayers. He faked it a little, mumbled through sections of the confession, the prayers of the people, and sometimes even began a response at the wrong moment. I started to watch for his head to raise up a little higher than usual and his lips to open, as if he were ready to cast out with his tongue for the missing language like a child trying to catch a snowflake. He knew the refrains of the hymns, but not the verses.

Finally, one coffee hour when I had fetched Ralph some cookies and a paper cup of coffee, I asked him about it. Did he have a prayer book? Or a bible? His face fell, sadder and more closed than I had ever seen it.

"No, I don't have a bible, though I sometimes get tapes."

"You read Braille, don't you, Ralph?"

"Pretty good, I do. But those things, those Braille books, are expensive, yes sir. I do OK," he had his smile back, was nodding, but it seemed kind of fake to me, an artificial resignation I recognized as meant to cover up real desire.

My buddy Mike Thompson, the son of the deacon, talked about it with me. What would it take? How much could it cost to get Ralph a Braille bible and prayer book? His dad did the research, and it got very serious. We would need hundreds of dollars. Saints Peter and Paul wasn't a blue-blood Anglican fortress of wealth by any means. Potlucks were festivals of Jell-O salads, hot dogs fried in dough, and tuna casseroles. Some Sunday school classes met in a basement cell with one tiny window outside the roar of the boiler room. But we figured it couldn't hurt to ask. The next Sunday we started our sales pitch at coffee hour. It was slow at first. One older man who wore western-style shirts with wide stripes loudly proclaimed that I'd not get a damned cent out of him. A sharp-chinned woman with a dead tooth in her grimace asked me how much I'd be putting in? I didn't hesitate.

"Twenty dollars. I'm saving up from my allowance money and mowing lawns for it," I told her, looking right in her eyes. It wasn't entirely untrue, as I did intend to put some money in. Deacon Thompson had warned us that we would need to pledge some seed money to get it going. After a long pause, she withdrew a thin embroidered wallet from her purse, unsnapped the clasp, and gave me a ten-dollar bill. She didn't smile, but put her hand on my head and wished me luck.

It took us six weeks to raise the money, which doesn't seem so long now, but at thirteen, was an epic task. The last dollars came from the wife of the man who'd yelled at us the first Sunday. She said it was just to stop us pestering everyone, honestly, but she winked as she handed me the check. We gave all the money to Deacon Thompson, who put in the order, but told us it might take eight to ten weeks for delivery. This is what we told the contributors when they skeptically asked us for a timetable. I had talked myself into a picture of how it would be, me holding my red prayer book up to read the post-communion prayer I had never memorized, Ralph standing there with his black Braille prayer book, one finger scanning back and forth across the page while he intoned, his voice grown strong, confident as he read along. I told it that way to impatient donors, who usually grunted and walked away placated, but not all with smiles on their faces. These interactions grew more strained as the delays mounted, and it was more and more painful for me to even be at church.

It was painful because that spring, Dad had insisted on coming out to the vestry, even though the bishop had told him in no uncertain terms that if he wanted to stay in the active priesthood he needed to keep his homosexuality tightly closeted. But Dad had already come out to the family, had announced his intention to divorce our mother, and seemed set on publicly leaving the priesthood. He got his wish right away; the vestry removed him from duty as soon as he was done speaking his piece, and he never preached from that pulpit again. He moved out pretty much simultaneously, coming back for boxes of his belongings once in a while when we weren't home. My mother and sister kept going to Saints Peter and Paul, even after the bank took the house and we moved across town to a rental near Alpenrose Dairy, but I went with them less frequently. I could feel the pity, revulsion, or shock of the other parishioners; everyone knew our story. It was awkward, shameful, and people were often circling up around my mother, reducing her to tears at coffee hour with their offers of prayer, cash, and concern while other congregants walked on toward the coffee and cookies pretending not to see her or hear her high-pitched sobbing.

The day Deacon Thompson and Mike presented the Braille bible and Book of Common Prayer to Ralph at coffee hour, I pretended I had one of my chronic stomachaches and stayed home. Mom gave me some of the story when she got back that afternoon. The prayer book came in four file-box-sized containers, running to some thirteen thick volumes, a detail I had failed to appreciate when imagining Ralph using the books in church. Mike and his dad had brought the boxes into the hall before the services. After mass, Deacon Thompson had called out for everyone to come around for the presentation of a gift. Mike sat Ralph down, and Mike's dad gave a short speech praising the parishioners for their generosity, and especially thanking Mike and me for working to solicit the donations. Sitting on the edge of my bed that afternoon, patting my shoulder, Mom said he spoke highly of us and did not linger on my inability to be there that morning. Then they helped the baffled Ralph open the first box and watched to see his reaction. "It was just wonderful," Mom said, in a voice I recognized as strained by a lie. I had been worried about that moment.

I could have gone to church. I knew the presentation was to be that day, though my mother did not. I chickened out for so many reasons. I hated the idea of embarrassing Ralph, and the idea that he would be obligated to say thank you, and that all the eyes would be on me. I was thirteen and liked attention usually, but in this case, just thinking about it made my skin crawl. Here was something I'd done that was actually sort of selfless, a goody-two-shoes, hey-look-at-me-doing-good kind of thing. I could imagine all the faces turning toward me, thinking some version of "poor kid with the gay alcoholic priest for a father, he's bearing up OK" with a mix of pity and revulsion. It really did make my stomach hurt.

I called Mike and got the less sanitized version from him over the phone. When Ralph opened the box, Mike said, he seemed flustered and even a little angry somehow. Serious. And then he said, "Well, I'll be," over and over again as he started to run his fingers over the pages. He was out of practice, as it turned out, and it took him a while to figure out what he was reading. And then he wept, the tears running down his cheeks. Mike said he sobbed and blew his nose on his white handkerchief and dripped tears on the off-white pages full of bumps.

I hardly ever went back to that church, and I never spoke to Ralph again. I thought I'd avoided ever having to see Ralph cry until I went back to the church to bury my father, who they'd welcomed home at last. Ralph was there, a little more stooped but basically looking the same. He was wearing a seersucker suit, perhaps the same one, crying as he was led out the door. I've never known his last name, and I'm sure now that he has passed, and I regret deeply cutting him off so long ago.

The first long-term effect, and the only one I can definitively attribute to the knife in the eye, is that when I used to box, a blow to my left cheek would often split the faint, hairline scar wide open. Over the years, as my vision deteriorated, eventually getting so bad that if I held my glasses at arm's length, they disappeared into the ocean of blur out there, so bad I couldn't walk safely on an uneven surface, couldn't see house numbers or highway exits even with my glasses, couldn't pass my van driver physical without some hints from the examiner about line three, my left eye led the way toward darkness. I had a bad eye and a worse eye, an eye so dim it saw colors differently, so warped it saw the perfect full moon as a smear of faint light. But that could have had nothing to do with having a knife probe my eye socket all those years before. One eye had to be worse than the other, after all, and though my left eye was the one the surgeon wasn't sure he could correct, in the end my cornea was thick enough to allow the degree of reshaping they needed.

So, in 2002, I did it, went under the knife and the laser for corrections. There were so many preliminaries: the drops, the bandage taped over one eye, the *Clockwork Orange* clips to hold the other eye open, the gentle tap that measures the internal pressure of your eye, the pressure cuff, which equalizes the internal and external pressure so that the microkeratome can slice an even 3mm flap into the surface of the eye. My heart was pounding when the surgeon instructed me to stay focused on the blinking red light as the pressure equalized, the blood stopped reaching my optic nerve, and the red light faded away to burgundy and then to deep purple and then to black.

Then the whir of the microkeratome—which didn't hurt—and the return of the light, and the bizarre moment when the surgeon delicately, with a tiny tweezers held in his steady hand, lifted the flap and opened my cornea to the outside air. The world solarized, turned metallic and grainy. The surgeon repeated, his hands gripping my head as tightly as a barber shaving sideburns with a straight razor—"keep looking at the light"—and then the laser pulses came with a cracking sound, like a Geiger counter in an old sci-fi movie. And then the detail impossible to reconcile, the one worse than the replacement of the flap, or the lurching of the motorized, computer-controlled table I lay on as it tracked with the laser to ensure proper aim, more memorable than the placement of the foggy bandage lens, worse even than the moment they started in on my remaining eye. This detail: the air slowly filling with smoke. I wasn't sure I was seeing it, but the aroma of smoldering hair was unmistakable, wafting over my face, lit by the pulsing red beams blinding me, burning away all that was wrong in my eyes.

When I got up from the table, half an hour later and $4,500 poorer, I had matching flaps cut into both eyes, corneas reforged by laser pulses, and cloudy bandage lenses serving as the scales that were to fall from my eyes the next day at noon during my follow-up. My eyes hurt, and my primary emotion was relief that I had not panicked and tried to sit up while the laser was firing, though the bile had risen in my throat and I might have chewed some silver slivers loose of my fillings. Sitting up, I expected the fog to be total and was surprised when the blue capped, blue-bloused, white-sneakered nurse handed me a little faux leather bag containing my eye drops, instructions, artificial tears in .01 ml plastic ampules, and my glasses. I was surprised because my hand reached out and grabbed it, because through the fog, I could see it. I could see the pattern in the linoleum, the door handle, and, as my wife guided me out of the building, the stairs, the tile work, the glass louvers on the front windows. While she drove us east on I-90, panel trucks loomed up outside the window, and I read their logos to her. At my appointment the next day, when they pulled the bandage lenses loose, Dr. Wilson, who seemed less interested in me now that I'd paid, declared me 20/30 and legal to drive.

Over the next two weeks, I put drops in my eyes four times a day, holding my eyes shut for a full minute after the first, and then waiting four minutes before administering the second. I kept my drops on the windowsill of the guestroom, and four times a day, I sat in the bentwood rocker by the window and diligently dropped cloudy and clear solutions into my eyes. During the four minutes between solutions, I stared out the window, every day able to see a little more, a little more clearly.

Since surgery, I have enjoyed so many common pleasures of vision. I have swum in a mountain lake and seen trout cruise fearlessly away from my shadow, watched the stars as I slept out at night, washed my feet in the shower and seen them get clean, risen from bed on a summer night and walked scarred and pierced but naked as I was born and been able to walk down the moonlit hall to the bathroom. I have woken to the world as a pattern that can be resolved as soon as I choose to see it, my hand clutching the blanket, the open bedroom doorway, the sparse decoration of the guest room across the hall, window beyond the guestless bed, apple tree swaying in the breeze, hedgerow beyond that, and blue sky peeking through the leaves. It takes only a few blinks to remember to see depth without straining past fuzziness, and it leaves me, almost every sunny morning, amazed at my luck.

Nearing fifty now, I am often struck by the good fortunes of being alive and of being able. Though I'm back to a mild prescription for distance and have to wear cheaters for very close work, I'm still daily grateful for the gift of sight. Whatever possessed me, as a child, to want to lose it? What did that poor, sad boy I was think he could gain with such a loss? To not see others looking at him? To be free of the sense that something inside was invisibly but irreparably broken? To earn the pity of others, escape their cruelty, have some dignified way to hurt? Blind is a noun as well as an adjective and verb, and perhaps that was what I really wanted—a way to hide from sight, mine and everyone else's, forever.

Ghost Story

I.

"Listen, can I talk to you about something?" Lash asked in a nuanced and serious voice. He could do that, set a grueling pace on a hot May afternoon and keep up a conversation that actually sounded like human speech, not a series of gasps.

"Sure," I managed, thinking he might let up a bit if he talked. Plus, we'd been friends and teammates for two years, an eternity in high school, and I'd been worried about him. Lash had missed a good deal of his senior season due to protracted and unexplained absences. Wiry, knotty-muscled, redheaded, and small-featured, he looked condensed somehow, all extraneous physique burned off. In the fall, he'd won the state cross-country meet, had a good shot at both the 3K and 5K titles that spring, and was training also for regional competition in the 10K, which we didn't even run in our league. But he was mercurial going from laughter to anger in a blink. One day he could run with long strides, as if his torso sat on top of a giant wheel that rolled along on the even ground beneath, and the next he was a cramped, crook-necked Quasimodo, his right arm lunging ahead of his strained face. This was one of the good days, and our five-mile workout began with an uphill stretch that made me acutely aware of certain fundamentals of kinematics, mass, inertia, gravity, friction, the pavement's equal and opposite reaction to me, the axiomatic increase of entropy as my joints wore down. Lash floated above these concerns, which for him seemed to be just one way of looking at things. I was just a skinny lad, but with Lash, I felt heavy, bound, and plodding.

With no discernible slowing of our progress, he explained he'd been having some issues with depression. In fact, he'd actually had to start a pretty aggressive therapy. He looked sideways at me chugging along to see how I was taking it. Actually, he'd had to spend a couple of days in the hospital, because he'd been mutilating himself with a razor. He used the word mutilate, as the shorthand "cutting" was not in vogue back in 1988—at least I'd never heard it. I expressed concern and sadness at this idea, and he nodded.

"I didn't try to kill myself or anything, but I couldn't stop doing it and I finally told someone." He said he felt good about the doctor he was seeing, and didn't feel so dirty anymore, but he still had bad days. He had memories he was still fighting, he went on, not looking at me. "When I was a kid, I was abused, Cris. Like sexually abused. Molested."

"Oh, me too," I said. It just popped out. There was a space of several strides in the conversation. I listened to the odd rhythm of our shoes falling on the road as it ran uphill, climbing away from the golf course on the left, and the wetlands on the right, the edges littered with trash and the occasional dropped three-ring binder some kid had lost on his way to school.

"Are you fucking with me?" he asked, his voice tight.

"No. Really. I was molested too. When I was seven or eight. Eight, I guess." Though no rationale for speaking had existed before I had begun to speak, one came to me. This conversation was all about making Lash feel less weird, more ordinary. My intrusive confession was about convincing him he wasn't alone. My intentions suddenly made pure and unselfish, a smug righteousness came over me. I went on, "I think it's pretty common, actually." I exhaled my way through some misquoted statistics I attributed to "an article I'd read," and it sort of worked. Lash thanked me, said it was a relief and that it gave him hope. As we turned into the aging suburban development called Windermere and strode levelly past clipped hedges and rock gardens, and elderly men in shorts watering their yuccas, Lash seemed to want the whole story, which I was happy to tell him. I began with the perpetrator, a family friend named Charlie.

"So it wasn't your mother, then?" he asked with a tone of disappointment, and my first real misgivings arose.

"No," I answered carefully.

"And was it only the one time?"

I became acutely aware of us, athletic young men, physically vibrant, competitive runners muscularly alive in that sunny hour, one of us deeply wounded, both of us haunted, but in very different ways.

II.

If you ask me if I've ever seen a ghost, my answer depends on which story I decide to tell. If I'm not sure about going into the details of being the object of someone's pedophilia, my answer is no, I've never seen a ghost, but once I heard something inexplicable, which I've always thought of as a ghost. It was actually the same spring of my conversation with Lash, just a few weeks later, when I was home for the summer and not yet off to my summer job spraying thistles and mending fence on a sheep farm outside Dundee. Dad and his lover, Joe Teague, and I had moved into a rented house on Southeast 27th and Morrison, just two blocks from the run-down Lone Fir Pioneer Cemetery, where some twenty-five thousand people were interred in a space two blocks wide by five blocks long. Some of the headstones there are from the turn of the century, with likenesses carved into the limestone. Some of the likenesses have been etched away by pollution and darkened by exhaust soot until they appear gaunt and hollowed, as if the deceased stood for his portrait sometime after he'd shuffled off this mortal coil. There were two good-sized mausoleums there, one with a chapel inside and broken stained glass windows letting the rain in. Another had lost its door, and you could go inside and sit on a slab of stone and give yourself the willies fairly efficiently, especially at night, which I did from time to time when we lived nearby.

Home alone on a sunny day, I didn't think of the cemetery until I went down to the basement, from where a loud rustling and thumping seemed to be coming. I found nothing at all down there in the dark by the water heater, but then I heard heavy footsteps above my head, treading across the main floor. There was only one stairway, so I yelled up, thinking that Joe or Dad had come home or that there was an intruder in the house, who had somehow, impossibly, gotten past me on the stairs. No one called back, but the footsteps kept moving, which freaked me out. I busted up the stairs, then pressed myself to the wall like the action-movie protagonist I dreamt of becoming. I went for the kitchen first and grabbed the good knife Dad always kept sharp, the knife he swore must never be used to cut cheese and that, when I did use it to hack off a slab of pepper jack, he claimed was never as sharp again. I moved into the main room of the house, knife at the ready in an overhand grip, but I couldn't hear anything. There were no curtains to hide behind, and not a lot of furniture, so once I'd yanked the closet doors open and nearly stabbed the coats, and returned to the kitchen to check that funny space behind the fridge in the breakfast nook, I was pretty sure I was alone. I was just about to put the knife down when I heard the footsteps above me again, in the bedrooms now, stepping regularly, heavily, with accompanying board creaking. A little sob escaped me. Transformed now from action-movie detective to that guy in the horror movies who's always walking backwards into dark rooms, I made my trembling way up to the second floor, where I went straight for my brother's rifle.

It was just a .22, but he had three ten-shot clips loaded with high-velocity bullets he used for target shooting ready to go on the shelf with the rifle. The clips made an authoritative sound when slapped into the slot below the mechanism, and the bolt sounded lethal enough. I suppose some people could tell from a distance that it was just a little .22, but it seemed like enough firepower to me. When I reached the landing, I dove past the bathroom door, hit my brother's door with my shoulder, reached into the closet and a second later had the rifle loaded and was stepping away from the door while I shot the bolt. It took me quite a bit more time to remember to flip the safety off. Armed and jittery, I continued my search through the remaining bedrooms and bathroom. I parted the shower curtain with the barrel; I swore fiercely as I imagined laying down suppressing fire. I even looked under Dad and Joe's bed, which always gave me feelings of distaste, as they kept a huge dildo in a shoebox under there, and a lot of rags. All clear. And then, of course, I heard the steps in the attic.

Five minutes and many goose bumps and sweat rivulets later, I had swept the attic, including the tiny space behind the chimney that I couldn't see around without jumping in there all at once, ready to fire away. I had a vision of myself then, in my running shorts and ripped T-shirt, my bare feet and firearm, stalking a noise in the attic.

"This is crazy," I muttered to myself, and it sounded crazy too, up there in the dust and heat. I left the rifle on my brother's bed and went down to the kitchen. Then I remembered the little balcony off my Dad and Joe's bedroom. I hadn't checked it. Now, whatever was up there would know about the gun and could get it, if it were a garden-variety crazy intruder, not some heavy-booted creature of the ether condemned to pace our house. I may have shed a tear at this point—it just seemed so terrifying—but I didn't have any basis in reality to justify my terror. I went back up there, talking to myself the whole time, and I checked the balcony, where only a few leggy marijuana plants were hiding, and locked the balcony door, and put the gun back in the closet, and went downstairs. When the footsteps started again, right above me, I turned on the stereo and cranked the volume. After a while, I sat on the porch with the door closed behind me. Never saw a ghost, but sure heard something strange that made me question my senses, made me worry for my safety, made me act comically like a horror movie teen. The experience reinforced my suspicion that there was more to this world than I could make sense of scientifically, that unknowable forces moved around me fating me to pain I could not avoid. But I didn't see anything that day.

The truthful answer and the story I tell when it feels safe to share it is yes, unequivocally. Absolutely, I saw a ghost once when I was very young. A perfect and horrifying sighting that has haunted me almost my whole life. At four, I shared a bedroom with my brother for a while in a little house on Sherwood Drive. We shared a bedroom at several points in our childhood, usually with the same dynamic of hilarity, cruelty, and horseplay. The standard was set early. I woke with my hand in a bowl of warm water, fought pillow duels as fiercely as I was able but usually got clobbered, was routinely beaten in wrestling matches, heard terrifying tales of the supernatural, teased and was teased, and sometimes listened to music late at night on my brother's radio. And one night when I was almost five, I awoke to the feeling of someone tugging at my toe, alternately yanking at it and tapping it. I groaned at my brother to leave me alone, but the sensation persisted. Raising up my head, I saw a small white triangle poking over the foot rail of my bed, clear in the streetlight's bluish glow coming through the window.

"Joseph?" I whispered, but when I looked over at his bed, his slack mouth faced me on his pillow, his white hair disarranged. Even as my breathing shortened into spasms, I could see his chest rise and fall. "Joseph?" I called again, but it came out quieter than the first time. The triangle at the foot of my bed grew taller, became a sheeted head. The cutout eyes came over the bed frame, and then the jagged mouth. Only blackness behind these holes, as if my white-sheeted ghost with the peaked head of a Klansman was not some shrouded specter, but a malevolent sheet itself, out to strangle me in its linen grip. It raised up, as tall as the ceiling, and it smiled, the sheet stretching to do it, and then it said incredibly, quietly, dryly, what ghosts say.

"Boo," said the ghost; I pulled the covers over my head and waited to die.

Leave the four-year-old boy trembling in his bed, too frightened to cry, paralyzed by fear of the perfect, iconic ghost. He'll wait for us to return—in some ways he's always there—frozen, poor kid. I've tried to think the whole thing through logically many times, but without much comfort. My experience was of absolute, heart-stopping terror, but what was reality? Was there someone under a sheet at the foot of my bed?

Maybe it was my brother after all who, having left a dummy of himself that I imagined I saw breathing in the gloom, cuts up a sheet, stands on a chair or stepladder or something, and scares me so badly the piss dries in my bladder. When I cover my head with the covers, he doesn't laugh, or make another sound, or ever mention it again. He is eight at the time. I find this possibility equally frightening, and also hard to accept. Then again, this *is* my brother, master of mischief, architect of cruelty, spy, bomb-maker, torturer of small animals, the same older brother who at twelve locked himself in the storage area under the basement stairs with a calculator, electric typewriter, and dictionary and hung a sign outside reading "The ENIAC is in." The ENIAC would accept written queries folded and passed through a hole in the door, and would go into a paroxysm of beeping, clacking, and humming before returning a type-written reply. Often the replies were cryptic or sarcastic, even insulting. The ENIAC provided definitions, did sums, and answered oracular inquiries with customary vagueness. It never spoke. After two hours of this, I couldn't believe my brother, whose attention span required regular injections of violence into any sustained activity, could keep it up indefinitely. I wrote out the message "The ENIAC sucks ass" and submitted it with some laughter. An instant later a fireball erupted out of the hole, rising to kiss the unfinished ceiling with a roar. I screamed from where I had fallen, watching little splinters of the ceiling joists glow for an instant before winking out in a haze of smoke. Without comment, the ENIAC spit out a typed reply—"Fuck You." I revered the ENIAC like Oz the Great and Terrible, even after I learned the trick (a lighter and a can of a product called Engine Start, a highly flammable aerosol spray), in part because I could have had my face to the little portal or the house could have caught fire, and in part for its disciplined silence. So it could have been my brother under the sheet, but it is a disturbing possibility.

More frightening are the other suspects. My sister, who would have had to come all the way downstairs from the bedroom she was afraid to leave at night, since her fever dream of imps in the hall, and then would have to break character by keeping a secret for more than two days? My mother, having lost it, just lost it from the constant chaos, decides to teach her youngest a memorable lesson in the tilted nature of reality? Or worst, my father, on a bender, inspired by too much reading of Christian mysticism, sneaks into his sons' room to try on the idea of possession? The worst part of all these scenarios is that I never took the cover off, but lay there waiting, trying to see through the mesh of the blanket, crying quietly. If there was someone under the sheet, he stood there a long time and then withdrew as silently as he came. When it got light, I made a break for it and ran to the kitchen where my mother stood, busy at the counter. She told me it was a dream.

Call it a nightmare. Call it a hallucination. Call it an impressionable youngster allowed to watch too many TV movies, flip through too many Caspar the Friendly Ghost comics (though he always seemed composed of marshmallow to me), or see one too many news programs on the KKK, a babe who dreams and can't separate the dream from reality. A much more reasonable option, but is it any more comforting? This dream had sensations of touch, sight, and sound, and even its own nightmare logic, the kind of calculus that dreams employ to assert their own reality while you lie there with your heart whumping in your whimpering chest. This dream was so vivid that for years every night's sleep became an exercise in dread, every bedtime prayer ("if I die before I wake") a plea that it wouldn't come back. With this dream began unbroken years of night terrors, insomnia so regular it became my normal to lose hours of sleep. I could not sleep without the covers over my head, could not face what was out there in the dark. I took flashlights to bed, begged to have the door left open, was reduced to infantile terror each bedtime. I did have nightmares about the ghost later, often, but none so riveting as the original "dream." In some ways, I find this explanation equally disturbing, even more frightening. What madness, that an innocent mind, left to its own devices, can hit on an image and scene, can call up a vision it can never forget?

III.

The ghost stayed with me for years, but then, miraculously, lost some of its power for a long time. We often had houseguests when my parents were married, usually relatives and clergy passing through, but also people in trouble who needed a place to crash. We had mothers who had lost homes and custody of children, a slew of alcoholics, teenagers who fought physically with their parents, foster kids between placements, the whole gamut. Once when I was twelve, we hosted a teenage girl who, I learned from my breathless mother, had been working as a prostitute. Vicky only stayed for a couple of days. When I heard she was coming but before I laid eyes on her, I imagined all sorts of scenarios where this brazen, sexualized succubus realized my potential as a lover and initiated me into the mysteries of coitus, and then told me how good it was to make it with someone for love, not money. I imagined these scenarios while my mom took her to probation meetings and bought her clothes. When I finally met her, she seemed about the saddest girl I'd ever seen. Her eyes were sunken in her pale face and she exuded a listless exhaustion, as if she'd been steamed. She slept—on the couch, in the guest room, in the tub—almost every moment she stayed in the house. I somehow found the decency to leave her almost completely alone. Or I was just shy.

Charlie, the adult child of some active parishioners who had found himself in some trouble, was among the refugees who took sanctuary in the Harris hotel. A longhaired son of the seventies, smoker of fragrant home-rolled cigarettes, beer drinker, guitar player, Charlie stood quite a bit over six feet, had long trembly fingers, a messy beard he fussed with absently, and large sad eyes. He stayed with us for a few days after his father, a locally prominent architect, had died suddenly of a massive coronary. My brother and I ferreted the details out of our mom. The architect had been sketching in his upstairs den when the attack made him clutch his chest and roll out of his desk chair. Lying there, in his final moments, he tried to signal his wife downstairs by tapping on the floor. She'd heard a faint tattoo, growing fainter, for some time before she realized it was a little series of three fast taps, followed by three slower ones, and then the three short "dots," if you will, again. He was almost gone when she got to him, purple in the face, still tapping SOS on the floor. Mom might have embellished a bit, but that's the story, anyway.

I was actually in the room where he died a few weeks later, a darkly paneled study with a modern-looking drafting table and a window through which I could see the steeple of Ascension Chapel poking out of the chestnut trees down the block. We were just "dropping by" to see how the widow was "getting along," which quickly turned into scotch and cigarettes and teary talk in a shaded house while outside, a sunny afternoon expired slowly, never to return. Once I'd slunk upstairs to the den—the death room—and had gotten down on the floor to see the actual spot (which to my disappointment was not outlined in chalk) there wasn't much to do. I looked at the papers still on his desk, eased open a closet to find it contained an aged upright vacuum. Quietly, I got down on my knees in the middle of the room, and then stretched face down on the carpet. I found my hand hovering over the floor, prepared to beat out SOS faintly. I couldn't quite do it though, mostly for fear of my parents downstairs, who would have something to say about my being up there at all, much less impersonating the deceased. My brother later referred to this as being a "chickenshit."

So Charlie was in town on and off after his dad died, but he wasn't the same folk-singing, laughing babysitter and campfire companion of old. A rift developed between him and his mother that left him in need of a place to stay. I remember he was going somewhere, California maybe, at the end of the summer. He had an air of impermanence about him, and even his extended stay with us was a countdown toward departure. He drank a lot and went out with Dad to do it.

Nights, as I've written, were difficult for me then. I liked to have someone read to me, and I would beg for more and more, reluctant for it to end. I needed the door open a crack, and the hall light left on. I had my stuffed animals handy, including a recumbent lion I had intended to name Leo, but my mother and sister insisted was named Aslan, having been so taken with the Christian imagery of the C. S. Lewis books that to have a stuffed lion and not call it Aslan would be somehow tantamount to refusing Jesus's love. Night after night, I lay awake with the covers over my face—it had worked the first time, and I couldn't sleep without it—waiting for the ghost's return. It was worse before we moved from the Sherwood Avenue house of the original encounter, where I had eventually been granted a little alcove upstairs as my own slope-ceilinged room. Outside my window, a neglected shade garden filled with ivy grew, and many nights I mistook my heartbeat's rustle in my ear as the footsteps of the ghost coming through the weeds. Even when I figured it out, I would still snap awake and cry quietly, sure if it wasn't this time, it would be the next.

The night I was molested, I was asleep under the covers when I heard something moving in my room. I was frozen, locked in place, as I heard it come to my bedside. Just as before, the ghost tapped at my feet. Then it moved up my ankle, past my knee. What would happen, I figured, having thought this all out many times before, is that the skeletal hand would either come to my throat and with an icy, implacable grip, strangle me while its master whispered something like "I told you I'd come back for you," which technically, it hadn't, the ghost having restricted itself to a more orthodox vocabulary, or the hand would come to rest over my thudding heart, which would give a little shiver like a bird dying in your hand, and it would be over. And the ghost was on my left side, where every child knows his heart is, and the hand slipped under the covers, and I prepared to die. Then the ghost went down my shorts. I felt a scowl on my brow as the spectral hand fondled my tiny penis, fully retracted by fear. True to form the hand was cold, and the ghost was muttering, but it also seemed to be crying.

An incredible thing happened then, when somehow my fatalistic vigil for my own death tilted into outrage. It happened quickly and powerfully. A sudden need to act overwhelmed my sense of impending doom.

"What the fuck are you doing," I yelled in a quavery voice. The hand snaked back. This was no ghost. I flipped the covers off my face to see Charlie, on his knees by my bedside, face half-lit from the hall light through the doorway, his cheek wet, wringing his hands.

"Sorry. So sorry. I thought . . . wrong room . . ." I could barely make out what he was saying but I was mad and above him, and after so much fear, in control of my words.

"Well, this is my room. So get out." He stumbled to his feet and lurched against the doorframe and padded down the hall. I got out of bed and shut my door tight. When I climbed back in bed, in the dark room, I had a strange mix of feelings—anger, yes, and a list of words I'd heard, like perv and homo and molester and weirdo and bastard, all rising into consciousness. And fear, what was to keep him coming back? Should I yell for my parents? But here is the strange part. I also had a sense of relief, intense relief. The worst had happened and I had fought back. I'd broken the spell, had banished the ghost. It took me a long time to learn to get to sleep, but as those night terrors began with the ghost, they began to end with Charlie. Somehow, I traded the fear of the molester, whom I had scared off, for the fear of the inexplicable phantom, and for a long time, that felt like a gift.

In the morning, I told my Mom about it and she put both hands on the kitchen counter and paused a minute, but didn't cry, not until I asked her what the hell he meant by "wrong room." Did he think a child had gotten into his bed?

"He probably thought you were someone else," she said, and then she cried, and said she was sorry and went on to say that Charlie was a homosexual—did I know what that meant?—and had trouble controlling himself when he'd been drinking. That was the end of it.

I didn't see Charlie leave the house; he may already have been gone. The matter, as they say, "was not discussed" for several years. It wasn't until long after Dad came out that I figured out my mother's explanation, though her confusion of homosexuality and pederasty has never really made much sense. In those days, I think she thought of all as a piece: the drinking, the violence, the men, the danger brought home to roost, night birds that hunted in the rooms of our home, if only for a little while at a time.

IV.

I saw Charlie again once, after Dad left and the money ran out and the bank took the house back in the fall of 1984. We had to move in a hurry, but we'd already worn out the generosity of most of our friends. Mom made a lot of calls and we packed haphazardly to drive boxes of junk one VW bug load at a time across town to the rental on Nebraska Street. At last, Mom scraped up enough to rent a truck for the furniture and found someone who could drive it. She asked me if it would be OK, and it was really the first time she'd mentioned Charlie to me in all that time. He'd been working as a mover, she explained. I think I snarled something like "As long as he doesn't touch me," but I would have had something snappy to say if she'd told me the Pope was coming to help, or a bevy of 38-34-36 playmates from my brother's stash of magazines, which I'd been perusing. I pretty much only had snappy things to say during that era. I was thirteen, my brother had left for college, everything was mixed up and embarrassing, and I had exhausted my limited capacity for grace in accepting favors. This situation, of course, was more than a little socially awkward. What do you say to a guy you last saw stumbling from your bedroom, his hand only recently withdrawn from your unformed childhood genitalia? I worked up a few accusatorial, combative phrases, practiced some shadowboxing moves, but none of that came into play. When the moment came, he was smoking a cigarette while he stashed the first load in the truck. He was paler and older and more tired than I remembered, but he was still Charlie, whom I'd always liked. When the hide-a-bed sprang open on the stairwell and lodged there, he cracked a few jokes and even encouraged my efforts to free it by climbing over the top and tying it closed with my belt. At the end of the day, he had a couple of cans of Oly with the rest of the crowd of volunteers, but declined the pizza Mom had ordered in. It wasn't hard to shake his hand when he left and thank him for his help. It had started storming hard, and when he went out the door he looked back once from the porch light's circle, the shoulders of his light blue work shirt turning indigo in the rain.

After Charlie left, I stole a six pack of beer and half a pizza and feasted with my buddy Mike Thompson in my new room. We cranked the stereo up pretty loud and knocked a can of beer on the carpet. While we were hurriedly ripping the carpet loose of its staples to hide the evidence, revealing a decent but unfinished wood floor beneath in the process, I told Mike who Charlie was; he'd already heard the ghost story on a campout the year before. We were raising a lot of dust from the carpet and its pad, and I knew my mother would also be upset about the commencement of the Harris impact on our new living arrangement, but she didn't really like carpet either, so I thought it would be OK.

"That must be weird, huh? Seeing that guy again," Mike suggested, and cleared some dust from his throat with a swig of beer.

"Just an asshole," I said. It seemed like what was expected.

Growing up in a Christian household, even one as unusual as mine, I had the virtue of forgiveness drummed into my head regularly. To make light of Charlie's assault on a child, on this child, seemed in the moment like the best I could do. And it's true, the conflation of Charlie and the ghost in my seven-year-old brain had made it easier for a long time to look at the silver linings. I was molested—a great fear went away. But what ghosts do is haunt us, trouble our sleep and our peace. Whether imagined or real, they can be a wellspring of anger, of bitterness like dark water to sink in. I can't dismiss the abuse, even just the one time, any more easily than I can dismiss my mother's decision to put Charlie back in our lives for a day. At my best, I can summon pity for him in his moment of weakness, for her in a situation so desperate and sad that she saw no other way. Unfortunately, I'm not often at my best, and as I get older, it seems to me sometimes that the best way to get rid of a ghost is to admit the shameful secret that I'm still angry, still frightened, admit that it haunts me still.

The Dogs

The dog I named Gremlin was the undisputed worst of the whole lot. Ugly, stinky, mangy, mean, a biter, not cuddly—it's difficult to report one good thing about that dog, which is, I guess, why we failed in our efforts to save him. That is to say, we failed to summon the necessary goodwill to keep him. Less euphemistically yet, we failed to resist the temptation to kill him. "Put him down" is the polite phrase to describe our choice, as in "we put him down," or even better, "we had to have him put down, poor dear." To give up on an animal and make that guilty drive to the vet is a common enough experience, but it was unheard of in our family. We were animal lovers, managing a menagerie of birds, lizards, rabbits, fish, and dogs for as long as I can remember.

When Gremlin showed up in the summer of '86, we were actually petless, down to nothing, having lost since 1983 a marriage, two dogs, the parrot, the house itself, both parakeets, my brother (off to college and the military, not gone forever) seven of the parakeets' chicks, the aquarium full of tetras, four chameleons, and three cats. Where before there had been a kind of Gerald Durell circus of children and animals in the rambling fixer-upper, now there was quiet in the rental ranch house on Nebraska Street where my mother and sister were starting over and where I still spent nearly half my time, though that was all changing. At first, Gremlin's arrival seemed a propitious sign that we were returning to the good old chaos. Thinking back, it took a delusional optimism indistinguishable from denial to see that dog as anything other than an albatross, a harbinger of doom, or at least the continuation of the pathetic status quo. But I was fifteen, about to start my sophomore year in high school, and prone to optimism.

In the winter of 2007, my dog Turtle snoozes by my feet while I scratch away with my pen and paper. She has been snoozing since I sat down in this particular old chair, good for reading or writing. When I made a move in this direction half an hour ago, she trotted in ahead of me with an excited jingle of dog tags and the back-over-the-shoulder glances she uses to pull you in one direction or another. She's a mutt of some kind, with enough blue heeler thrown in to make her vaguely dingo-like in her spotted, brown/black/grey double coat. Incredibly—to me—she is between eleven and thirteen years old. Mary found Turtle at the pound in our first year of marriage, when she was looking to surprise me with a dog.

We braved a heavy dark rain the night after she found Turtle, drove out to the pound on the far east side of Portland where Mary had spotted her, but we found out that she had been taken to a run-down shopping mall where Animal Control was using a vacant storefront to sucker passing window shoppers and their children in to meet a few highly adoptable pets. They would be closing within the hour and for some reason, weren't picking up the phone when we tried to reach them. We drove out at speed, scattering shoppers in the rain-slick parking lot. We found the place fast enough and stepped into a clean, open, well-lit, quiet space where only a few kittens and a majestic German shepherd were in plain view. Feeling our momentum evaporate, we looked around for a moment before dispiritedly asking the exhausted looking animal control guy at the desk what had become of the heeler mix. We supposed she'd been adopted already?

"Her? She's in the back. She nipped a kid this morning."

"We'll take her," I said.

After the touching scene where she came out of the dog crate in the supply closet with her head down and tail wagging, tried to lick us, rolled over for a belly rub, shook, demonstrated that she already knew sit and down commands, after we paid our registration and signed papers and got our certificate for spaying or neutering at participating veterinarian offices and a short length of yellow nylon rope to use as a temporary leash, I walked her out across the echoing mall floor and carried her up the escalator in my arms. While Mary dashed into the local Petco for essentials like food and flea dip, I sat in the back of the car with my dog and talked to her around the lump in my throat and petted her, and actually fell asleep with her curled up on my lap. True, it's unbelievably sappy. I hadn't even known I'd been missing her.

Animals, and particularly dogs, I'd argue, let us feel and express love and longing in a purer form than does the everyday society of humanity. I am frequently greeted by my happy, barking dog. While I roll her over to rub her belly, I lean close so she can almost lick my face (which I sometimes encourage by pretending to lick back) and utter a kind of broken record of infantile glee which runs something like "Oh, Turtle, Oh yes, the Turtle dog, who's the Turtle dog? Who's my girl? Is that my girl? Isn't this the best dog? You are the best dog, Turtle dog. Yes. Oh, Yes. And you have the stinkiest breath, don't you? You do. You're the stinkiest dog. Good girl. Oh, nobody pets you, do they? You never get any pets. I know. Tell me all about it. I know. It's so sad. Turtle dog, how about a cookie? Dog biscuit? A biscuit!" This scene, replete with funny voices, can in fact repeat itself several times in one day at my house. When I see my brother, perhaps every year or two, the conversation is more muted. We get out of our cars, walk toward one another, call out, "Hey, Bro!" and have a long hug. During the hug, we tear up, so that when we are done after twenty seconds or so, we let go and say a kind word or two in hoarse voices. "Good to see you, man," we might utter, and then, embarrassed, we begin to make fun of each other (age, hair loss, tendency to hurt one's ribs while hugging, etc.). Try and imagine the situations reversed.

Gremlin had another name, back when an elderly gentleman took pity on him and adopted him as an ugly puppy. I don't actually know that he was an ugly puppy, but I suspect so. He was that unfortunate kind of mutt who appears to be a mix of two breeds by surgical means. His front half was pop-eyed, stumpy-legged, snaggle-toothed papillion, while his back half was bull terrier, thick-thighed and six inches taller. Walking, or rather scooting, he was like a steroid-driven drag racer with lowered front and jacked-up rear, but without the impression of speed. When he stood up to beg, he was the shape of a bowling pin, tapering at the top. If you saw him dancing around grunting for a scrap of food from the front, you might think miniature *Tyrannosaurus rex*, with those vestigial claws hanging uselessly.

The elderly gentleman, for whom perhaps this unlovable Franken-stein's monster of a dog had provided great solace in the last decade of his life, had raised Gremlin (possibly named Hero, Scout, Champ, or Rex in those days) on a diet of steak—steak precut into bite-sized strips the lucky creature simpered from his master's shaky hand. I'm being ungen-erous, I suppose, as it was probably a sad and lonely little ritual, but it gave me whole new reasons to dislike the animal. These were the days of Mom's frequent unemployment and habitual hemorrhaging of our meager financial resources. The era in which my brother and I fashioned a throttle linkage out of an Erector set piece for the Volkswagen. The times when we frequently ran out of gas, because we never put too many dollars out of immediate access by converting it to fuel. In eighth grade, we'd gone a long stretch without water service; the phone was always in danger of being shut off. In supermarkets, I used to stare through the glass at hunks of meat in a gangly parallel to the little kid at the bakery case ogling éclairs. That the little malformed sausage-dog grew up tiring of New York strip was a setback in our relationship, though to judge by the dog's teeth, fur, and crooked spine, I had probably gotten the better deal nutritionally.

The circumstances by which Gremlin came to us were of course the reason we took pity on him even temporarily. A parishioner with an RV-sized heart had been taking care of the elderly gentleman in the last months of his life. She helped with hot meals and company and coordi-nation of visiting nurses, and when he grew too ill, she adopted his dog. Almost immediately after, a drunk was ejected from a bar one evening just as she was passing by the door. He saw her, and according to wit-nesses, knocked her to the ground with his fists because she was looking at him. He kicked her when she was down, and stomped on her when she curled up, just hard enough to fracture her spine and paralyze her from the waist down. She was a big sturdy woman, nurselike, but when Mom and I visited her apartment she was broken, her face lumpy with bruising. She hadn't yet mastered the wheelchair, and her legendary capacity for taking on the sorrow of others seemed exhausted. Mom prayed with her while I looked at all the different kinds of plaid used in upholstering the furniture, browns and yellows and greens. While Mom caught her up on church gossip, I played with the mangy dog who snarfled and wheezled around underfoot. He harfed and wheezled because his teeth and nose were so scraggled and scrunched up that he suffered a sort of permanent canine apnea. Despite the revulsion I choked back, we took him home. He was so ugly, I watched him with amazement. When I put him in the back seat, he nipped my finger. As we drove away, I examined the little bite and noticed that my hand smelled like death, like I'd been petting a stuffed dog improperly tanned whose leather and stuffing were rotting away.

Those who know me well might think that I am omitting the detail of smacking the mutt around after he bit me, though these days I'm likely to discipline a dog with a) the side-to-side shake, b) the submission roll, c) the gentle under chin cuff, or d) some other Monks of New Skete—approved method of being your dog's best "friend." That I did not open a can of whup-ass on the ungrateful goblin in the back seat no doubt has much to do with my pity for his previous owners, but also with my own dog-guilt, that feeling of deep regret associated with the death of a dog you have not always treated well. Mine has grown worse over the years, especially connected to my family's long, miserable experiments with miniature schnauzers, especially to the first of them, Gustav.

Given to us by staunch parish member and amateur breeder Joanne Boyer, Gustav grew to be a fine example of the breed. We docked his tail and cropped his ears, and after he survived that torture and the tape came off his head, he became a classy little salt and pepper with his grey beard and alert audio equipment. We might have been letting the house fall apart, might not have clothes that fit or cars not in danger of repossession, but in Gustav we had a little purebred who looked the part. One rainy fall day in 1981, my brother and I both stayed home sick from school, and my mother left us in each other's tender care. At some point that afternoon, probably when I had given up bouncing a tennis ball in the little strip of drier driveway pavement under the eaves, I failed to shut the side door tightly. Later on, when the dark had settled in and I was actually napping with an open book next to me, my brother yelled up the stairs that I had killed the dog. His actual words were something like "Nice going, shithead, you killed the fucking dog," delivered with just the right catch of emotion. When I didn't respond, he elaborated angrily that Gustav had been hit by a car. This was exactly the sort of thing he was always doing to me, so I returned to my dozy reading, but not without unease. I came downstairs finally when I heard more commotion, car doors slamming, my sister crying, and saw the dog dead on the parking strip, the headlights illuminating the purple mess his head had become.

For years, when plagued by unwanted erections during elementary and middle school, I could conjure the image of Gustav and experience a rapid detumescence in part connected to the frequent reminders from my father that he loved that dog and I had killed him. We buried him back by the compost pile and then went inside and watched the *Muppet Show*. I laughed at the funny parts, which made me feel even worse.

My guilt for the second schnauzer, Wilhelm Alexander (named Wilhelm by Joanne in honor of the newly born Prince of Wales), is almost as bad. Dad insisted the dog be called Alexander for reasons he never made known, in the same way he insisted I be known as "Sean," my middle name, not Chris or Christopher or Cris, as I later preferred. Alexander survived the abuses of the Harris children, from the comic— blindfolding one dog, attaching it to the other at the tail, and then tying in the aging double-yellow-head parrot with homicidal tendencies—to the deliberately cruel, which may have included explosives, air rifles, household appliances, and sprinklers, alone and/or in combination. He also lived through an actual runaway/dog-napping case that lasted for months.

Alexander was actually a pretty rotten dog: untrained, spoiled, and not very bright. Knowing what I know now, this is no surprise; schnauzers are notoriously sensitive. They grow neurotic when subjected to loud noises (firecrackers? AC/DC on the stereo?), corporeal punishment (holding the dog in one hand and beating it with the other the whole distance home from where you've finally run the little bastard down?), and a constant diet of domestic discord. Fact is, Alexander ate compost, rolled in muck, peed on the floor, and ran away every chance he got. When he finally did make what appeared to be his final getaway, no one could be definitively pegged as the culprit who left the door open, but this time I had a good alibi. In his immediate absence, we did all the usual things, like calling shelters and running newspaper ads and putting pleading posters up on telephone poles where they melted away in the rain after a few days. We also took the unusual steps of prayer offerings to Our Lady of Walsingham and driving around with one or another of us half out the window, howling, on the theory that he might respond. I have several surreal memories of being driven to strange corners of Portland, half-singing, half-howling out the window with my mother harmonizing at the wheel. Once in northwest Portland, passing under the 405 overpass, two homeless men came out of the shadows and howled back. Later, I wondered what they thought of me, tongue lolling, paws on the sill, commenting on the bleakness out there.

As an adolescent, I tried to smile grimly at misfortune, to experience loss as more proof of my own toughness, which I have been known to confuse with hollowness. I frequently muttered my apathy to the mirror, declaring my lack of love for my parents, siblings, friends, anything and everything. "I never liked that dog anyway," I'd say, at first only to myself, but as the weeks went on, more publicly. A gender divide opened wider in the house, with only the women continuing to believe, keeping the ads running, driving across town on calls of a sighting, praying. I'd long since given up and gone camping when he returned, victim of a hideous scheme. He had been "found" by a nefarious suburban couple only a few miles away who had "needed" to shave off all his markings to get rid of mats and fleas. An observant (some might say slightly suspicious) neighbor had made note of the new dog next door and as the markings grew back in, grew ever more convinced that she had a crime on her hands. Finally, she called the number in the ad. Mom called Joanne. Joanne called the police, and all parties converged on the scene. The policeman, browbeaten by Joanne, made the couple produce the dog for inspection and took down their pitiful story. While the officer did not hand us the dog—thus earning another long tirade from Joanne—he did seize it as contested property, turned it over to animal control, and fined the couple for failing to report finding valuable property. After fighting the humorless pound vet, who insisted the dog was too old to be ours until we brought in a littermate for comparison, the dog was sprung. It's a heartwarming story of faith, endurance, neighborliness, and a love that knows not the cynical, stony male heart. A story where simple loyalty between dog and owner brings the best together and punishes the guilty. Or, if you subscribe to my father's point of view, it wasn't Alexander we got back, and even if we had, we'd robbed those good people of the dog they'd taken in and taken care of, whose fleas were atrocious and did have matted fur that no one ever groomed. Besides, we were fined for failing to register the dog, so who were we to be celebrating justice?

In any case, my mom declared that we would not go through *that* again, and so it came to be that in the winter of my freshman year, I dug a deep hole behind the red twig dogwood and retrieved Alexander from the deep freeze where my mother had placed him until I could return from a weekend at a friend's. Saying goodbye to the stiffened miniature schnauzer, tongue discolored from the poison he'd drunk, I turned him over and read my mother's driver's license number tattooed on his groin in a string of blue numerals. She'd loved that dog, even if the rest of us hadn't, and I buried him good and deep.

It is with respect, admiration, and bone-bred affection that I now reveal the proto-canine, Benjamin—the original salty dog, the survivor—my own childhood amigo, likeable mutt of my youth, the dog one priest judged "the ur-dog" when he saw Benjamin systematically extract a scratch behind the ears from each attendee at a clergy conference. Oh, Benjamin, I miss you still. I do not remember his Christmas arrival, but my siblings often shared that the stocky black and white Cocker/Poodle mix fit in our father's palm as a puppy that morn. I do remember that in his first year, he could jump prodigiously to snap treats from an outstretched hand. Not being tall at age five, I had to climb a garden wall or a stepladder or climb onto a table to give him a challenge. And I remember not being allowed to approach him after he got hit by a car on Sherwood Avenue that year. He broke both back legs, fractured his hip, and damaged his spine. We used to say that he'd broken everything but his tail, though in fact it was always a little crooked after the accident. He still jumped, once he'd mended, but never as high, an early object lesson in decline.

Our family history teems with stories of Benjamin. Benjamin growling from the prow of the boat when the bull orca broke the surface, his dorsal fin rising up out of the water of Plumper Sound and my father gripping the gunnels in fear. Benjamin crapping not just on the obnoxious neighbor's lawn but on their doormat. Benjamin in his middle years walking blithely through the traffic on Yamhill Street, undeterred by honks and yells from his rounds on the other side. Benjamin barking when Dad, deep in his cups, declared we'd "have a little uproar" and commenced to slapping his black leather gloves together. Benjamin howling over my mother's voice as she sang out for us to come home. Benjamin outliving the puppies meant to be his replacements and attending their burials with disaffection. He seemed old from about my tenth birthday, though Dad always called him "a randy old fucker" whenever he had to go on antibiotics for prostate infections. Benjamin knew no tricks, would not come to his name unless he wanted to, would not fetch, and while affectionate, could be totally oblivious to us if he had something else on his agenda. He liked to have his belly rubbed and ears scratched, but rather than beg for attention, he merely appeared in his gravitas and received his due.

As Benjamin aged, I began to approach his napping form with morbid fascination, calling his name (despite the fact that he barely responded when he was awake) softly but with increasing urgency. Sometimes I had to get down on my knees and hold my ear to his nose to feel him breathing. By the time I was fourteen, it had gotten pretty bad. His breath stank as if he were rotting from the inside. He got in a fight with a sexy German Shepherd bitch who, interrupted from her snacking at the pile of garbage bags behind the kitchen at the Nebraska house, had seen fit to bite through Benjamin's muzzle, knocking loose a tooth I removed by twisting it free with one hand while holding his mouth open with the other. We had to treat him for shock, and while he shivered on the heating pad, I thought he was a goner, but he recovered. He developed a hypersensitivity to the fleas that infested our home-sweet-home, which spurred him to chew the fur and skin from his rump until, in desperation, we made diaper-shaped bandages out of old sheets to frustrate his efforts. We changed them whenever the fluids soaked through. And the old car accident came back to haunt him—his hips and back would lock up until he convulsed on the floor. Did we put him down? No, we got him powerful painkillers that made him a puppy again (until he'd try to do something athletic and end up crying out like a burned child) and, as a little pharmaceutical bonus, sparked the cancer-like growth of canine warts, one of which grew to the size of a plum on the back of his ear, and then went on to grow to peach size and pull his ear up in an expression of perpetual false alarm. Hairless, the wart was really more like a nectarine than a peach, but grey, mottled, and hot to the touch. I'd bring a friend home and watch his instant total immersion in the Harris gestalt as he stepped into a squalor of dirty laundry, dirty dishes, half dismantled electric fireplace (the kind with the rotating cellophane that simulates flames), ants crawling in and out of the sugar bowl (but only into the honey pot) and was greeted by a mangy, scabby, stinking mutt with a tumorous mass hanging from his ear. "Oh, that," I'd explain. "It's a canine wart."

But despite these indignities, the randy old fucker wouldn't die. In fact he never did. After my sister graduated and I'd had enough of that household's particular style of neglect and moved in with my dad, Benjamin's time came. He did not leap in front of a speeding car, yelp out his last in a thunderstorm, lick his master's hand and die, or attempt to mount one last purebred female five times his size. Instead, he just walked away one afternoon when my sister's boyfriend was watching the house. I see him just getting up, stretching, and wandering out some open door, shambling across busy Shattuck Road to the old Alpenrose Dairy, where he spent the afternoon walking among the noble, chewing cows. In my mind, it's a sunny morning with fog in the creek bottoms, and he is eventually lost to sight as he makes his way through the lush grass.

By 2010, though Turtle has probably logged hundreds of miles of walking trails and running the roads, I stop taking her out with me. She has gotten a little too stiff and footsore for the whole day slog, and limps around afterwards just like her owner. But she still chases squirrels and groundhogs, and as her vision weakens, she chases things entirely of her own invention. She has gotten a bit deaf, which eats into her once impressive ability to do a whole array of tricks for amazed visitors. We teach her hand motions instead, which she responds to well. Somehow she knows that when the clock strikes five it is time for her supper, still tolerates the pet ducks that nibble her tail, makes peace with the rooster and even the couple dozen quail we raise one spring. She learned, between ages eleven and thirteen, to fetch a tennis ball. She is still in good health but, of course, is aging.

One dark morning that year, I come downstairs to the kitchen and put the kettle on. By the time the clicking of the burner has given over to the whoosh of blue flame, she is there, sitting by her bowl. From the tin in the pantry I scoop out her breakfast of kibbles. She sits, waiting, until I tell her "OK," which sometimes I have to shout or signal with a thumbs-up. As happens more and more often, she wants to go out, not eat, and trails me through the house as I fetch coat and gloves and hat. She whines with her nose against the cold glass of the kitchen door while I stomp my feet into snow boots. I open the door, and then the storm door, and then the screen door of the porch, and she's off, running a tight curve in the powder, head up, on the lookout for rabbits or squirrels. She sees something by the chestnut, and while I trudge down the driveway to retrieve the paper, my head still thick with sleep, she's darting around the yard, to all appearances free, and young and tirelessly happy, the snow kicking up at her heels.

Looking at her, I think what everyone thinks, I guess. How precious some things are, even or perhaps especially, the cast-off, the abandoned, the survivors by luck and grace. I think of how, with a dog, you see life in miniature, the timescale of birth to childhood to adolescence to adulthood to middle age to decrepitude, all of it compressed until you can almost understand what it is to love something you must, like all things, make your peace with losing.

Sometimes, not often enough, I give the dog an extra cookie.

As for Gremlin, from age fifteen, I'd had it with being unpopular, a loser, an outsider. I'd stopped going by Sean, leaving the whole soft-vowel sibilance of that name behind. I'd saved my money and purchased contact lenses and clothes a step closer to the right ones. And I was determined to begin my sophomore year properly by acquitting myself at pre-season soccer, where I tried to look the part with green nylon shorts, homemade sleeveless T-shirts, and bandana headbands. One afternoon, frustrated by my lack of foot skills and my difficulty getting new cleats broken in, I padded around the main room of the Nebraska house in a foul mood. My brother was home from college and had enlisted in the Air National Guard to pay for his continuing education. I sat down at the piano bench with a bottle of beer he handed me—our mother tried to set limits on the beer consumption, but we just broke them at will. Leaning back against the keyboard, I tucked my blistered, aching right foot underneath me. At that moment Gremlin—who had neither given nor received much affection thus far in his stay with us and had taken to hiding underneath the piano bench—went, as we said in the eighties, *postal*. Despite his warped posture, his mange, his snaggle teeth, his clumsy forelegs, he succeeded in latching his jaws onto the toes of my right foot, sinking his rotten little teeth in deep. He held on even as I whipped my foot forward with him clinging like a weasel, hanging in midair from my foot while I screamed. Gremlin finally flew off, spinning end to end across the room, a leaden little sausage of misshapen, unwanted, widowed/widowered dog. He landed with a thud behind the couch. He lived, but he'd made his enemy.

In horror, I cradled my right foot atop my left knee. The bite was real, a row of oozing puncture wounds between the ball of my foot and the pads of my first three toes. Though my brother was laughing from deep down in his gut, tears running down his face, I was thinking of cramming this foot back into my cleats and running two practices the next day in the wet grass. At stake was not just the infection I actually did come to suffer, but more painfully, my ability to keep the old, familiar, chaotic animal world of my mother's house—where chameleons rested on the schefflera, where the parrot ate the ficus leaves, where the biology class boa-constrictor was always welcome over Christmas—to keep that world separate from my other life, where I denied its messy existence.

On one hand, I feel more dog guilt for my advocacy of Gremlin's destruction than for any other dog sin. It's true that I could not let go of the subject until the matter was settled to my satisfaction. I used foul language, logic, and threats of spending even less time at the house. It's also true that my mother didn't need too much convincing, as if she too was ready to put all of it—the dogs of the past, our duty to victims of age and violence, our squalid service, our wacky originality—behind us, to act fiercely for once, and assert our capacity to pursue our own happiness, whatever the cost. She made the appointment, and she took that dog away, and the vet put Gremlin down.

Moving Out

I've done very few brave things in my life, though I've worked those few heroics into some pretty good stories. Now that my teaching also includes directing an outdoor program, I come across more risk than I used to, but none of it seems very real. I mean, my knees certainly shake when I'm up on the ropes course, and my heart gets up in my throat when I crawl into a snow shelter for the night, but in the first case I'm roped in, and in the second, it's toasty in there after a while and I light a candle and watch the steam from my breath build up near the roof. In fact, the snow shelters we build up in the Allegheny National Forest are the type called quinzshees and have walls twelve to eighteen inches thick; their interiors are absolutely dark, absolutely quiet, and compared to the snow whipping through the night air outside, they seem homey little refuges where you and your companion can stay up talking or playing cards from inside your sleeping bags until you get drowsy. The bravest thing I've done as an adult was propose marriage, which felt a lot like jumping off a cliff. It had the same after-this-step-you-cannot-go-backwards feel to it.

The bravest things I did as a kid were within a year of each other. After eighth grade, when I was fourteen, my mom, understanding my pain at not returning to Pender Island and feeling that I needed a male figure in my life who didn't from time to time reflect on the merits of going out in drag, arranged for me to sail from Seattle to Vancouver, BC, with an old family friend who was taking his twenty-two-foot San Juan there and back. Ray was one of the many Episcopal priests my parents had divvied up in the divorce; Mom got him, though I always thought he and Dad got along really well, drinking scotch and laughing through their beards around many a campfire in my childhood. I was excited at the prospect of the trip—anything to get out of the house and break my deadly routine of lawn-mowing, tanning, and trying to get someone to do something fun. I also yearned for Pender and couldn't stop thinking of special places I wanted to visit. Dad called me at Mom's house on Nebraska Street a couple of days before Ray was to pick me up.

"He likes boys, you know," he said, matter of factly.

"Dad."

"You need to be careful. I'm telling you, the man has a thing for boys. Watch your ass. He will."

"Jesus, Dad."

"Do you have a knife? You should bring a good knife." This wasn't the kind of news I could really discuss with anyone except my brother. Everything was set; I would crew for Ray, he would take care of expenses, I'd catch a ferry to Pender where our old friends the Bowcotts would meet me and put me up in their cabin. Now I had to contend with the creepy thought of Ray, his little beady eyes waiting to assault me, licking his lips under that bushy mustache. Though weaponry was really more my brother's thing, with his help, I decided on a show of force. I strapped the good survival knife, well balanced for throwing, in its clip-on nylon sheath to my ankle, and I practiced a quick draw. The nunchucks needed to be visible, so I made sure I was working them as fast and violently as I could when Ray showed up with a resigned look, as if to say, "Look how you've grown, into a sullen teenager."

He commented on my habit of clipping the knife to the shelf next to my bunk with the blade loosened in the sheath by informing me that piracy wasn't too big of an issue in the Pacific Northwest these days. I gave him a look.

The trip up was eventful; we hit six-foot swells in the Strait of Juan de Fuca, had to motor through Active Pass after midnight to catch the tide, and kept on through the night with the phosphorescence glowing in the roil of our wake. I saw an enormous tidal whirlpool, a ring of foam around flat water with a knot of flotsam (or is it jetsam?) spinning around and going under in its center. Dolphins leapt out of the water at one sunset, keeping pace with the prow. Ray did encourage me to sunbathe nude several times, and did so himself, but it was only creepy when I thought I caught him playing with himself on deck one afternoon. He was probably just scratching. In Vancouver, we went to a meeting of the local rotary in Chinatown, where Ray and I were the only white people and the only English speakers at our table. We ate and ate whatever came around the lazy Susan. I missed a bus that made me miss my ferry to Pender and sat alone for hours in the ferry terminal, growing increasingly worried that I couldn't get in contact with anyone on Pender to tell them I'd be coming in late, after dark.

The whole trip was like that, full of moments of unease. When I arrived in Pender, traveling solo, I trudged up the boat ramp in an outward show of confusion, but I assumed that no one would have gotten the message. To call the elderly owner and manager of the Bowcott's cabin, Mrs. Pollard, was not an option this late. So I started walking, lugging my bags, figuring I could walk all night if I had to—it was as good a way as any to stay warm. Pender is more developed now, but in those days you could walk miles between houses and farms. There were two main roads on South Pender, and the Driftwood Inn (always changing owners, never changing) was at the crossroads, so I wasn't going to get lost. I got about half a mile before a pickup stopped; a youngish guy in a baseball cap told me to throw my bags in the back with the big German shepherd who was panting peacefully and looking out at whatever the headlights and brake lights illuminated of the brush along the ditch. I didn't hesitate much, and it turned out the driver was headed to the government wharf just a quarter mile from the Maples and the Bowcott cabin. At fourteen, I had begun to learn that it was best not to talk too much, and so we rode along in relative quiet, listening to an AM station that played country. After a few minutes he asked me how I came to be walking and I told him my friends hadn't met my ferry, but that I knew where their cabin was, having been here so many times before.

"I used to know a guy who stayed up at the Maples who had kids about your age. He was a priest from Oregon. Wore sandals all summer."

I laughed and wondered at my luck, to have found someone who knew us already, found him right out of the dark on a country road. "In fact," he added after a bit, "he blessed my boat for me." Suddenly I remembered him and his unusual concrete hulled boat, a deep-keeled ocean-going monster painted red and black. We shook hands, which seemed unnecessary given that I was already riding along in the dim light coming from his dash, motoring through the gentle curves of the island road. He dropped me off at the gate of the Maples and turned his headlights back up the road, leaving me in the dark again, but less alarmed at the prospect.

The cabin turned out to be empty, no Bowcotts at all. Though their cabin had power, I didn't know how to turn it on and so lit a candle I found on a saucer by the window, laid my sleeping bag out on the couch, and rifled their shelves for some crackers. The icebox held mustard and ketchup, pickle relish, and an onion, so I knew they had been there. The situation seemed in some ways totally insane. No one actually knew where I was, I had little money and apparently, very little food. No phone, no car, no bike, no boat; just some books, a survival knife clipped to my ankle, and a pair of nunchucks in my bag. I fell asleep feeling strangely happy, like I was on a grand adventure.

In the morning, my hungry belly woke me up a little after five. I killed some time setting up my tent behind the cabin, thinking the Bocotts would surely prefer to find me there than squatting on their couch. At six-thirty I started the long walk to the Driftwood Inn, where I figured to buy breakfast, some groceries, and some time on the pay phone.

I knew the road well, having walked and ridden it hundreds of times over the years. Almost nothing had changed along its length; my steady stride brought me around the curve to the government wharf, where the dirt pack always seemed well oiled and not as prone to dust, down the little hill past driveways leading to houses on the ridge whose interiors I'd never seen and to beach lots with trailers or A-frame cabins whose owners I knew by sight. A bit farther and the big, old, grey barn whose hayloft I'd played in many a hot day on the way back from buying ice cream. Way down past the fields, shimmering with morning heat and dew now, stood the tidy little Driftwood Inn, with its mini-grocery counter, ice-cream counter, and lunchroom.

When I walked in, I felt like a very young child again, but one playing the role of a man. I decided to splurge on a sit-down breakfast, though it used up a chunk of my money. Eggs over easy, sausage, wheat toast and coffee, I told the waitress/clerk/cashier whose accent seemed somehow southern to me, like she'd spent time in Georgia before developing her own twist on the Canadian "eh?" I didn't and still don't really like my eggs over easy, but it seemed the right thing to order, and I even mopped up the yolk with my toast, chasing it around the edge of the crockery till I'd made a clean plate. I resisted the urge to explain my situation at every opportunity, though I almost cracked when I asked if there was a payphone I could use. I felt like explaining the whole thing to the operator who helped me place a collect call home to my mom, but was also beginning to feel the eyes of the waitress on me. Perhaps I'd counted my money too carefully, or lingered overlong in deciding on the hot dogs, buns, saltines, and kippers I bought as provisions. She watched me, thinking maybe I was a runaway or a troubled youth of some stripe, while the phone rang without answer in my ear. I thought about it for a while before I did it, but in the end I called my father, whose outrage was predictable. He would be in touch with my mother, with the Bowcotts, with Ray Anderson, and Mrs. Pollard before I made it back to the cabin with my groceries.

"I'll be fine, Dad. It's fine. I just wanted to know when the Bowcotts were coming. Everything is totally fine." He raged some more on the other end of the phone, but it was true. I would be fine, and I would accomplish what I'd hoped to do on this leg of the trip. Over the next three days, while my dad figured out that my mom had assumed the Bowcotts would be on Pender the whole month and hadn't cleared my arrival date with them, and that she had been frantically trying to get a message to Ray, and that the Bowcotts were due in mid-week and were worried about me, I read my books, built campfires at night, walked the beaches, dug clams and cooked them and ate them, wandered in and out of every old haunt on the property as if taking stock of all my memories of Pender. I did not, however, bathe except in the salt sea, so that when the good Bowcotts did arrive with a car full of groceries and lots of apologies about the mix-up, my hair was matted and stiff and my sunburned skin crusty with salt all over.

None of these adventures were the first of the two bravest things in my childhood. They were larks, crazy stunts, definite high-wire acts, but with a visible net. It was on the way home, when Ray realized we were running out of money from the higher-than-expected moorage fees, the higher-than-expected cost of feeding me, and the unexpected expense of my drinking half the beer, that bravery was required. When I returned from Pender and Ray told me we'd be leaving Vancouver as soon as his conference ended, I got the sense that he was no longer too thrilled to have me along. Difficult, little, suspicious man-child with the thirst for the Molson, I'd been too much for Ray before my father started leaving hate-filled messages for him at his conference, which came to him in the form of yellow notes pinned to the conference bulletin board. Some of them had a lot of underlining and question marks penned in. Though Ray always said it was the rapidly diminishing funds that made our choice, I've always thought it was my family's rougher edges that convinced Ray to pull out into Rosario Strait against a small craft advisory, while the fishing boats were heading in to safe harbor.

The sky got as light as it was going to get until the storm broke by about six, and then the grey rain settled in. We were cutting across the strait to the Gulf Islands, taking a slightly more direct route in order to spend a night with friends in Long Harbor. The big swells came at us from the south and west, with little whitecaps dancing all over them and clapping into the boat from all directions. The wind was right for a fairly direct tack, and we sped into the waves, both of us on the high side, soaked from rain and spray, the prow raising up and slamming down with a shudder when we topped a big wave. By eight o'clock, we were in the thick of it and had to point more into the wind; it was taking us too far, so that small waves were breaking over the sides of the gunnels. Shouting, Ray said we'd be battening the hatches pretty soon, and I laughed, having never understood what the term actually meant. It was only seconds later that the first big wave hit us.

A small boat bounces around on the waves, always bobbing up happily. Down in the trough of a six- or eight-foot swell, our little twenty-two-footer would suddenly angle up like a plane taking off and shoot up the face of the coming wave. But the waves had gone from six to eight to something more like ten or twelve, or maybe even fourteen feet, Ray said later. There was no longer any surface of the ocean, only caroming hills, peaks of dark water rushing and lurching. At the top of a wave, you could see over to the next big one and the one behind that, and then in the valley, you could fight your heart back down your throat while you waited. At the crest, the eight-foot waves would break over the bow, splashing all around us like in the scenes from movies where the sailors are holding tight onto the lines and for all the world it looks like someone just stage left is throwing bucket after bucket of soapy water on them. When we hit the first of the larger waves, the face proved too steep. I watched the wave closing in and the boat tilting, and incredibly, for all the crashing around below deck in the cabin and the feeling that I would fall back off the stern, the wave still wobbled and foamed high above the prow. We went through the top three feet of that wave, which felt like being in a fire hose, or so I imagine. It is exactly like being buried up to your neck in the sand when a three-foot wave smacks you in the face. I could only have been under water for a moment, but I knew instantly that I had not been splashed, had not been sprayed. I had been, along with Ray and the deck of our vessel, entirely submerged for a moment, and I just about pissed myself.

Ray started yelling as we fell down into the trough with a rush and a slapping of waves. Ray had the tiller in both hands and was trying to angle us to face the next wave—clearly capable of turtling us should we take it broadside—but also managing the fact that that when we caught a hard gust of wind, that too would take us over. He was yelling for me to close the hatches, to shoot the bolt and lock us outside. Later, he explained that the boat was everything for our survival, and that if the cabin flooded and she sank, she could do us no good inside her or out in the water. He also pointed out that the boat wouldn't maneuver if she took on too much water, and then we'd be smacked down for sure. At the moment though, he was screaming at the top of his lungs for me to grab the plywood door and slide it into the groove and pull the fiberglass cap down over it and shoot the bolt home, closing us off from the only shelter we had. Belowdecks was awash in seawater; I saw my books floating next to my bunk as soon as I put my head down there. The hatch was floating next to them, and I scrambled back up and placed it, but not before another wave tried to take it from me, tried to knock me flat.

As soon as I had it in place, Ray had me tie myself to the jib sheet with a bowline knot through my life jacket, and I knew it was serious. Then came the hard part.

The wind grew steadily stronger, strong enough that we were living in a constant spray from the whitecaps, and always pitching with its gusty force. We put a mile of slack in the jib right away, relying on just the mainsail, but we couldn't motor effectively. We had a little outboard, and its screw churned a couple feet below the surface. As we tipped down every big wave, the propeller came out of the water; it whined loudly and smoked. What we needed to do, Ray yelled, was reef the main. He talked me through it. I would have to get out of the cockpit, up onto the deck. I would have to crawl a few feet across the fiberglass to the mast. I would straddle the mast, gripping it with both arms and legs, and then I would uncleat the halyards, lower the jib, and then lower the main until he could reef it against the boom. He would do it, he explained, but he needed to stay at the tiller, which was true. The tiller jerked around in his hands though he gripped it till they were white and braced himself against the opposite bench of the cockpit. I relate this as a sort of calm discourse, and in reality, we were outwardly calm. We screamed to be heard over the wind and water and the motor, and Ray's face was deadly pale around his eyes gone so wide. When we hit the bottom of each trough with a crash, my nuts would ache with tightness. Once, the boat shook so hard we could hear our belongings flying about down below. We thought we might have hit a giant waterlogged tree that was menacing us on our way down and up the waves. Water crashed all around us, but we had no choices. We couldn't turn to go back in these waves without risking taking one broadside. We couldn't sit still. We had to get across the strait. And though I was crying with fear, I did what he told me. The deck was slick, and waves were still coming over it. I slipped once all the way to the low side rail, the water roiling six inches below it. And I got a hold of the mast and wrapped my limbs about it like a tree I would shimmy and I got the halyards uncleated and I lowered the jib and I lowered the main until Ray, standing at the tiller, one hand holding the boom, looped a cord through a grommet to make the main a more manageable size, and then I got back. I looked out at the water only once while I was at the mast, and it was like nothing I've seen, though I've dreamed it many times since. I looked out at it, then finished my job and went back to slump against the warmth of the compass. This was the bravest thing I ever did in my childhood. I'm sure I learned some lessons about persistence or faith or something, but that's not the truth of the story, which was just that I saw death all around me and felt fear like a leaden chill in my veins, but tried anyway.

The storm lasted about four hours, during which time we made a crossing that had taken us closer to twelve hours in the slack winds of the night two weeks before. When the storm broke, it disappeared, rolled away like a curtain and left the sea blue and full of foam, the sky a brilliant hue with white clouds scudding across. We were a couple miles off course, but tacked back to a different channel that would get us into the islands. It was like waking from a nightmare. We motored on and took turns bailing out the cabin. We hauled wet sleeping bags and clothing up on deck, where the wind was giving way to a light breeze and the sun was drying out everything. Muscles in my back and abdomen were trembling with exhaustion from keeping myself upright in the surf. We were both bone tired. We made sandwiches with lunch meat and bread that had stayed dry in the cooler, and broke out a couple cans of cold beer to celebrate our survival. I took a turn at the tiller while Ray napped near the piles of drying gear, and when I got hot enough in the sun, I looped the tiller in a taut line to hold our course and went down below for another beer. I stepped into a foot of cold water.

"Ray?" I called up topside. "Hey, Ray!"

"Yeah?" he yelled back, his voice sleepy and irritated. I paused for a second before I asked, because it seemed like I should know, but exhaustion was on me like a heavy blanket.

"Didn't we already bail out the cabin?"

"What do you mean?" he called back, and I knew we had, not even an hour before.

"The cabin's full of water, Ray." It only took us a few minutes to find the breach. Up there in the forward sleeping berth, the cabin was dim, and once my eyes adjusted, I could see the sunlight and shadow of the waterline on the hull. When we found it, the crack glowed a greenish yellow as it admitted both light and water. The latter seeped from it and trickled down the side to join the ever-deepening indoor pool our boat now sported. We had cracked the hull about two feet below the water-line, right up on the prow, where the hull took the brunt force of the waves.

Under clear skies, in fair wind, we had to call mayday. We maintained radio contact with houses on the shore while we bailed and sailed on for Long Harbor, where we motored through a sea of jellyfish so thick it almost jammed the propeller and spent three expensive days in dry dock before sailing on home.

I had first heard the term AIDS that previous fall of 1984, when I was in eighth grade. My sister brought the news home from high school, where she had learned about it in a junior year sex-ed course. The way she passed it on to me and my mother was a little breathless and more than a little simplified, but correct in its essentials. A new disease was on the march out there, infecting gay men all over the country, especially in San Francisco and New York, but even in Portland. The disease, she explained, knocked out the immune system and then the affected died from infections. There was no cure. Eventually our conversation became apocalyptic, warning that though no one had proven it possible, mos-quitoes could pass it on to everyone and we would all die of ordinary ailments, maybe acne or a cold, but some part of me stopped listening at that point and kept repeating the facts to myself. I suddenly became very interested in immunology and all things related to HIV, once the term became common. AIDS encircled us in no time: TV coverage, *Newsweek* articles with 3-D renditions of killer T cells being co-opted, pamphlets in the guidance office, and always the rumor mill, which churned out monkey sex and government programs as origins of the plague, a Typhoid Mary named "Patient Zero," and the famous story where after the one-night stand the guy wakes up short a kidney—no, wait, wrong story—he wakes up with a skull and crossbones drawn in lipstick on his mirror and the message "Welcome to the World of AIDS" blocked out beneath in smeary letters. Every urban legend is in its heart a cautionary tale, but at that age, I believed everything I heard.

Dad went through a really bad flu that winter of 1985, the kind of flu that knocks you out of work for a week and makes you rethink your every breath for a few weeks afterwards. None of us thought much about it; Dad got sick a lot and always had. He worked really hard, smoked a lot, had asthma, and though notoriously strong in the back and round-shouldered with labor, he was horribly out of shape. The illness threw off the quality time weekends for a bit, which I didn't complain about, as the awkwardness of being dropped off or shuttled over by a sibling never went all the way away.

I usually enjoyed myself on these weekends, but it took an effort. Then Dad parted ways with his lover Darrell, and after a couple months living alone, moved into a vacant room in an apartment on Northwest 21st Avenue, where our old family friend Thom Jones lived in a splendor of fussy antiques, leather sofas, Bang & Olufsen stereo equipment with laser-guided linear tracking turntable, hundreds of houseplants, hardwood floors, and the majority of wall space covered in paintings, framed prints, shadowboxes, and even an enormous display of mounted butterflies. Northwest Portland was a hot spot not yet colonized by the yuppies and high-end boutiques that came to gentrify it into mediocrity; it was funky Cinema 21 and the Gypsy and a fish market run by dour lesbians, microbreweries that looked and smelled like breweries, used bookstores, and dozens of tiny hole-in-the-wall cafes. Dad had moved past cooking for a downtown bar and grill and back into polymer chemistry, landing a job at a high-tech firm with the wacky idea of making erasable compact discs. All in all, he seemed to be getting his shit together.

The next fall, just a month or so after I had my adventure on the high seas, he called to tell us he was HIV positive. He didn't tell me directly; he spoke with my mom, who immediately broke down in tears. Her explanations, twisted by hysterical grief, were not wholly inaccurate. That he would die of the disease was true, in the end. That she would prevent us from seeing him was untrue from the moment she said it; she never tried to stop us. He might have a year or two, she said, which at that point wasn't out of line with the experience of other HIV patients around the country, who went from positive to symptomatic to lesion-addled and pneumonic to dead inside of three years. Dad didn't know how long he'd been positive, but he suspected the bad flu was seroconversion, the harbinger of things to come.

I made my decision to move in with my father very shortly after we learned his status. I know I talked it over with my brother, but mostly it was a decision I came to on my own while walking the dog around the block in the rain night after night. It took me a long time to make good on the plan. First, I stopped trying to avoid my court-ordered weekends. Then I begged out of a Thanksgiving trip with my mother and sister to Idaho and instead spent the long weekend with my dad in the apartment while Thom was off in Seattle, trying to restore his fortunes.

I was terrified of this extended visit I'd arranged. I can't even order the fears I had running around inside me like mice. There were semi-rational fears (this man is a drug-using, alcoholic, sexual deviant who used to beat you when you did wrong—stay away!) and irrational fears (you will fall under the sway of the satanic pro-homosexual cultural influences of the household. Woe! Woe!). There was the fear of contagion all around me. Dad, a chemist by training, was meticulous in maintaining sterile conditions in some areas, like the kitchen, but kind of sloppy in others. He hated to waste bath water, for instance, so would call for me to use his once he was out. I often found ways to avoid the bath, but sometimes had to stand there, hyperaware of the garish orange and blue tile work, the patina on the brass fixtures, the occasional floating curly hair, and sometimes I sank into the warm water feeling doom upon me. I knew not to touch his razor or toothbrush, but what about his hairbrush? What about the toilet seat? What was the proper containment response when he nicked his finger with a knife at the kitchen counter and a drop of blood fell on the cutting board?

And there was the fear of change. I had the man pegged, had had him pegged for many years. He was the man in black, the bad guy, the loud yeller and fast slapper, the drunk, the dopehead, the man of false promises and excuses. He was the one who didn't pay the child support, the dreamer of expensive dreams, man of rages, thunderstorm after thunderstorm. What would it cost me to question that role? What would it change if he turned out to be someone different? What if—the evening when we made a simple supper of grilled cheese sandwiches, spicy tomato soup, and garlicky green salad, consumed at the apartment's tiny kitchen table under lamplight, and then had easy conversation over blue mugs of coffee while a rare November snow lightly coated the icy street outside—what if that was the truth of the whole thing? What if it was all about the easy morning ritual of making the coffee to his exact specifications and pouring two big tumblers of orange juice and bringing the glasses and the coffee to him while he shaved at the mirror, and together drinking down our glasses of cold OJ before having the first sip of bitter coffee and saying "aah" in unison. Who would I be in what story then?

It wasn't all noble intentions. With the fear and risk came distinct advantages. Dad did seem to be going somewhere, where Mom was an unemployed deadbeat constantly in trouble with the landlady and the utilities. Because we couldn't and didn't pay for garbage service at the house on Nebraska Street, I was free to burn our refuse in an unused trash can out on the patio, which I did because I liked burning things and I hated the rats that tunneled through the piled-up black trash bags waiting to go to the dump, but the practice left me with the aroma of melted plastic and ash. Here's a picture of squalor: a teenager prodding vulcanizing Styrofoam with a half-burned yardstick in his unmown backyard before going off to prep school. Because we failed to pay our water bills for some time, we went a week without water service, carrying buckets of water from the neighbor's hose to flush the toilets. Carolyn and I broke into the school gym, prying the catch loose with the blade of my pocketknife to shower before school, shamefully, in the dark, mildewy locker rooms. Our ancient Volkswagen bug broke down regularly and in embarrassing locations, like in the driveway of a wealthy classmate hosting a class party. Our best clothes were hand-me-downs, which came to us washed and neatly folded in brown paper bags from our friends the Bassists. Everything we had seemed cheap and broken to me, and I didn't know how to fix it. Of course, I could have tried washing dishes when I dirtied them instead of piling them in the sink where the ants crawled over them. I could have, I suppose, started doing a load of laundry every day instead of adding to the pile outside the bathroom, a pile where the dogs slept and fleas could literally be seen jumping with the naked eye, a pile visible from almost anywhere in the tiny ranch house. I was sure moving in with my dad would turn me around, make me the kind of self-sufficient fellow who knew how to deal with adversity and could find monastic simplicity in poverty, the kind of guy who would take any job to have a job and be moving up, goddamn it, never mind if it didn't pay as well as the unemployment benefits currently feeding the kids. But my empathy for my mother remained nascent and poorly formed, while my keen sense of self-interest dominated my thoughts. I wanted to know my father while I had a chance, having never really had one I recognized before. And I wanted security, cleanliness, regular feeding, a sense of progress. I made my choice and moved in with my dad in the early spring, though it meant moving through scenes of teary pleading, scenes of my brother interceding on my behalf with his dramatic line—"He's fighting for his life, Mom!"—which made us all pause in confusion, followed by forced smiles while I loaded my few boxes into his car and drove away.

When I got back from my sailing trip, I told the story of our misadventures so often that I etched into narrative all the twists and turns, the missteps and close calls, both large and small, until I had a story an hour in the telling. My friends would ask me after I finished, "Would you do it again, knowing how it would turn out?" I'd always say, "Sure. Of course. When do you get a chance to do something like that?" But in reality, my sailing trip was overshadowed by fear and the real risk of harm, and the sense of being a burden on the adults who had to put me up and put up with me. When I think of the waves breaking over the boat, I still get the shivers in an unromantic, gut-tightening way. Would I go out against a small craft advisory in a small craft again? No, to tell you the truth. I wouldn't.

Ask me sometime, would I rethink my decision to move in with my dad, knowing what I know now, that he would live for ten more years, that I would watch him thin down to nothing as his friends and lovers passed away, as he lost his ability to work a job, as his garden grew to be too much, that I would move into a household so depressed and fearful that mail was rarely opened because it likely contained bad news, where, when I was a sophomore, my dad might go out for a beer and return three days later? Would I do it knowing that he would give me the kind of discipline to take care of myself, which I felt such a need for, but also a teary sense of fragility that makes me weep at classical music? Would I do it, knowing that it would hurt my mother more deeply, cause her to question her own abilities as a parent, and divide our family further into the girls and the boys, a division that widened until my sister was disowned, a split still healing all these years later? Ask me sometime, but you know the answer already.

Roommates

When the sun came through the windows, I woke with the distinct feeling that I had sand in my eyes and chalk in my mouth. When I turned my head to read the clock, some portion of my brain complained mightily and commenced to pound in time to my heart. Ah, I thought, I'm hungover, and the night, so recently ended, came back to me in pieces. It hadn't been a huge party, but twenty teenagers in a building with an unofficial no-kids policy can be challenging to pull off, especially if they arrive with cases of beer and shopping bags of gin, vodka, and tequila. Dimly, I remembered one loud girl yelling from the apartment balcony at a squad car on 21st Avenue—"You fucking fucker fucks!"—and having to have everyone sit perfectly quiet for a few minutes until the hubbub in the street died down. We'd also had to monitor the stereo volume. Thom's system was a powerhouse and could just about take the paint off the walls if you cranked it. I made a habit of turning it down two notches every time I passed it on my way through the crowd into the kitchen.

The sunlight did hurt my eyes, but I had to admit it was beautiful. The apartment's main rooms unfolded spacious and open, separated only by a massive stained beam on the ceiling. Both rooms had built-out dormers with huge double-hung windows facing the street on the west wall, and the midmorning sun came streaming onto the hardwood floors through the windows angling north. The dining room dormer had a door of small panes on the north side, which led to a narrow balcony between the dormers, just big enough for a couple of chairs and a bougainvillea. Soon after Thom headed up to Seattle for an indeterminate stay, Dad had taken down all the blinds, so nothing obscured the views of the west hills and the bustling streets beneath them. Stained oak built-ins dominated the dining room. A buffet and glass-fronted cabinets filled the east wall, and an oak table and chairs filled the middle. In the living section, a chesterfield sofa, its quilted leather shining warmly, faced upholstered chairs across a plush rug. Because almost everything actually belonged to Thom, almost everything matched and had the quality of fine antiques. I walked across a fantasy of unpainted wood, glass, sunlight, leather, and paintings. That morning, bleary as I was, I looked out at the good fortune I had fallen into, the trappings of taste and means all glowing in the morning sun. Four of my best friends snored in the back bedrooms, and a pyramid of beer cans marred the ambiance slightly, but I could imagine myself a young man of privilege in that apartment. My father was out of town for two full weeks and I had the place to myself. I was sixteen years old.

The two years we lived in that apartment together proved difficult in many ways. Money was very tight, and Dad had fallen into a depressive habit of just putting all the mail in a drawer unopened unless it had red FINAL NOTICE stamps on it. He was stoned so often and so deeply that it was sometimes impossible to have a conversation of any kind with him. He went out with lots of different men, some kind and friendly, some creepy and frighteningly friendly. Against the forces of disorder, he erected a fortress of routines covering the making of coffee, orange juice, salad dressing, the placement of cups, the precise method of vacuuming, the watering of plants, how we answered the phone, the organization of the refrigerator, the organization of the pantry, the organization of records and books and tapes and silverware. Regulations concerning laundry, if written down, might rival the laws in Deuteronomy in scope and specificity. Case in point—his lunch, which he ate every day, without variation, for over ten years: cheese sandwich, apple, and an orange. The cheese sandwich was made with Tillamook cheddar, two slices one-eighth inch thick, cut from a two-pound brick. He had explained, in some detail, what to do.

Take two slices of bread to which one has already spread a thin layer of Hellman's mayonnaise, careful to cover each slice out to the edges.

Cheese slice one is to be placed in the lower left of the bottom bread slice.

Slice two is cut in half, and one half lined up with the right edge of slice one to create complete coverage of the bread's lower area.

The remaining half, rectangular in shape, is halved again along its long axis, and one of these resulting strips is placed above the original slice.

The remaining strip is halved again, this time along its short axis to fill in the space above the original first half of the first half.

The remaining eighth of a cheese slice is halved again and eaten in two neat bites by the sandwich maker.

Bread slice two is now added. See Wrapping in Wax Paper for detailed instruction on the next steps.

Deviation from this plan was unacceptable and could result in huge arguments, yelling, the pounding of fists. On one hand, I loved the structure and found that it took away all kinds of stress because I always knew, with considerable precision, exactly what I was supposed to be doing and how. On the other hand, the consequences of lax adherence to instructions were severe. Dinner could become a sullen silence or a tirade if the napkins were folded improperly. The entire day could be shot if coffee was ground too fine or too coarse.

But along with these difficulties came an astonishing freedom. In the fall of 1986, when I was yet to turn sixteen, I could and did request the apartment to myself on a Friday or Saturday night. All night. Why? Because, I explained, I had a date, and I wanted to bring her home. After all, he made the same request of me from time to time, and I always graciously spent the evening elsewhere. Each time I made this request, he would grin, and say yes, and remind me where the condoms were. Just in case my wildest dreams came true.

On any given Saturday, once my chores were done, I could walk out the door into the city to sit in coffee shops or see movies or browse bookstores. Friends were almost always welcome for dinner, or the night, or the weekend with or without prior notice. I had no curfew, though the expectation was that I let him know where I was, unless it was late, in which case he'd rather not be woken by the call. We were like roommates as much as we were like father and son, roommates who trusted each other with a lot of the truth, who learned to talk for long hours about politics, religion, science, food, movies, and even the changing of the leaves up on the hill. Strangely, he often treated me as an adult, and I sometimes treated him as a child. I remember vividly a frank conversation we had at the dining room table where he laid out a plan for building a small ecstasy production lab in the kitchen and going into business with a dealer he knew. He pointed out the astonishing profit margin, but I kept getting stuck on the risks of prison, drug violence, or at least, loss of custodial rights. He agreed with me in the end and thanked me for my input. I remember another night when, choking back tears, I asked him to smoke less pot, because it made him into someone else, someone blunted and dampened, someone I didn't like. And again, he thanked me. These moments were difficult, but I mostly remember them with something like pride, because he gave the opportunity to mature, and I often handled that opportunity better than anyone, including me, expected. For instance, when he took a two-week trip back East during the fall of my sophomore year, he handed me an envelope of cash for food and told me to take care of the place.

When my friends finally woke to the smell of the coffee, the day had clouded up a bit and the sunlight had taken on a weak, pale color that made it hard to look at the outside world. Or maybe our hangovers were just that bad. We made an enormous batch of scrambled eggs with ham and onions in it, and ate at the table with the stereo playing in the background, just like we would have if Dad had been home. At some point while we were cleaning up, I looked out the window and saw, at the tables outside Delilah's Cafe across the street, what looked like a beautiful girl about my age. We clustered around the window with our coffee cups, trying to get a better look and competing to describe her attractiveness in more and more expansive terms. We turned down the music and carefully opened the balcony door. It was a really small space, but we crowded it and squinted against the sun to see her. She was blonde and had taken off a light-colored coat that hung on the chair behind her. Her sweater was tight in ways that made us appreciate her figure and wish she would stand up for a moment so we could see her legs. She sat with an older woman in dark clothes and sunglasses, whom we guessed was her mother. Four stories up, we were close enough that we didn't want to make a lot of noise, but still too far to really see the girl well. What to do? The fantasy was to ride the elevator down to the lobby, walk out the door and around the corner and just approach the girl directly. Maybe get a phone number, or even better, invite her up for a session on the sofa. Had she been alone, I have no doubt that one of us, in our groggy sense of invulnerability and teenage boy egoism, would have done just that, probably with so much laughter that she wouldn't have been able to understand. But with the mother, or guardian, or armed escort present, the prospect of it all going horribly wrong seemed to outweigh the risk. We really needed more information. Back inside we talked it over—should one of us go on a recon mission? Buy a latte across the street and check out the situation? Should we all go? If only we could see her more clearly!

We looked through the big buffet drawer, where a lot of Thom's miscellany still lay jumbled together, but could find no binoculars, opera glasses, or telescopes. But then I remembered my brother's scope. He had spent a lot on a fine, high-quality scope, a big black bulging thing almost eighteen inches long with adjustment knobs for wind and distance and God knows what else. But we had to be really careful not to knock it out of calibration or he'd probably kill us with his bare hands when next he came home from college. There was absolutely no discussion of removing the scope from the rifle—couldn't be done without him knowing. Instead, we rushed back to the closet where his things were stored, and being the host and brother of the scope owner (and attached rifle), I asserted my privilege of the first look. I assert with absolute conviction that there was zero hesitation or conversation on the part of those assembled as I took the rifle out onto the balcony, set the barrel on the rail, and scoped out the girl. My left hand cradled the barrel, my right went naturally to the trigger.

There she smiled, clear as day, zoomed in enough that her face filled my vision. She brushed a strand of hair from her eye with her right index finger and I could see the red polish on the nail. She laughed, and stuck the tip of her coral pink tongue out between perfect white teeth. I felt like I could almost hear her—a throaty alto quick with the jokes. I was narrating all this in a whisper to the boys behind me, who kept calling for a full body scan, but I was stuck on that face, that beautiful face still revealed mostly in profile. I wanted to see the color of her eyes, and then she turned my way for just a second, a little flash of dark blue before she said something to her companion. Then she turned back with a strange look of alarm, looking up so I could see the hollow of her throat. Her brow furrowed above eyes so dark as to be almost purple in the cross-hairs. I had my first misgiving just a second before she screamed and jerked herself out of my vision. I hit the deck myself, the rifle cradled to my chest, whispering "shit oh shit oh shit" to my friends. "Get down, get the fuck down!" I hissed to one boy trying to see what was going on out there. I closed my eyes and could see, for a moment, how it must have looked, the scope glinting above the rifle barrel, the stock up to the shoulder of the sniper on the balcony across the street. I could hear a siren out there in the distance, which was normal this close to Good Samaritan hospital, but still scary. She was probably calling the cops right now, who would no doubt arrive with a full tactical unit, a SWAT team in battle helmets toting assault rifles who would rappel down from the roof and swing through the windows boots first. Or she could be paralyzed with fear down there on the sidewalk, crying and trying to make her mother believe her that there had been someone there, a rifle-man, taking aim.

We did the most mature, reasonable, adult thing we could think of at the moment. We put the rifle back where it belonged. We turned off the stereo, component by component as trained, and shut down the cof-fee pot. Quietly, avoiding the windows, we found coats and wallets and keys. We did not run down the stairs, but rather, waited silently for the elevator, and then rode it to the basement, where a side door let us out into a parking lot off Johnson Street. We walked the first block south reminding ourselves not to look back, turned the corner, and then ran like hell, cutting through the park, the back alley of Temple Beth Israel, the access lane to the old folk's home, across the cathedral parking lots and on and on until we got downtown and were safe.

We spent the day partially on the steps of Pioneer Courthouse Square and partially at our favorite coffee shop in Old Town, Le Patisserie (upstairs from the astonishingly appetizing aroma of a mesquite grill at the street level restaurant), and as our numbers dwindled, partially wandering through Saturday market and partially doing a poor job of some homework at the Anne Hughes cafe in the back of Powell's Books, where it was always tempting to go look at beat-up copies of Vonnegut novels instead. At the end of the day, as the streets filled with evening shadows, I walked back to the apartment alone. As I figured, no tactical response unit awaited me, no plainclothes detectives in trench coats, no squad cars, not even a note from the landlady. Just the sticky lock of the heavy door to the American Apartments, and the echoey tile of the lobby. I punched the elevator button, and just like always, the cab descended with a hum and its gate crashed open and closed behind me. As always, I fumbled with my keys a little in the shadows of the hall.

Inside, I turned on lights and the stereo, went to the kitchen to see about dinner. I remember so clearly the sense of not knowing what to do next, standing in front of the fridge. After a minute, I put some leftover soup on the stove and spread some books out on the dining room table. After another minute, I picked up the phone and called my mom. She had the TV on and was settling into the Sunday dinnertime routine, cooking some soup or casserole from leftovers, laughing at the Disney movie with my sister. I think I managed to sound casual when she asked how I was doing. I know I tried.

Found Money

When the first twenty-dollar bill blew up against the rail, Joseph made a sudden dash, snatched it up, and held it triumphantly for our father, too slow that time. In that instant he regressed from moody, worried nineteen-year-old to immature ten-year-old so powerfully that he was still shaking his head about it that night when he told me the story. Finding a prize, the finding worth as much as the prize itself, the grin of the lucky child. It was a poignant feeling as well, because he and Dad were walking the waterfront as part of officially designated "quality time," which always felt like the opposite of childhood innocence. Back in the thick of the divorce, such time was court-ordered and now was technically optional, but our parents had a way of requesting time with us that seemed pretty official anyway. This stroll along the waterfront drew to a close an afternoon that might have included a movie or lunch at a greasy spoon, or even just hours of walking and talking—getting to know each other again. Given Joseph's ability to walk and talk without interruption, usually with a serious, wrinkled brow while he is listening, there probably wasn't anything else on the agenda, just a long walk through Northwest Portland's neglected industrial area, finishing up by traveling south down the waterfront park, then catching a bus back to the apartment on 21st and Johnson. They would talk about serious things, the heart of their relationship, their future plans for careers and imagined lives as they walked out this spring day, a bright chilly afternoon with gusts stripping the occasional cherry blossom and dropping it into puddles on the concrete from the morning rain. Down on the waterfront, the river looked hard and glassy in the sun, with infrequent white caps from the wind.

In spring of 1986, I had just moved into Dad's apartment and was still navigating the hazards of our new relationship. Carolyn and Dad were still speaking, though already heading for their ultimate estrangement. Joseph was staying at Mom's run-down rental by the Alpenrose Dairy, where he had a '55 Chevy in pieces strewn all over the garage and lawn. Dad was offering to take him in, sans white-trash, shade-tree-mechanic habits, but Joseph was wary. So they walked and talked it all through the way Joseph still likes to do, and Dad smoked half a pack of Camel Straights while the blocks and miles rolled by.

Northwest Portland was grungy in those days, a zone of warehouses, disused rail lines, homeless people living under overpasses and in shacks, machine shops that mostly stood idle but occasionally flung their doors wide to show someone intent on making showers of sparks with an arc welder. Ivy grew thick over brick walls and boarded windows. Riding my BMX bike around in those streets, the only people I saw were wearing coveralls, or many layers of coats, or expressions of surprise to see a kid down there not riding a skateboard. When I visit Portland these days, I can never quite reconcile my memories of those blocks, full of the smell of the breweries, with the glossy "Pearl" development that sprung up in the area, square miles of glass and steel galleries, condos, high-end restaurants, coffee shops, primary-colored trolleys bearing loads of richly dressed patrons while Teslas cruise slowly, looking for rare parking spaces. Back in the mid-eighties, you walked through the area to get in touch with your brooding, melancholic, looking-for-a-fight-you-wouldn't-even-mind-losing side of your personality. I know Dad saw it the same way: a treat for lonely, angry, cynical people to find a whole neighborhood that looked like they felt—abandoned, labyrinthine, beat-up, and scary. Like a lot of my friends, I shot grainy black and white stills down there by the roll.

And Waterfront Park was no better. In fact, it held more danger, because so many violent and desperate people populated its neglected spaces. A network of homeless shelters, food pantries, and soup kitchens grew up around both ends of the Burnside Bridge, stabilizing a population that took up residence underneath and around it. You could reliably see really down-and-out people there, and be offered drugs, sex, and an ass-kicking during a short jaunt. Which made sense, in a way, as the park wasn't really a destination or even a connection between destinations. No one had yet built exclusive marinas, Japanese American internment memorials, luxury hotels, interactive fountains for kids to play in, or mixed-use housing along its length. The river itself was a Superfund site just upriver at Oregon City and downstream at the shipyards. Old guys, mostly Black or Asian, fished from the banks here and there, to the amazement of passersby who would not touch the water, much less eat anything caught in it. Portland, in its pre-tech-boom glory, had many places like these, atmospheric, edgy spots where you walked looking for trouble or at least the sense of trouble.

So on a gusty day, buttoned up and avoiding eye contact, Dad smoking as he walks, Joseph listening or working something out, they walk along the river. A twenty-dollar bill, scraping and tumbling, blows down the pavement and catches on the fence rail just before it would sail out over the water. Joseph leaps forward and swoops it up, grins at his good fortune. While he's gloating, Dad laughs and claps his hands in encouragement, secretly wishing he'd seen it first. They walk on, all smiles now, and stuck to the leg of a park bench, on Dad's side this time, is another bill, crisp, green-gray cash. Dad guffaws as he nabs it. Then does this thing with his hips we all found embarrassing, switching them back and forth in glee. He defended this habit as "earthy" when challenged. I'd call it "raunchy" or just "gay" but that only encouraged him. I know that in that moment on the waterfront, when Joseph was enjoying the sheer normalcy of a competitive father/son moment, the gesture would have crossed the line, suddenly revealing Dad in his butch glory—heavy mustache, tight jeans, leather jacket, black watch cap and boots, shaking his ass while laughing and holding a twenty in the air. There weren't a lot of people around, but I'll bet Joseph had one of those sudden reevaluations of his situation, especially since he and Dad looked so different. I'll bet it felt like every single person in the park was wondering whether the older guy in the leather or the young, athletic, tall guy with the white-blonde, feathered hairstyle was the customer.

Then everything changed as they noticed movement at the edges of their vision, other pale bits of paper fluttering. My dad had a deep philosophical objection to running, but he leapt into action. In a moment they were both running upriver, grabbing at twenties that bumped and scraped across the pavement in the wind, tumbling out over the water. Try not to imagine the Hollywood version, with confetti clouds of currency, but there was money in the air, landing out in the Willamette's clay-colored waves, money sticking in puddles on the concrete, money inciting the few bench sitters to their feet and making them snatch at the air like kids after dandelion fluff. Dad and Joseph yelled encouragement to each other, and then it was over a minute later, with no bills left but those sinking in the water.

Dad had managed to grab $80 or $100, Joseph a bit more, not huge numbers, but enough to have them bragging like pirates in the apartment kitchen. We were drinking a pot of coffee and prepping dinner, thick pork chops Dad had stopped and bought on the way home, a garlicky green salad with tomatoes, a pot of black beans, broth thickened with spices and flecked with cilantro. I kept asking about the event, spurring them on to greater detail. Twenty years of inflation has turned $200 into a few tanks of gas or a trip to the vet or a fancy dinner out. But man, at fifteen, it was way huge, some fifty hours of manual labor if you could find it and get paid under the table. Two hundred bucks was thousands of weeds pulled, for instance, so I couldn't get over the fact that no one had jumped into the water, especially as both Joseph and Dad were great swimmers, unlike me, who always faked the crawl and really, still do.

"I'd have kicked off my shoes and jumped right in," I say, shaking my head. "What a waste." They both look at me. Talking it over, they share their theory that it was probably a deal gone bad.

"Probably drugs. Cocaine maybe," says Joseph casually. My eyes fill with slow-motion shots of men in dark suits and thin ties, extending steel briefcases to each other, when one pulls the MAC-10 from under his jacket. I pictured him as red-haired, with a hairlip like our friend Danny O'Malley, and he sneers before pulling the trigger, unleashing not separate gunshots, but a stream of fire and ricochets, jets of blood spraying out into the air. And then the third man behind the lamppost! The guy with the pistol and laser scope! They are trading shots and running out of the park, into the alleys by Skidmore fountain. The briefcase full of unmarked bills, its covers pocked with bullet holes, lies open on the pavement, the lock sprung. The sounds of gunfire and sirens recede in the distance, and the breeze lifts first one, then another bill loose from the case. They tumble down the waterfront a few at a time.

"Did you go look?" I ask, afraid of the answer.

"I already told you, idiot, that we got out of there. Something bad was going down, and there wasn't any more money coming."

"I'd have gone and looked," I say.

About a year earlier, my mother had received a check in the mail for $1,000, I think from her uncle Kingdon Swayne, whom I had only met once, at my grandmother's funeral. I remember him as rather jolly for the occasion, pink face and balding silver hair above a powder-blue suit. Mom often mentioned him as the one in the family with money. His check came at a good time, as we were experiencing what newspapers refer to as "financial insecurity," the kind of broke that takes the fun out of poverty. We were used to calls from collection agencies and envelopes marked FINAL NOTICE. We did not expect new anything at all, nor vacation trips, nor allowances, nor much else that was exciting (except that cast-off things were always arriving at our door, and they were often exciting—a television that had no knobs, easily solved with a pair of vice grips, a bag of hand-me-down clothes). But right around this point things had gotten kind of bad. The clutch went out on our 1968 Volkswagen bug, so Mom learned to shift without it, though this involved a lot of gear grinding if you were doing anything tricky, like downshifting to go over a speed bump at the entrance to your elite private school. We would cheer loudly when this happened, my sister and I, though mostly out of embarrassment. More often we walked to or were dropped off at the back entrance to the school, a chain-link fence and gate at the end of a maze of curving roads, cul-de-sacs for a future development that remained a field of mud and weeds for several more years. Often the gate was locked, so we would scale the fence, or if Carolyn was dressed up, walk around it and come through the woods, arriving on campus like little Appalachian refugees to the land of au pairs and BMWs.

The water company made good on their threat to not give us water if we didn't pay them for it, so for a brief period we struggled to make do. This had happened once before, but in the summer, when a kind neighbor actually offered to run his garden hose across Nebraska Street to our front yard, where we could fill buckets for cooking, bathing, and flushing the toilet. But this was the fall, that stretch where Carolyn and I showered at school some mornings, which also involved walking down through the woods to the gym. Its heavy metal doors had a lot of play in their hinges, so if I leaned hard on the side with the doorknob, the socket in the strike plate would open up enough that I could slip in the blade of the lock-back knife I'd taken to carrying and release the latch. The door would swing open on the dark expanse of the basketball courts. Carolyn had to walk all the way across the absolute black to the girl's locker room entrance, and then up the stairs where a gray glow came in through dusty skylight windows. It took courage and ingenuity and a general regard for cleanliness to go through this ritual, but mostly it felt shameful, and Carolyn made me promise not to tell my friends that she was showering in the locker room in the fall of her senior year because no doubt, they would ask why.

Being broke is about not having choices, I guess, but there are choices you think you are making, ways of dealing with the lack of options. Really, they are solutions; the choice was to solve the problem in the short term at least. At a certain moment though, with rats in the piled-up garbage sacks you have chosen to haul to the dump—later, when you have more cash—rather than pay for garbage service, with ants crawling over your face in the night, with the friendly landlady beginning to threaten eviction, with the rock-hard loaves of homemade bread and endless pots of soup, you arrive at a pretty constrictive feeling.

And then, an envelope with a thousand-dollar check in it. We all knew what was owed to whom and where that money should go. I didn't read the bills, but Mom answered questions about finances candidly, and frequently went through a sort of budgeting exercise at the table. I think she was glad to have someone to talk to about it. So I knew, and Carolyn knew, and Mom must have known that going out to dinner—even just Chinese at the suburban strip mall on Beaverton Hillsdale—was an utterly unjustified extravagance. She would not be dissuaded, would not actually engage in debate. Cheerily, a little brittle in her cheer, she led her protesting children to the car and started driving. The bug also needed an alternator—lights, windshield wipers, and the radio could not be operated simultaneously without a metronomic static and dimming of the lights with every sweep of the blade. You had to turn off the radio on steep hills to avoid stalling. We trundled on through a steady, cold drizzle.

A cold coke with ice. A scotch. A cup of coffee. Kung Pao chicken, sweet and sour pork, egg-drop soup. A steaming bowl of fluffy white rice. Refills from the fountain. A second scotch. A warm-up for my coffee. A vegetable shrimp stir-fry. All of it brought to the Lucite-topped table on big platters. Plastic chopsticks in paper sleeves. Fortune cookies. Outside, the dusk deepened to full dark. The rain was cold and relentless, but it was steamy and warm and womblike in the restaurant with its heavy use of dark red fabric, and I should have been happy. But this panicky, anxious side of me was doing simple arithmetic and starting to mutter my results. Five bucks for this and $7.99 for that and $3.50 twice, and pretty soon we were looking at $60, blown. Pissed away. Carolyn looked near tears, either at the wastefulness or the prospect of a fight breaking out. Mom lit a cigarette and brought her left foot up to her chair seat, draped her left arm elegantly over her knee, palm up, the cigarette extended between drags. She looked into the middle distance as if pretending that we didn't exist.

We argued on the way home. My position that we could have eaten for a week on that money was not hyperbolic. Mom took a higher plane of argument. It was a gift, she said. Found money. When the world is generous to you, you have to be generous of spirit yourself.

"Lighten up," she said. We dropped Carolyn off at a phone booth at the bottom of the hill. She had two quarters and planned to call a boy. She didn't want me pestering her to get off the phone at home, and planned to talk as long as she wanted for that twenty-five cents. The other quarter was to call home for a ride if it got too late to walk. We had school the next day, and it was already late, but Mom let her out and we drove home listening to the wipers whine back and forth across the windshield.

Midway through Thanksgiving morning, with Dad's apartment windows steaming up and the activity level in the kitchen growing more intense by the hour, I announced I was heading out for a run. Cross-country season had ended just a week or two before, and my team had won third at the state championship. Things were turning around for me in my sophomore year, and running was a reliable source of esteem-building pleasure. Plus, I reasoned, if I headed down to Marshall and headed West up into the hills, I could eventually climb up into Forest Park, hit Skyline Road, come all the way north to Burnside, and drop back down the hill to 21st and come home. I didn't have a map, but guessed it was about seven miles and steep enough to take over an hour. Past experience had shown me that I would be entirely forgiven that hour of solitude, a stretching session, and a long, hot bath; also, the general post-run fatigue might get me out of significant kitchen duties that were clearly stressing my father out. Family holidays in this era tended to go from sad, tense occasions in the morning to angry exchanges in the afternoon and could reliably be expected to culminate in slamming doors and hurled gifts before evening fell. Already, there was an edge to Dad's instructions to his lover Joe about stuffing preparation, and an urgency in his musings about when my brother would actually arrive.

"Oh, for God's sake, Renne," Joe would cackle, his Texas coming through even in exasperation. Miraculously, Dad would apologize and laugh. Though I tried not to get too attached to the men who would suddenly become a part of our lives and then just as suddenly disappear, I liked Joe and wanted the day to go well. He seemed to find us, the family, more funny than sad, and had a way of letting Dad play a maudlin version of himself that was more easily handled than the depressive one. So I swaddled myself in heavy sweats and headed out.

The run turned out to be a lot longer and a lot more difficult than I had imagined. The temperature started in the mid-thirties, and I was plenty warm as I ascended the hill through a cloud of misty rain. At the top, wet snow blanketed the roadside. Rain turned to intermittent hail. My knee started to pain me at every left step, and I frequently had to walk or stop and stretch. My sweats turned into massive sponges and seemed to weigh forty pounds. I laughed weakly as I stumbled along Skyline Boulevard, soaked to the bone, slogging through. Two and a half hours later, I came down Burnside making slightly faster progress than

I would have made crawling. The gutters were full of melting hail, with channels of water sluicing through them bluely. Outside of The Gypsy—a venerable cocktail lounge on 21st—I saw a wallet in the gutter. It was a large, maroon pocketbook sort of thing, with a snap to keep it closed. The street, I noted, was deserted. I picked it up, unsnapped it, saw credit cards and ID and a checkbook and $47 dollars in cash. I had the money in my pocket and was bending down to replace the wallet in the gutter when I had a pang of doubt. I walked the last couple of blocks, debating whether to keep the money my own little secret ("It was empty when I found it, ma'am. Scout's honor") or replace it and hope for a reward. I knew what the smart thing to do was—I'd almost done it already.

Dad buzzed me in and opened the door for me, shrieked at my dripping sweats, and grabbed me a towel. Both he and Joe had changed their clothes, made a fresh pot of coffee, and seemed in a much better mood. I took their suggestion to find a dry shirt and jeans myself, leaving the pocketbook by the telephone. I tried to regale Dad and Joe with the story of my run (they nodded along, and Joe even said "Oh my" several times, but they were just being polite) and then went to call the number on the soggy checks. I had to put my finger in one ear to hear the phone, the two men behind me were laughing so hard. The owner was overjoyed to hear from me—the checkbook was their business account. She was still in the neighborhood visiting friends, and could be over in a few minutes. I gave her directions and hung up. I padded into the kitchen, all tender-feet and stiff legs to get a cup of coffee.

"Well," Dad said, suddenly serious.

"Well, what?"

"Did she ask about the money?"

"No. Just about the checks and credit cards." I was puzzled about this myself, having a hard time imagining not being concerned about my cash.

"What are you going to do?" he asked. A trick question in a way. There was only one correct answer, I knew. It wouldn't do to keep even part of the money. I had put it all back in on the way upstairs, I couldn't take it out again.

"Maybe she'll give me a reward or something," I said. Dad's reaction was inscrutable.

The owner buzzed a few minutes later and I let her in, telling her I'd meet her at the elevator over the squawky intercom. The American apartments had a lot of old-fashioned features that were highly marketable later, when the building turned into expensive condos, like hardwood floors and balconies with French doors, high ceilings, octagonal-tiled bathrooms and kitchens. It also had old-fashioned features that were less marketable, like the intercoms, which were ancient phones with separate earpieces, and the wonderfully unreliable elevator with the brass gate that crashed open and closed, through which you could observe the elevator shaft passing. Both the outer windowed door and the gate had to be fully closed before the elevator would respond to a pushed button. This delay allowed other apartment dwellers to summon your elevator if they hit the call button on their floor before you punched your selection inside the cab, which added to the horror movie ambiance of the place—you come in late, call the elevator to the dark, echoing, marble lobby, and it descends, empty and lit by a flickering bulb, down to a sudden halt two inches above the floor. You step in, allow the outside door to swing shut and then wearily, you close the gate and the cab leaps into motion! You can't stop it without making its alarm bell sound! Captive, you ascend to the sixth floor, where a hollow-eyed elderly woman in a nightgown waits. The elevator could also do tricks like stopping between floors, or below the basement if you had too many friends or heavy pieces of furniture in it. So I waited for my visitor there in the hall in case she had trouble, and tried to look friendly. I held the pocketbook in my left hand, ready to pass it on.

She was tall, a bit weary looking, in her mid-forties. She had a firm handshake and heels that clicked on the tile. I handed her the pocketbook, explaining where I'd found it and apologizing for it still being pretty wet, though I'd put it on top of the radiator while I waited for her. She thanked me for calling her, explaining that she and her husband owned a small restaurant, and that without the credit cards and checkbook for the business, they would have had a pretty miserable weekend. While she spoke, she unsnapped the pocketbook, reached in, and pulled out the bills in a stack without looking at her hands. She held them out to me without mentioning them in her explanation of the hassles of closing accounts and getting ID reissued and how I'd saved them a lot of time.

"You sure?" I said, looking at the money.

"Absolutely," she said, and thanking me again, got back into the elevator to go. She waved as it dropped down out of sight. I walked back to our apartment door, still open and issuing Bach at a high volume, feeling both happy for the money and slightly guilty for having almost stolen it. I blew it on books, coffee, and music over the next couple of weekends, and that assuaged the guilt.

It seems that everyone has a found money story or two to tell. Something about the situation proves a celebration of good luck and often a test of character. The universe hands you some scrap of good will and you have to figure out what to do. I had a boss who tells the story, in his lovely Carolinian twang, of finding a fifty-dollar bill on his way to school. He holds his hands out, shaking, to mime his reverent posture when, his little third-grade voice near tears, he gives the money to the school secretary, saying that he's found it and doesn't know what to do. Later, after the principal highlights the story as an example of good citizenship in his morning address, the child is beaten by his classmates on the playground. "You idiot!" he remembers someone jeering as he lay on the pavement. "You could have bought a minibike for that!"

In college, when Mary and I were broke, we'd troll the ATM at Kimbark Plaza in Hyde Park. The wind came right up 53rd Street from the lake as a steady pressure and could gust just as the cash fluttered down into the tray. More than once, we'd found a ten or a twenty among the leaves that eddied up behind the brick pillars outside Kimbark Liquors. Such providence, we'd say as we carried the beer or wine back to the dorm, where we shared it with friends. And the glory of childhood summer mornings, when a search through my Sunday clothes from winter, hanging all askew in my closet, could result in a dollar bill—no doubt meant for the offering plate at some long-ago service and thoughtlessly forgotten—still neatly folded in a pocket. Or, even simpler, walking to the store with no money on a hot summer afternoon, hoping and hoping to find four cans or bottles in the burning street to redeem for their nickel refunds, which in Oregon could turn into a twenty-cent popsicle staining your face blue on the walk back home. Purer still, stumbling empty-handed and with no hope at all down to Dickson's Drugs in Montevilla—where the widow Dickson turned a blind eye on depressive kids hiding behind the comic-book racks on rainy fall afternoons, where you could escape for the whole of the doldrums between 2:00 and 5:00—and finding, in two separate sidewalk cracks, two pennies. Just enough for a Jolly Rancher candy, a tiny bit of sweetness handed to you when you needed it. And the rules for found money have always seemed consistent and sound to me—you spend it freely, share it without stint, find some thankfulness and wonder to go along with the cash. Those afternoon discoveries of ten or twenty dollars in college always ended in evenings or laughter and drink, watching the sun go down among friends recounting their good fortune.

When Dad died in 1995, it fell to me, as the son living in the house, to make the call to his life insurance company in order to "submit a claim." I understand the phrase, but it gave me pause, especially the connotations that come with submit (you give something to a higher authority) and claim (what you suggest will be ruled on in terms of its veracity). So much in my life was utterly, incontrovertibly, unchangeably true. The evidence was all around me. I dreaded the process, which I imagined might be cumbersome and involved, but got in touch with that plodding, stoic attitude that can make a grieving person a slow juggernaut. It took a lot of sighing and shuffling of papers, but I made the call. It was a policy set up through Portland Public Schools, Dad's last employer, and I knew about it because I'd helped him change the beneficiaries about a year earlier, right about the same time he'd added Joseph and me to the deed on the house with rights of survivorship, to keep the property out of the estate. He'd wanted to split the life insurance evenly between Joseph and me, as he'd wanted everything not specifically willed to anyone split. Carolyn, officially disowned in unambiguous language, was cut off completely.

It turned out to be a low-key call. This was about five weeks after the funeral. Mary and I had flown back to Iowa, packed up our apartment, driven to Appleton for our wedding, driven back down to Iowa City, filled up the U-Haul trailer, and headed west to Portland, all inside of three weeks from Dad's death. We were cleaning and dealing with the garden, and in tiny increments, the mountains of paperwork. I'd made a lot of phone calls by this point and gotten better at saying what needed to be said with what I hoped was an honest, but not overly emotional, tone. At the insurance agency, I spoke with a startlingly perky receptionist, who established my identity, instructed me on mailing in a death certificate, and reviewed the beneficiary information and mailing addresses. It was pretty painless.

She called back about ten minutes later, breathless.

"Mr. Harris, are you sitting down?" She seemed genuinely concerned. I was in fact still sitting in exactly the same spot, but for some reason felt like standing. She'd never know.

"Yes. Is there a problem?"

"Well," she began, with a fairly unbusinesslike, almost conspiratorial whisper, and then proceeded to narrate her perusal of Dad's file as if it were the most exciting thing she'd had happen in a long time. Maybe it was. She'd found a second, much larger policy of which I was named as sole beneficiary. It took her awhile to get through the business of bringing in her supervisor and double-checking the protocol before she shared the actual news. Meanwhile, I'd headed to the kitchen in search of coffee. I paused then, in the doorway, and looked down into my empty cup. I asked her to repeat just the pertinent bits, the total number of policies (two), the payment on the second policy ($90,000) and the beneficiary (Christopher Sean Harris).

"We should divide it like the first policy," I said, I hope firmly. At this moment, her breezy, intimate, Prize Patrol mien vanished and she became all business. It was a relief. At her urging I repeated my request several times, and once again to her confirming supervisor, and it was read back to me as well.

"It's what he wanted," I said at one point.

"Are you sure?" she asked back.

"I'm sure," I said. She pointed out that both policies had had their beneficiaries confirmed on the same date—if he'd wanted to change both, why would he only have completed one?

"I'm sure," I said again, though of course I've never been sure. He could have meant it as some surprise reward, some special treatment. If that were true, I guess I got the message whether I kept the money or not. But it's a safe bet that he just fucked it up, signed one form and took a long hit off his pot pipe, threw them both in an envelope and went to bed. And what were my options? Talk it over with someone? Opt for greed and a dirty secret from my brother? Try for both the birthright and the blessing?

I've never told him, unless he's reading this, because I couldn't find a way that wasn't about me being the self-righteous kid who could have had the minibike. And I don't think about it too often, except to remember how easy it was to let it go. Joseph and I bickered about other parts of the inheritance, things both little and big, squabbles I regret, but that part, the extra policy no one knew about, I let go of it like found money, a gift from the world when I needed it.

I come back to the apartment on a bleary Sunday morning, nearly noon but seven am dusky in the quiet fog. Back of my headache and watery insides is a night drinking whatever there was to drink—light beer, sloe gin, rum and coke, screwdrivers, black Russians, white Russians—at two different parties full of hysterical high school students. He will ask me, I know, if there was drinking, and I will tell him the truth. This is our arrangement. We do not interfere in each other's weekends, but we do tell the truth. He is forty-six. I am sixteen.

The little foyer inside the apartment door is dark, and down the hall the bathroom light is off, but he's in there; I can half see his seated figure on the toilet—"the throne," he calls it. His bare legs stick out from beneath his robe. I call out that I'm home and he replies in a strangled voice. I move to the door of the bathroom as he's standing up, flushing, pulling on his briefs. The crotch is stained with blood. "Jesus, Dad," I say and shiver.

"It's nothing serious." He is ashamed, weary to have to tell me. "A little rough sex, that's all. I'm just bleeding a little from my penis." He has been in the emergency room much of the night, explaining to doctors that his partner blew air down his penis and ruptured something so that a slow, steady drip of dark blood has, without much pain, reminded him moment to moment of the choices he's made. He has been HIV positive for over two years.

This is a moment of such wrongness, such danger, such not-okayness, such absurdity, that I feel a smile break on my face, a laugh begin in my throat. I ask, "Are you going to be all right?" and he looks up at me sharply, alert to the tone in my voice. "I mean, if not, there's always amputation . . . I can get the scissors."

"Not on your life." He scowls and smiles at the same time, eyes bright.

"Is there coffee? I need coffee. I'll make a pot of coffee." Not long after, I bring him a cup where he's slumped in a chair, sitting on a towel, his cigarettes and lighter on the table next to him. He grunts by way of a thank you and doesn't tell me to keep my feet of the couch when I lay back on it and close my eyes.

. . .

Apron Strings

It's a story he likes to tell, has always liked to tell. At his graduation from high school (I have a picture and so know what to see: his crew cut, bow tie, roguish grin, sparkling eyes back in June 1959), his young mother waited to give him the present. First he opened envelopes from aunts and uncles with five- and ten-dollar bills inside that represented significant sacrifice, wheat and wool and saved wages, dents in bank accounts slow to recover. Then, his mother's gift. In telling the story, he shapes the long, thin box in the air. I imagine it as white, the cardboard perhaps scuffed from a previous use, the kind of box you might use to gift a tall set of beeswax tapers or a single long-stemmed rose.

My grandmother, Eileen Saling, née Harris, née Kelly, all my life seemed ageless, with crinkled crow's feet and rosy cheeks. Her teeth were always white, and she never complained of pain save to say "Gotta hitch in my git-along" with good humor when rising with effort from a comfortable chair. If she seemed sad, or to always be slowly turning away, isn't that likely my own projection? She laughed with her head thrown back, just like the rest of us. She never suffered a gray hair to remain undarkened. While she grew stern with my brother and me on a few notable occasions, as when I fell through the ice on the creek out at the ranch, or when we ate every last crumb of breakfast cereal in her cupboard as a snack one afternoon, she seemed largely beyond anger with grandchildren, even though her youngest daughter was my brother's age and she was all of forty-six when I was born. It is hard for me to imagine her ever as cruel, or subtle, or calculating. But we Harris folk of eastern Oregon, Irish mutts one and all, have our love for outmoded idioms, which perhaps explains everything.

"Bread and butter," I mutter automatically when a lamppost passes between me and a walking companion. "Wreck of the Hesperus," I sometimes sigh under my breath, looking at the kitchen after dinner. I demand a penny when I give a knife as a gift, grow cross when anyone speaks before drinking to the toast, want roast beef and Yorkshire pudding for Christmas dinner, and occasionally even yearn for mincemeat pie with hard sauce. So I should never have been surprised by her, long-suffering and kindly though she was.

The box is light, weightless as tissue paper. He stands tall at the dining room table in the suit he has bought with money saved from an assortment of jobs, all kinds of old-fashioned jobs with hyphenated names belonging to another era: slash-crew, ranch-hand, soda-jerk, paper-boy. He is thinking of going to college in the fall, as he's been encouraged to do, has a summer job as a fire lookout that will give him his tower in the woods, his panorama of glass, his precise records and radio to monitor. He opens the box and understands the shape of what is coming to him. He would have it no other way.

He tells me the story for the last time in the early spring of 1989. I have applied to five colleges, all private schools, all with tuitions in the tens of thousands of dollars. I have extracted from him the financial information I need for the FAFSA and have penciled in a photocopy of the maddening green form before transferring my calculations, again in pencil to the form itself, before overwriting them in ink and erasing. I have no college fund and have saved only a hundred dollars or so toward the future, though I am tutoring middle-schoolers and working as a legislative aide at the capitol in Salem one day a week. We sit at the dining room table where he enjoys a cigarette and waits for the fresh pot of coffee to finish its throat-clearing rumble in the kitchen before we get busy clearing plates and silverware. His lover Joe, always restless, is up rattling around, talking himself into running down to the corner store for a package of cheap cookies we will gorge on after the dishes are done and we can plunk ourselves down in front of *Star Trek: The Next Generation* and laugh together. I have heard the story before but am in no hurry. I know the ending and know it can't repeat itself exactly in our situation, but am resolved to do what I can to keep the family story alive. My brother joined the military to pay his way through school. My sister works full time in a private clinic to pay for her nursing-school classes. I feel resolve solidifying in me like iron reinforcements to my spine, or perhaps bands of steel around my heart.

"I opened the box, there with all my relatives, everyone watching. There were sheets of tissue paper carefully folded over what felt like nothing." He milks it, smiles in mock puzzlement. "Finally, I open the paper, and there are two long cloth bands, narrow rolled cotton bands, of a light blue I recognize instantly. They were her apron strings, and they were cut." He leans back and smiles. The coffee pot gives a long death rattle, and he gets up to grab the carafe from the burner. Wordlessly, he grips my shoulder when he refills my cup.

Three months later I board a ferry in Seattle with a steerage ticket, negotiate the ragged crowds jockeying for the best spots in the solarium, and find a deserted side deck piled high with coiled ropes the thickness of my arm. I lay out my sleeping back between two coils and wait for the ship to push off from the dock. After two days, I disembark in Petersburg, Alaska, and make my way to the cannery, walking past a bald eagle pulling a McDonald's bag from a trash can. I join the ranks of young men and women trudging up the low hill to join the workforce. Three days later I work my first eighteen-hour day in the fish cannery.

When we speak over a crackly pay-phone connection two weeks later, he wants to know where he should put my stuff. Confused, I ask why exactly is he boxing up my belongings?

"We rented your room," he says flatly.

"Jesus, Dad. You rented my room already? To who?"

"To whom," he corrects, and then tells me the lodger is one Duck Luvv, a recovering addict thus renamed after senselessly swimming away from the Portland Police, who rescued him from his suicide attempt jumping off the Morrison Bridge into the cold water of the Willamette River. I've met Duck a few times and believe him to be the exact kind of nutjob who would try to jump off the Morrison Bridge and rename himself Luvv. "So I'll just put it all in boxes and you can sort it out when you pack for college," Dad says to my silence.

I don't call for nearly a month, by which time things have changed. It's a record season up in southeast Alaska, and I've earned a spot on the night cleanup crew. I'm pulling down seventy to ninety hours of overtime a week. I've got a cough I can't shake. Duck Luvv no longer lives at the house, if he lives at all. Joe found him lying on the carpet one afternoon, turning blue, no pulse, with the heroin needle still in his arm. The EMTs had his heart going when they took him away, but that's the last detail I ever hear. Dad has moved my boxes back to the room, he explains. I tell him I'm glad to hear it. On payday, I send him a check to send to the university, then get a few hours' sleep before the next shift.

My Father's Idea of a Story

"Simple story," he says to me.

"Simple story," I say back.

"I heard this when I was just a boy," he says. "Just a little kid hanging around the barbershop. I'll tell you this story, you'll see what I mean." He waves his bottle out over the unfinished patio, now darkened by dusk. We have been working on it all day, out in the sun, and now, my father and I are sitting on the porch where it is cool, and we are drinking Henry Weinhard's, still locally brewed that summer, and smoking cigarettes—him Camel Straights, me Marlboros; he calls mine bitter, I call his insane, we both give it up after a couple more years—and eating hamburgers with rye bread and mayo and tomatoes and salt and pepper.

"Simple story," I repeat. We've fallen into a conversational rhythm, a little hilarity. We've been making good progress through a six-pack; I'm twenty and tobacco makes me feel dizzy, so at this stage of the game I'm repetitive. Keeps him going.

"It's about an industrial accident involving trains."

"I've heard this, I've heard this. C'mon, Dad, I just ate hamburgers." This is a true statement; I can see the grease all around on my plate, and I know this story, drunk kids sleeping on the tracks, decapitated and footless after the passage of the train, or worse, it's the one about the guy who falls asleep in the car and wakes up in time to see the grain dumping in on top of him and drowns in wheat, his grasping fist turning blue above the harvest. He's full of these.

"You haven't heard this one. It's not gory."

These stories of his. He tells them over and over till they turn into a kind of familial oral tradition and you find yourself passing them along to drinking buddies or airline passengers who then, to your surprise, react towards you as if you were this patriarchal figure handing out wisdom, as if you had stepped into the person of your father and spoken with his sermonizing voice.

"I'm telling you. A simple story, no gore, then you'll get my point."

"What point?"

"My point. The point of this conversation. What I've been trying to express."

"If you didn't always speak in parables, you'd probably get your point across faster. The problem with parables is that there are only so many and you've got to twist them around to make a new message, that's what the problem is." He can't help it though, too many years in the priesthood.

"Be silent, child. Listen to my words." He raises an eyebrow in imitation of his own angry face, draws off his cigarette. I laugh. "Silence! Simple story."

"Simple story." I'm not getting to him yet.

"A man works in the rail yard. I don't know what he does, make something up, quick."

"He checks for hoboes."

"Too authoritarian, something humble."

"What's the time period here?"

"Turn of the century. Maybe a little earlier."

"OK, he runs around with a long pole switching the tracks. He's a switchman. Does that sound right?"

"It'll do. A switchman. Good. He's passing between two uncoupled cars, a thing you should never do. Don't open your mouth like that, I'll tell you why. Because to couple them they have to ram the cars together pretty hard. These couplings are stiff, massive affairs. They have to stay together. So, as he's passing between them that's what happens. They ram one group of the cars into another. He's way down the line so he doesn't know what's going on. It all happens very fast. The cars are rigid of course, the force travels without being eaten up by slack or springs or anything."

"An inelastic collision, kinematically."

"Yes, yes. An inelastic collision. At the moment it happens, he's passing between the two sides of the coupling."

"Time out here, old man." I make a T with my hands, shake my head. "You said there would be no gore, did you not?"

"Hush. The cars couple inside his abdomen, and he's stuck there a foot off the ground, run through by this huge, huge piece of machinery." Dad holds his hands out making a circle ten inches wide. "And, he's conscious."

I suck down some cool beer while he pauses dramatically and looks out over the patio. Down on the street a maroon caddy, stereo booming, glides by with an angry teenager at the wheel. It's like that in our neighborhood all summer, or was until the forces of gentrification turned 14th Avenue super white, super wealthy, and deadly quiet. Back in the early 90s, we hadn't thought of ourselves as the tip of that spear, but there you go. I wait till Dad is just about ready to speak, then I interrupt before he can even begin his first word. He's still on the inhalation but I'm ready.

"So. Simple story. Fictional dream, reasonably vivid and continuous. Central character in a causative situation. Now resolution. With some complications along the way of course, for art's sake."

"No complications. Well, I guess this counts as complication. They bring a doctor, he determines that the wound is fatal. Genius doctors. No way can they remove this train from the man, it's the only thing holding him together. Moreover, his pain isn't bad, as it seems to have busted his spinal cord. Does that suffice as complication?"

"Sure, sure. So it's fatal. The end? Or is there resolution?"

"There is resolution, of course there's resolution. He's hanging there, still conscious. The doctor—you may imagine him in appropriate small-town doctor attire if you wish."

"Black coat, not too good but very formal. I'm getting monocle, but that seems too European. Black bag, anyway, horse and carriage, beetling brows, a slow way of speaking, pocket watch."

"Right. So the doctor relates to the man his options. He can wait it out, bleeding to death slowly over the course of several hours, or they can unhook the coupling and he can die all at once."

"It's a dilemma story. Feathers and lead, is that it? Rock and a hard place, Scylla and Charibdes. Father, the cup is too bitter."

"Really. You don't have to make it so dramatic."

"You're the one bringing the doctor in to give him his final choices."

"Christopher Sean," he says, exasperated, shaking his head. "I haven't even got the wife there yet."

"There's a wife?"

"And children. Two boys. Young."

"Six and eight?"

"Seven and ten, how about. Add an infant girl for gender balance. He asks for them, you see."

"I'm not trying to be a smart ass here."

"Heaven forbid."

"I'm not. But."

"Always a but with you. You have a question, a doubt? You can't follow the story?"

"I'm just missing the point, I guess. All this romantic sentimentality. The doctor, the wife and children. He asks for them?"

"He asks for them. But you're imagining violins, aren't you? You've got some black and white, jerky frames with curlicued storyboards running through your head. You've got close-ups with heavy mascara blinking away tears that look like freezing rain drops. Am I right?" He sighs, finishes his cigarette and flicks the butt off into the sand pile to one side of the excavation. Wags his head. "All that tuition and you're stuck before the talkies."

"You can only blame yourself. It's your story."

"Listen. There are no violins. It's hot, dusty. Grown men are standing around swearing palely. The doctor sends a young lad running to town. Friends of this man, this injured victim, can't take their eyes off the blood welling up around the iron, the slow drip of it . . ."

"You said no gore."

"Someone kicks a dog away. The smell is all the smoke and metallic steam and tar of a railroad yard with whiffs of coppery blood—you can smell it, by the way, makes your nose hairs curl—whiffs of it and the smell of excrement—"

"Jesus, Dad. I just ate. You've got dogs and blood and now—"

"Excrement. He's voided his bowels. You want realism, I try to provide. Pass the matches."

I pass him the matches; he lights up. He's on a roll now. Having fun. He draws hard, continues.

"It goes on a while, this scene, the men staring. People bring him water but he can't drink it because he's breathing in gasps."

"Is he going to ask why his father has abandoned him?"

"Enough. Someone, a worker, asks hoarsely how long this has to go on. Eventually the wife is there, and the kids. The priest brings them—"

"What priest? You've got a priest in there now."

"Well, there's got to be a priest. Just some country priest brought in to give rites."

"Catholic or Protestant?"

"Good question. This is outside of Pendleton. Could be an Irish Catholic family, could be Scotch Presbyterian. Those are the options. Let's say Catholic. He brings the children forward, who are scared almost silent in their weeping. The priest tries to hold the mother up when she appears to stumble, but she brushes him off. Stands straight. The Father mutters away in Latin and makes his obscure signs, but no one pays him much mind. The man with the train through him, he says goodbye to his family, he tells his wife he loves her, and then he tells the doctor to uncouple the cars. They set the coupling from where it juts out through his back, signal the engineer, who pulls the throttle on the far away engine and the engine pulls, and the pull shoots through a series of almost inelastic collisions, as you pointed out, to the coupling in the man, and the cars part. The man falls to the ground and dies, no doubt rather messily. The end."

"The end. Simple story."

"Simple story. An industrial accident, a bit of bravery on all sides. Death." He drinks from his beer, puffs at his tobacco which glows more and more in the fading light. Looks out over our work for tomorrow. He can be dramatic when he wants to.

"So the teaching will be revealed by the master now?"

"What teaching?"

"Your point. You said you had a point."

"Well, that's it. That's my point."

"You exasperate me, old man."

"That's my job. I'm your father."

"Hmm. Simple story."

"Simple story. A man is hurt, fatally. He chooses to end it quickly, but not before he can say goodbye, not before he can finish things. His family, they are afraid but they come and witness the end. The institutions of such stories are there, the doctors, the priest, the working men, the friends. If they were absent, it would be some tragically missing element, don't you think? The whole thing, that's my point."

"Hmm," I say. I stay quiet while he gets up and carries our plates inside. I sit there with my thoughts and inherited vices. Does this mean he will stop taking his medication? Am I to understand this as goodbye? Is there some other meaning to this besides that my father thinks there are certain stories that hold the whole world? After a while he comes out and sits down again. He puts his hand on my shoulder. I think to wait him out, but after a few minutes he just points to the shadowed patio and says, "We're doing a good job on this, you know that?"

Closing Joe's Eyes

In those last days, nothing reached him completely. His catheter went red from blood, his left eye began to droop, his breathing grew more and more irregular. Dad and I smoked on the porch in free moments, knowing the time would come soon, but remembering that we had believed that for almost three weeks. We discussed his condition frankly, shaking our heads and exhaling. We compared observations with a clinical pride that allowed us to talk about him without hurting ourselves, like finding a way to speak with glass in your mouth.

On December 7, 1992, Joe and his doctor had admitted defeat. While the cornucopia of drugs he ingested every morning were slowing the disease, his condition still deteriorated month by month, and all the toxic chemicals made his days shimmer with dizziness and his nights full of restless moonlight. He stalked the house in a white T-shirt almost every night for the last year of his life. He decided to have done with all the drugs, blood tests, nausea, sleepwalking, the pain, and the waiting. He accepted the disease and came home to die.

When I returned home for the Christmas holidays, I entered a house of silence broken by squeaking chairs and coughing. Joe's sickroom was merely a futon in the plant room at the southwest corner of the house. The idea was to let him lie among his bonsais, our enormous ficus, his jade plants, and the philodendron starts we had made the summer before, that he might draw some comfort from the relics of his life as a gardener and a nurturer of growing things. The gesture was revealed as largely symbolic when I discovered the plants' condition. They crawled with aphids. Brown licked at their dry leaves. In the spectacle of a life crumbling, the small things suffered the worst neglect. Forgotten, many died with their keeper. He ordered them removed from his room as one of his last attempts to control his own space.

On that first afternoon of my return, Joe directed me in pruning the ficus. The tree had grown unattended to fill the entire room with spindly, long branches. Joe pointed a shaking finger and ordered me to cut. Even in his reduced state, unable to rise without assistance, he still possessed his acid wit and clear sense of how a plant should be directed and shaped. I moved slowly, making sure that I was pruning the right branches. My dad shrieked from the kitchen periodically to try and slow us down. Joe would shake his head and murmur angrily, "That man. That man."

That night, and most nights, we ate in the dining room without Joe. I never could shake the terrible strangeness of eating with the door of Joe's room visible, his bed still while he tried to rest. His chair never seemed quite empty; our conversation seemed quite forced.

Evenings were the worst. Joe spiked a fever every afternoon that robbed him of his senses and patience by nightfall. It was in the evenings, in the dark of the sickroom, that Joe might cry out for it all to end.

"I wish . . ." he would begin and then gulp down a sob. "I wish we could get this over with."

I held his hand and whispered back to him. "You take your time, Joe. We'll wait for you."

Twice in the last nights of his life, Joe asked me to hit him over the head with a hammer. Both times I laughed at him, but he wasn't really joking. The roof of his mouth had flaked off. Bedsores were developing. He could no longer swallow without pain. He cried out at night for water and company. He refused all painkillers, even aspirin, believing them to be prolonging his struggle. His patience wore understandably thin.

We did what we could, and what he would let us. One day we carried his sloppy weight up the narrow stairs to the bathroom so that he could take a hot bath. All through the adventure he attempted to help, offering to put his feet down and take a few steps, pushing off walls with well-meant shoves that twisted my back painfully. He swore under his breath, and grimaced as if angry until we lowered him into the tub. Then he smiled and closed his eyes. He soaked for about an hour, relaxing and letting my father wash him. Down in the kitchen, drinking coffee, I could hear them giggling and splashing, and I smiled at their lack of embarrassment. When it was time to bring Joe back down, he had no strength at all. We carried him like a stone, and he cried all the way down the stairs.

Our Christmas, as my father wrote in the announcement we sent out in January, was outrageous and bittersweet. I decorated the ficus. We paraded the Christmas roast through the sickroom, and Joe even managed a few bites. We ate with him until he grew too tired and then adjourned to the dining room. Earlier in the day, we had opened presents at the foot of Joe's bed, as he requested. There were many cards for Joe, but few gifts. What do you give a man who has days to live and is too tired to eat or listen to music? There was a donation to a hospice project, a food donation to Somalia in his name, and a CD by the New York Gay Men's Chorus titled *Love Lives On*. It featured impassioned voices and the most painfully sentimental songs. Fragile as we were, when we played it none of us looked at each other, aware of the embarrassment of tears. "I'll Be Seeing You" continues to be a song that unmans me in three bars.

There was an accident involving Joe's catheter one night. He pulled it loose in his sleep and soaked the sheets so thoroughly that urine seeped down past the absorbent pads and into the egg-crate mattress we had bought to reduce the risk of bedsores. Changing the sheets and pads was routine; we did it almost every day. The egg crate was another matter entirely. To wash it we carried it up to the bathtub, and though both of us had nagging doubts, as if we were forgetting something important, Dad and I lowered the foam mattress into the hot water. We saw our error immediately. The egg crate was designed to be hydrophilic, and it sucked up the water like a two-hundred-pound sponge.

Straining our backs to lift it, we wrung the foam. We let it drip dry. We blew fans and heater vents on it. We even took every towel in the house and tried to blot the water out by stepping on it. Four days went by as the mattress dried, and we kicked ourselves for our stupidity. I felt terribly uneasy whenever I had to touch the thing. As its dampness folded around my arm or hand, wafting an odor of vinegar and bleach, I could not help but shudder. I held my breath, afraid of contagion, though I knew the risk was nonexistent. I was afraid but ashamed to tell my father. I certainly wouldn't tell Joe that each time I grasped his hand or held his water glass, I shook inside, terrified that he might be contagious. It seemed both irrational and yet very rational to be afraid. I washed my hands every chance I got, often clear up to my shoulders, and that is what I remember most, wanting to hold Joe, wanting to help him any way I could, and being afraid to touch him.

On Boxing Day, I sat by his bedside reading the paper and drinking coffee while he slept. I'd been there a long time before I noticed a change in his breathing, and I put down my paper to see him open his eyes, swallow thickly. "Cris," he began, then stopped to grimace.

"I'm here, Joe. Joe, I'm here." I leaned in close, but I could feel my heart speeding up, afraid that this was it.

"Cris, I don't know what is wrong with me. I just can't seem to get my dick hard anymore," he muttered, with an air of bewilderment.

"Well, thanks, Joe. Thanks for sharing." I found my smile while he closed his eyes, face still puzzled, and went back to his dreams.

Go back, back to August. Summer of '92 broke all Portland's records for heat and drought. All our lush grass turned brown and dust followed the passing of cars. Other than the cars, there was no breeze. In the heat of the day, the city's children watched TV and drank soda from sweating aluminum cans. But I had promised Joe and Dad that I would transform the backyard through landscaping as payment for my room and board, so when I could I dug and carried and drank beer in the sun. Joe, who had not worked in over six months, occasionally found himself blinking against the light and heat, watching me cover myself with dust. Dirt made my legs black and stuck to my chest and sides like dark bruises on the sunburn. I steadfastly refused his offers of sunscreen, hat, and work shirt, preferring to burn and overheat all at once. If he came out for more than a few minutes, he would put on old Levi's, now many sizes too large, a long sleeve shirt, and a straw hat. He had a chronic problem with skin cancer, made worse by the failure of his immune system and the carcinogens in his medication. The sun made him sick to his stomach, so he never stayed out for long.

Joe stayed close to the television around noon, eating yogurt and tortilla chips and watching *Perry Mason*, *Matlock*, and *Hawaii Five-O* without really paying much attention to the plots. He laughed at the shows nonstop and shouted advice to the characters in a voice that declaimed his Texan origins. I often stopped by the kitchen see how the shows were going, have a glass of ice water or a sandwich. Joe always gave me good but muddled advice on whatever project had me stumped. A gardener by trade, he had a lifetime of experience to share with me but was unable to articulate most of what he knew, or unwilling to make the effort. Lying on the tired couch in the kitchen with all the shades down to keep out the heat, he watched the screen flicker and every week he seemed a little more bitter, a little more tired.

Evenings came and Dad returned from work, all bluster and viciousness. Joe and I tried to stay out of his way, just parking our butts in front of Star Trek with a bag of chips and some salsa. We often tried to make dinner for Dad, but as he was a self-proclaimed control queen, we could never produce a meal he could be happy with. Joe's attempts occasionally resulted in catastrophic failures. He would burn the rice, or over spice the chili, or just not make enough food for three men. In this way, our dinners were ruled by the disease. Joe's cooking had suffered, and both of their food tolerances had changed drastically. Garlic, once a staple in our household, was prohibited, as were jalapeños, chili powder, and even strong onions.

We often ate in front of the TV, watching *MacNeil/Lehrer* and chewing without saying anything. A rising Bill Clinton dared us to hope for change in November, and we were often riveted by his talk of nationalized health care and economic prosperity and social justice, which he made seem like simple programs just waiting for someone to implement them.

When I did not go out with friends, I sometimes sat on the front porch and smoked with Dad, discussing our grand landscaping plans. Sometimes Joe joined us, and occasionally he even had a cigarette. Nights usually ended for him and Dad between 9:00 and 10:00. Joe, sober for ten years, had begun to take a glass of sweet Manischewitz

Seder wine before bed, on his doctor's orders. He hated the stuff, but choked it down anyway. To sleep better, to sleep at all.

That summer we built the patio in the mess of the front yard and talked a lot. Never did we speak of the fact that we were both watching Joe with love and concern, but also with fear. We watched to learn what the future held, what we could expect. Some nights I sat out on the porch alone for a long time after dark. Some nights I found my old man already there, and I sat down beside him without a word.

Back further, to the first great crisis of Joe's health. When my phone rang on November 2, 1991, I was sitting on the floor of my dorm room with my girlfriend, drinking wine and watching a candle flicker. My father spoke to me in the low tones he had practiced in his years as a priest. He was calling from the hospital. While he related the details of Joe's condition, explaining that Joe might die in a matter of days, that I should consider coming home for Thanksgiving because he might not make it to Christmas, my candle went out. Just a coincidence, but the dramatic effect made me shiver. Joe had developed a form of TB, just as the news of new TB strains in New York and San Francisco were making headlines. While he did finally recover enough to collect on my father's promise to take him to Mexico if he lived until spring, that protracted illness signaled the beginning of the end.

His stay in the hospital ended soon after he improved enough to try and leave his ward by force. He woke in the middle of the night in need of pain medication. When he rang for a nurse, he received no response. Believing that he was the victim of homophobic discrimination, he ripped the IVs from his arm and crawled his way to a wheelchair. He made it halfway across the hospital before someone got him back to bed. The incident became one of his favorite stories.

My father was less amused by Joe's escapade, but told a different story just as often. On Halloween, the night Joe was hospitalized, five neighborhood children and their mother rang the doorbell, even though Dad had turned the porch light off. Frantic from helping Joe in and out of cold baths to keep his fever down, trying to wash towels and talk to the doctor on the phone, he was understandably grumpy with the trick-

or-treaters. But as he gave them each a bite-size Milky Way candy bar, they said, "God bless you."

"Well after the first one, I was offended," Dad always says, "but after the third one I realized they meant it. When the fifth one smiled up at me, I started to weep. And I accepted their blessing." When he told this story he invariably shed a tear. Joe would snort if he was around, Dad would laugh and stomp his feet, and I'd denounce them as "crazy old faggots." We had some good times.

In the end, he died away from us. His long-lost cousin Shirley had come and said her goodbyes and returned home to Texas. Dad had been called back to the office and had arranged for twenty-four-hour hospice nursing. The twenty-eighth was my twenty-second birthday, and I had gone out for as long a time as my few friends in town would take. I returned late, but mostly sober, and feeling guilty for not being by Joe's bedside. The night nurse had arrived in late evening, I guess, and we made our whispered acquaintance in the light of his portable reading lamp by Joe's bed. He seemed like a nice guy, quiet. Joe was breathing more easily; the labored choking breathing that chased sleep away from the house with its long pauses between exhalation and rattling inbreath had eased. I squeezed Joe's hot, dry hand before I headed to bed. I awoke to my father's keening cry, which he sang out over and over again.

It was around nine in the morning. Dad had left for work and arrived there to receive a message from the nurse to return home. It was as if Joe had waited until none of us would be watching. I took a brief sobbing hug from Dad, his face wet and still smelling of his shaving soap. He got on the phone and commenced telling friends of Joe's death and called the mortuary service where everything had been arranged. I heard this from the old captain's chair I'd pulled close to Joe's bed. The hospice nurse slipped out almost immediately, his work done. Alive, Joe had the face of a laughing gnome, his cheeks shiny and red, wispy white hair poking out from under a cap. He mostly had a beard for the years I knew him, and tugged at it when he laughed. His eyes were bright, always bright, whether crinkled up with laughter, or stretched tight with anger, or shiny with tears. Now, his face slack, chin dropped, his eyes were wide and I could see for the first time the paleness of their cornflower blue. Someone came to the door, a family friend, poked his head in and put his hand on my shoulder before joining Dad in the kitchen. The coffee grinder whined.

Joe's eyelids were stiffer, waxier than I imagined, and I felt clumsy and scared. In the movies, you just pass a hand over the face of the dead man and like a magic trick, he goes from staring to sleeping peacefully, but my chin was wobbling and my hands shaking as I reached out my right hand, first and second fingers extended in a V, and placed them on Joe's eyelids. I tracked my hand down, pushed the top lids into contact with the lower, then watched them crawl halfway open again. It took me several tries to get it right. On the last try, I held my hand there, feeling the orbs of his eyes underneath the paper lids underneath my fingertips, and then I stepped back from the bed, afraid I'd done something wrong, overstepped my place. The house was growing loud with talk, louder than it had been in months. I set my jaw and walked away from the bed, having done what I could that mattered.

• • •

*A day comes when we just sit, me in one of the old captain's chairs,
my dad propped up in his bed. He wears a funny little fez he calls his
"house hat" and a tattered, old, blue bathrobe. Throughout the morning I have been reading him the accumulated personal mail and taking
dictation. Old friends have written, and some old enemies too, former
opponents in church politics, lovers, co-conspirators, I have typed brief
letters of response and printed them and given them to him three at a
time to sign. He has said two dozen goodbyes in a morning. Now the
noontime sun is coming through the sheers of his bedroom windows.
Outside, the spring advances, swelling buds, blooming daffodils, new
green leaflets. The mud of Portland's winter begins to dry.*

*I've ironed a shirt and polished my shoes and put on a clean pair
of jeans. He tells me I should wear a jacket when I go out to my old
high school, where I hope to have an informal interview with the Upper
School Head; she might hire me the next fall when I am through with my
graduate work. The plan is to be here, in Portland, watching over dad or
taking care of his estate. It's a sensible plan, well thought out, realistic.
He recommends the darker of his two Harris tweeds. The lighter one fits
me better, but the darker is a finer coat. He makes me spin around in it
where he can see, gives a grudging smile of approval.*

"Take that one back with you," he says. "Take them both if you like."

*"I might," I say easily. And this has become easier over the years, plan-
ning for the worst, accepting the truth. The truth is that he will never
wear them, nor any other sport coat or tie or blazer or pair of slacks,
again. "You want some tea?" He nods. I come back with his tea and a
cup of coffee for myself, take my seat by his bedside next to the ficus. In
the tree's giant clay pot is a glass jar, tightly lidded, with cigarettes and
an orange peel to keep them from going stale. I ask for one and he nods.
We sit and watch the light in the smoke, sip from our cups. He is tired
now, too tired to talk anymore, so we just sit, sit and wait for the time
when I'll go.*

• • •

Darrell

My father's first lover after my parents split: Darrell, a tall, thin, long-nosed, long-fingered, red-bearded, balding queen who, when he danced to The Who's *Tommy*, moved with a rock star's unhinged pelvis and the hand movements of Indian sacred dancing. His rolled his eyes and gave a look of mock surprise to create a coquettish affect. "I'll tell you how it is, honey," he was fond of saying as preamble to a story of his drinking and using days. He had a beautiful tenor voice that never cracked or sounded a distinct falsetto. He never, in all the time I knew him, spoke harshly or cruelly to anyone. He had bred horses, acted, hit bottom, kicked heroin, climbed back up, sang in the Portland Gay Men's Chorus, which he referred to as the PGMC, as it appeared on really tight T-shirts, coffee mugs, and posters throughout the household. Dad sang in the chorus too—it was de rigueur for gay men of a certain age who had come out not so long ago.

All this was somewhat secondary, from my point of view, to his Doberman, Court Jester, who went by Courtney in the extended metaphor of gender ambiguity that dominated the household. Courtney ran about ninety-five pounds and could cross the park or the parking lot so fast that when I raced him, I would find myself flat on my chest with a growling attack dog on my back before I even reached top speed. It seemed an act of teleportation. He had other tricks based on this ability. You could be walking him in the evening, his absolute black coat making him an indistinct glossiness in the shadows between streetlights, when suddenly your wrist would burn. You would look down to discover that the leash you'd looped your hand through had gone from evenly slack (Courtney never pulled on the leash) to just gone, with only a burn from the nylon to prove it had been there. If you caught up to Courtney in time, you would see him shaking a rag doll that used to be a cat vigorously back and forth. If you got there too early, you'd also hear a surprisingly loud cracking and popping as he rendered the feline devoid of long bone structure in the first ten or fifteen shakes. When he was done, he'd raise his head as if he'd just heard your calls and fall back into heel position as if nothing had changed, as if he hadn't demonstrated that your hold on him was a matter of his own choosing and his apparent goodwill was a pose of politeness that he could, when pressed, abandon to reveal his true nature as an attack-trained killer. I loved that dog.

Courtney: he allowed me a place to look, a chore to perform, a creature to talk to in my own terms during the painful court-ordered, quality-time weekends I spent at Dad and Darrell's apartment. If I felt sad or out of place, not knowing how to be in this place that seemed normal when I knew that all manner of depraved sexual and drug activity was stinking up the shadows behind each potted plant, it was always OK to talk to the dog. And as far as Courtney was concerned, I was pretty cool, given that I actually liked wrestling with him, even when he could raise up on his hind legs, put his front paws on my shoulders and tip me over backwards like a wooden boy divested of animus, no matter how I tried to resist.

To a certain degree, Darrell played the same role. When he and Dad picked me up for the first weekend, I recognized Darrell first, though I'd never met him before. They climbed out of the tan Nova the church had given Dad and which he had kept when they forced him out of his pulpit, and I didn't recognize my father. He had shaved not only his beard (which he'd done before, no big deal) but also his trademark mustache, the focal point of his face, the bushy center of so many of his gestures. He had all these signals, twirling an end in laughter, combing it down with his thumb and forefinger in thought, tugging at a grey hair in frustration. Now his face was smooth and wet, pink looking, and eerily familiar, like a distant relative I was supposed to know on sight and thank for last year's lovely Christmas present. It didn't strike me until years later, looking at a photograph of those times, that part of my discomfiture may have been the recognition in his uncovered face of my brother's face, my sister's, my own. In any case, I stared without full comprehension as they put their arms around each other's shoulders and walked up the drive to the steps and the door. On the left, in a tan leather coat like my father's, with a flannel shirt like the one my father wore on days off, walked a man who seemed impossibly cheery, full of bright news and intent. His blue eyes were fixed ahead. On the right, the taller bearded man with the stretched face, tight T-shirt and tighter jeans seemed mostly sad and worried. When he saw me watching through the door window, he smiled warmly, but briefly, and with a haunted look. The clean-cut man in my father's clothes seemed to me entirely dangerous, unknown, and false. Throughout the brief conversation on the steps, with my mother crying and asking about the support checks, Darrell looked around, looked for someplace to put his eyes where they would cause no shame or anger. Dad was still Mr. In Control, saying "Margaret" so that one could hear each letter, as if it were a title. In his fixed smile, I recognized danger before I recognized the man. In Darrell, I saw someone as clearly uncomfortable as I felt myself. We hit it off right away.

Unbearably difficult moment made right by Darrell #1: Back in their apartment, a run-down, two-bedroom off Alberta Avenue—long before it became a trendy grunge neighborhood with good art and great burritos and then another example of brutal gentrification, back when it was just known as a blighted, poverty-ridden neighborhood where Portland's Black community held on—Dad pounded on the wall to shut up a woman's scale of grunts and moans. Once in a while, after a particularly long chain of steadily rising uhhs, she gave out a "yeah, baby" that sounded like an advertisement. It was the third time that afternoon she had strutted up the walk in her short skirt and overcoat with a man and the third time the bedsprings had sung their song. She looked old to me, as old as my parents, and neither she nor each of the furtive men who accompanied her to the door smiled. Though the evidence seemed and still seems clear, the idea that sex for money was occurring on the other side of the patchy plaster had no reality for me. The women looked as distant from the forbidden pleasures I imagined as did the secretary at my middle school: plump, affected by gravity in evident ways, and persistently pissed. Dad was not amused; he fumed and trembled with anger, spilled his coffee, swore, and, as I mentioned, pounded on the walls. After a while, it came to me that he was ashamed about the neighborhood. At thirteen, my own moral scale of sin and shame made this seem unreasonably bizarre. Whores, poverty, bad furniture—trifles. Actually letting the world know that you took it up the ass and were moved to tears by show tunes, International Male catalogs on the coffee table—those things deserved shame.

Darrell sauntered over to the stack of records leaning against the wall and pulled out an album whose cover depicted the bulging crotch of a man's jeans. The Rolling Stones—Sticky Fingers. I knew the Stones. My brother was a fan of the British invasion, and I knew the Stones were basically cool. I also knew that my father disapproved of rock and roll, though he had a soft spot for ABBA and the folk music of Nana Mouskouri and Gordon Lightfoot. Darrell was laughing to himself as he put the needle down and cranked up "Brown Sugar." He danced around the living room in his tight jeans and T-shirt, snapping his long fingers, matching Mick Jagger's range with his own. He laughed and laughed. I didn't understand at first what he was doing. Racist jokes, comments, or TV programs were, like rock and roll, explicitly banned from my Dad's hearing, but he didn't stop Darrell playing the song twice, loud enough to make the speakers distort to a rumble on the heavier bass notes.

A few minutes later the woman next door left for the rest of the day, with a door slam her goodbye to us. Darrell was in a good mood for hours after that, and kept the stereo humming with his favorites. I petted the dog and listened as he and Dad bantered in the kitchen.

Winter of Great Rice: When I was in eighth grade, monstrously young and old, I often stayed with Darrell and Dad. Their new apartment was in more up-and-coming northeast Portland, very near Lloyd Center, then an aging shopping mall on the verge of recovery. The apartment complex was an early fifties affair, with a three-story Tudor façade facing Multnomah Avenue. You entered through a gated breezeway into a much-neglected courtyard where ferns and rhododendrons competed to engulf a moss-covered sculpture of some saint. The saint had too much moss and algae on it to be very inspirational; not a whole lot of sun got in there. To my eyes, it was a little magical garden, a secret shrine. Tudor details, like half-timbers and peaked roofs, disguised what were essentially ranch-style barracks that encircled the courtyard. Dad and Darrell's place was on the east side and was actually smaller than the Alberta place—a one-bedroom with a galley kitchen so tight that you couldn't turn around with a drawer open. Smaller maybe, but to me it was a huge step up. Just north lay the fashionable neighborhood of Irvington, where classmates of mine lived in arts and crafts bungalows and had access to their parent's liquor cabinets. Just west was the vast labyrinth of Lloyd Center, with its open-air ice rink, endless music shops, and a movie theatre. Best of all, to the south, Sullivan's gulch beckoned.

The gulch was, basically, an old railroad easement in a dried-up creek bed. The vast majority of it contained Interstate 84, six lanes of stalled traffic behind concrete walls forty feet in height. From the highway, the walls just seemed like guard rails, but they hid the valley behind them, where a rarely used track still ran and hoboes camped. The creek itself had long since been diverted into culverts and concrete pipes way upstream, and this was before the city built a high-end municipal light rail public transportation system that gleamed itself through the gulch at fifty-five mph. In the mid-eighties, the gulch was forgotten real estate, a place for the homeless, graffiti artists, and kids who dreamed of themselves not as scholarship students at elite prep schools across town, but as serious urbanites with angst, heavy angst. It helped to have an attack-trained Doberman with you, by the way. I got no shit in the gulch as I wandered up and down, past modern camps of blue tarps and tents, past survival shelters built of rotting wood and thatched weeds.

Darrell and Dad would always feed me a big meal before turning me loose on the town with my friends. We ate this great lemon chicken just about every weekend, usually with broccoli and heaps of rice on the side. The chicken was so simple: rubbed inside with salt, pepper, and thyme; doused with the juice of two lemons; crusted with as much dried oregano and thyme as needed to cover, the whole thing roasted on a bed of sliced onions until crispy gold and the onions a caramelized lem-on-thyme succulence. The broccoli was steamed with nothing but salt and pepper on top. And the rice—mountains of fluffy white rice. Or else we had stir-fry, or beef with rice, or rice with butter and soy sauce. Rice pudding became conspicuous as dessert, as did fried rice at breakfast. Veteran of the great oatmeal month of 1979, I became suspicious.

In '79, after moving to the first and last house my parents ever owned, in the rock-bottomest days of my dad's alcoholism when my mom tried to keep up with him, we had an unusual number of emergency room visits: Joseph's rake tine through the foot (it didn't spring up and hit him with the handle like in the Three Stooges, it just punched on through his white sneakers and there was a whole lot of bleeding); Carolyn's migraine; my stitches after the wrestling match on the night of the earth-quake—which is really a whole other story. A minor earthquake shim-mied the den where my unsupervised brother and I had been watching *Dallas*, and after the public service announcements ended, leaving us with powerful feelings of invulnerability, the images shifted to campaign adds targeting Reagan for his asinine "trees cause pollution" stance. We raveled up into a quick wrestling match, which I lost when my forehead met a brass drawer knob. Our parents discovered me on the bathroom floor, where an overflowing shower provided a nice cooling puddle of water to lie in while I contemplated my dying words.

Maybe it was those emergency room visits, or maybe it was other expenses—the dog's prostate; the furnace; the architect who drew up the fantastic and never realized scheme for a remodel of the unfinished attic into an adolescent child's paradise complete with spiral staircase, skylights, pocket doors and our own shower; Dad's asthma attack so severe he spent a full week in the hospital cranky for cigarettes and whisky. Who knows. It's a little hard to pin it down, but there was a day when we'd had oatmeal for breakfast, for lunch, and then, impossibly, for dinner. As I dipped happily into the sugar and reached for the milk, I had a "just wait a second, buddy" sort of moment, when I realized I'd been eating a whole lot of oatmeal lately. I was usually pretty happy to subsist on sugar, milk, and gooeyness, but it came to me that one could get pretty sick of it after a while. Mom laughed off my accusations that we were starving. She pointed out that we still had a lot of government surplus peanut butter and cheese, so what was I talking about, starving. Honestly.

On a side note, government surplus food is a superior product. Unassuming with its white labels and black stars, inside one discovers cheddar that has aged in some endless warehouse somewhere, achieving a sharpness and subtle creaminess. And you can keep your gourmet, fresh-ground peanut butter—give me the gallon jug and a wooden spoon to stir the oil back in for half an hour, secretly avoiding the pure, rock-hard peanut puree on the bottom that, when uncovered at the end of the month, makes a delectable treat on a crusty piece of toast with a spoonful of super-sweet government honey made by, I figured, government bees who did everything with earnest diligence.

But the rice—the rice was a challenge. Life at Dad's was frugal, but it wasn't till the Winter of Great Rice that I realized how little of that fiduciary discipline was optional. We baked bread in coffee cans, saved all vegetable scraps for soup stock, ate almost no meat, took the bus or walked to the grocery because the truck (the Nova had expired by this point) slurped gas and had expensive breakdowns regularly. The luxuries of the house were cigarettes, coffee, and huge quantities of marijuana, which no doubt ate into the budget, but made Dad and Darrell deeply content with poor quality food in large portions. Of these luxuries, I was allowed the coffee, as much as I liked to drink. My dad's cheerful ability to live on nothing always gave me a sense of pride and security. While my mother's financial struggles seemed to produce squalor, desperate measures, and depression, Dad's produced a military tautness. Everything was swept clean and scrubbed whenever I was there, because Dad felt he could afford no disorder. The knives were sharp, the house plants watered and fertilized, the walls freshly painted with Dad's labor and the landlord's dime for the paint. My reaction, even to the fifty-pound sack of rice next to the fridge, was to learn how a man reacts to adversity—like a monk, like a hermit, with attention to the little things.

Of course, I didn't know the half of it.

What Courtney could do: Sit. Lie down. Fetch. Take a running man down, even my older brother the track star, without hurting him. Unhinge his jaw to open his mouth all the way. Wait as long as you told him to without going too far. "Stay" exactly where you told him to, even if what you'd meant was "wait" because you were catching a bus downtown and wouldn't be back for hours and didn't expect to find a very sad-looking dog sitting in front of the door when you came home, a dog who didn't come lick your hand because, you see, you had told him to "stay." Completely destroy the quiet order of the house if you tried to vacuum while he was inside, by vomiting and shitting all over the carpet. Kill cats. Lick wounds vigorously—which my father let him do to a scabbed knee repeatedly until Dad, wondering why the damn thing wouldn't heal, found out the dog had given him a staph infection. Chase cars. Theoretically, go for the femoral artery or the jugular on command, a thing his sire had once done when, in Darrell's drinking days, a totally stoned buddy had broken in, startling Darrell where he sprawled semi-comatose with vodka, only to have his femur crushed by the hundred-plus-pound guard dog dangling from his thigh. No barking, of course.

Death Sentence: Dad was diagnosed as HIV positive after a bad flu in February 1985. He always claimed that "Darrell brought the damn shit home from the baths," but who knows. They were both pretty scared and sick in the beginning there, and things became tense in the Multnomah apartment. I spent a lot of time walking the dog in the gulch. The last dinner of the winter, and the last I attended before Darrell moved out, was my favorite lemon chicken. Before eating, we three stood around the table in the little nook off the kitchen. What I later came to understand as terrible synthesizer music only appreciated by the tasteless and the stoned, by a Japanese artist who called himself Kitaro, spun its trance-y web in the living room. The rice was steaming hot before us while Dad said a blessing unusual in its gratitude not just for the immediate meal and day and weather, his usual formula, but for extended friendships, for loves that have been, for goodbyes. We squeezed hands and said amen and then I looked over at Darrell and saw a drip on the end of his long, long nose. "Just a tear," he said, with a hoarse voice hard to understand. This was how I found out that Dad had asked him to leave. Courtney was hit by a car down by Lloyd Center that same week, but I didn't find out about that for a long time, when one of my "whatever happened to" queries was answered with the reply I've learned to associate with truly bad news: "Oh, didn't I tell you?"

Bank Robbery: Of all Dad's friends who struggled with HIV and got sick and died, or got better for a while and then died, Darrell was the one I worried about the most. I saw him at the PGMC concerts that Dad still dragged me to over the years, where bearded men wept at sweet renditions of "The Rose" and "Somewhere." Darrell, who had used to appear in drag, or with an usher's solemn black pants fitted as if he'd sewn them on his body, or in a state of affected hilarity, appeared wholly cadaverous. Still the center of attention, he was often surrounded by well-wishers who, like me, were shocked at his thinness, the rottenness of his skin, the yellowing of his eyes. There was always talk of who could put him up, give him a decent place to die, but Darrell had become a little private for that. He kept working intermittently, as his health allowed, and ended up in a low-income housing project in the Hollywood neighborhood, across the highway from the hospital. Year after year, as I graduated high school, went off to college, went to graduate school, I'd ask for news of him. It was always the same—he was always just about dead, having lost all his belongings, having just spent a month in the hospital, having lived on the street for a few days and gotten sick again—without a lot of hope.

Dad of course had moved several times, working through a string of lovers until he ended up with Joe in the little house on 14th Avenue, not far from the Alberta apartment that was slowly being surrounded by a gentrifying neighborhood, working families of color pushed out by white couples with BMWs and a knack for flipping houses. And Joe had ended up dying in December 1992, and Dad was getting sicker and sicker himself. One day during my first year of graduate school, when I called home often to keep in touch with the man who was so clearly headed downhill, he told me the news about Darrell. He'd robbed a bank.

Dad's story was that Darrell robbed a branch with three other dying HIV patients, all without health insurance. Their plan was to a) steal enough to get down to Mexico and buy treatment with their loot so that they could live a few more months, or b) get caught and become wards of the state, receiving full medical care in the county and state lockups for as long as they could live. They were serious and had guns and ski masks. Dad seemed embarrassed by this detail, as if it were "too much." Darrell drove the getaway car, except they never even got away from the curb in front of the bank. The ultimate irony was that the state declined to jail them, and instead gave them ten-year probation sentences and turned them loose on the street, where they had even less of a chance. The way my dad told it, Darrell became a hapless character too unlucky, too brash, too crazy, or maybe too vital to die nobly.

In my second year of graduate school, when Dad was fading pretty perceptibly month to month, getting IVs full of drugs dissolved in lipids through a catheter in his chest, saving sputum for the home-health nurse to check, unable to rise from his bed for days at a time, he gave me some other news about Darrell. He'd had a remission. A total fucking remission. White blood cell count climbing, weight increasing, steroid treatments helping him build muscle mass. He was still in the wheelchair he'd had to start using full time when he'd dropped below one hundred pounds, but there was light at the end of the tunnel. He might soon be strong enough to take the DDI, DDC, AZT cocktail that was helping people live on. Dad had grown too weak for the drugs; he would never survive their toxicity. I visited him in March when he called and said it might be best for me to come home while we could still talk. In May, while I was putting in a raised bed for an Iowa City widow who paid me as much for the company as the gardening, I got the call that I needed to get home. I was in Portland by the next morning.

He died less than twenty-four hours later. My brother and I got to sit with him a little, helped him sit up and lie down. He fell in and out of something like consciousness and smiled at us several times over the course of the day. His eyelids drooped, and it was impossible to get any water past his lips. He could not speak, or didn't try to anyway. His coughing seemed weak, and ineffectual, and came less and less. Still, he smiled at us, and it seemed for a while there that things weren't so dramatically wrong. The morphine pump beeped every now and again, and he relaxed a bit each time. During her midday visit, the home-health nurse talked us through what we could expect, and we paid diligent, clinical attention.

It is hardest for me to recall setting up our beds in our father's room, spreading blankets and pillows on the floor. It seemed so cozy, warm, and together, so eerily like camping out together, or setting up for a sleepover when we were kids. We said as much, keeping it light. By dark, we were lying still, not talking, listening to his breathing, and I think I even drifted off briefly.

Within three hours, such a short time, really, Dad's breathing began to falter. He gasped, shuddered, stopped, gasped again. He was drowning in the foam of his lungs. We held his hands, one on each side, Joseph and I. We resisted the urge, which I could feel all across my neck and shoulders, to help him sit up; we knew that would just make him suffer longer. In my other hand, I was punching the morphine pump as fast as I could, and it beeped distractingly while Dad tried and tried to give up the fight. It went just like the doctors had told us it would, in terms of the Cheyne-Stokes breathing, the convulsive efforts to rise, the sudden coldness of the extremities right at the end. What they couldn't tell us, of course, is that we would find ourselves able to keep looking. They didn't warn us that our throats would knot so painfully and our faces tense like drum leather, and words that had no meaning—encouragement, assurances—would squeak out of our mouths between breaths. And that we wouldn't know what to do when it was over.

Darrell came to the funeral. I didn't recognize him at first. He was huge, bloated on the steroids to well over 250 pounds. Where before he was tall and thin and long featured, impish and quick and animated, now he was ponderous, grave, stentorian in his speech, and he walked very slowly with a silver-headed cane. Getting him a cup of coffee from the caterer's silver tea service and walking it over to the chair where he seemed a sink of gravitas, sucking all light into his black mock turtleneck and trousers, I discovered that I hated him brightly and deeply, without justifiable reason, without an ability to hide it. He eyed me warily as I served him, and I withdrew. For some reason, it wasn't just that he'd lived and Dad had died. It wasn't just the possibility that it was his promiscuity that brought the disease home—a possibility made irrelevant by the fact that they were both fucking around with whatever chanced in from of them so that it was only a matter of time, a foregone conclusion that one would bring it as a deadly gift to the other. And it wasn't just the fact that Darrell had let Courtney get killed, had let him run around loose because he was too lazy to walk him. At bottom, in that moment I hated him for being false in all ways, for not really being the steady friend I'd seen him as when my father was changing so fast I couldn't keep up, for not being the disciplined trainer and breeder of German dogs who carried lethality with their friendliness, for not really having been on the edge of death after all, or so it seemed. And I hated him for taking all the sympathy and attention from the many guests who knew them both. When I got a second alone in the kitchen, leaning against the sink, I shook with it, my anger. But when evening came on and Darrell got to his feet to leave, I walked him to the door. I even gave him a hug and felt the tears rise back up, just when I thought I was done with them, while I put my eyes against the fabric of his sweater. His eyes were wet too when we let go, and he nodded his now massive face, heavy with flesh, before turning to the stairs, placing his cane ahead of himself with each step.

One More Version: It would be kindest to leave him there, I suppose, in his tragic stature, the weeping young man behind him. But in fact, I ran into Darrell once more in Portland. It was that same summer after my dad died, a hot, dry afternoon beginning to cool as the sun edged lower. Outside the Safeway on Weidler, not a half-mile from the old Multnomah Street apartment, still standing squatly for a few more years amid the packed-in toney condos and mixed-use developments going up everywhere, I recognized the big man in the wheelchair as Darrell. He looked even paler, and more bloated than I'd remembered, and rolled along the concrete with slow purpose. His eyes were set back in the flesh of his face, mostly hidden by that beard, and I don't remember a thing we said, only that it was strangely uncomfortable and that I couldn't tell what Darrell thought of the person I'd become. I balanced my groceries on one hip, probably inquired about his legs. I do remember trying to say something pleasant, but really, at that point I wanted him to vanish, to be annulled from history and let me alone. Two years later I spent a few minutes staring at his picture in the paper, not on the obituary page or the rap sheet, but on the society pages, smiling broadly, standing tall at a fundraiser for a hospice house whose services he no longer needed. I didn't know what to feel—relief or happiness for him I suppose would have been best—but I thought about who and what survives, and strangely, I thought of that dog running in the park, pounding hard at the earth under his feet, his whole body free and in motion.

Smoking

The guy was understanding at least. His voice came over the line in a sympathetic tone. He arranged to come over, look at the stuff, and give me a price. While I waited for him, I blew off some steam in the garden, pulling more thistles, tearing out an azalea gone dry and brittle in the June heat. In the wasteland of morning glory, chickweed, and dandelions, all the carefully laid raised beds grew only weeds and dust now. Around 2:00, he pulled up in a blue hatchback. His name was Stan. He had a neat beard, was tall and lanky, wore a dark green shirt, pressed, I imagined, for the visit. I had on cutoffs and a tank top, and probably didn't present the grieving son image he was prepared for. But what are you supposed to do? Sit around all dressed up for the rest of your natural life? There were weeds to pull and the basement to clear out, and a lot of stuff to get moved out of Dad's bedroom before we could paint it, put curtains in, and move out of the sunroom where we'd been sleeping since we arrived with our U-Haul, five days married. I shook Stan's lank and skinny hand. That fit. He offered condolences; I looked at his shoes. Drug dealer shoes, I thought to myself, though they were just loafers. We went upstairs to Dad's room, where all the windows were open, though that sickroom smell still persisted, and would until we scoured everything with TSP and spread sealing layers of paint. Stan turned his lip down, and stood in silence for just under a minute. He knelt down on one knee next to the purple bookshelf and took the five bags of dope in one hand. To me, they looked like jumbo, restaurant supply size bags of oregano.

"He didn't smoke much of this last batch, I guess," Stan said.

"No. His lungs got pretty bad there at the end."

"Yeah, it's mostly all here."

I waited, listening to the sound of a lawnmower drifting out the window. I wasn't going to make an offer or anything. I had zero personal experience with this sort of thing.

"Well, your dad paid me a hundred bucks for each of these bags. They're what we call "hundred-dollar baggies." There's just a little gone here in this one bag, so I can resell this for around $475 and give you the money." Stan looked directly at me for the first time when he made this generous offer. He had deep, slow brown eyes that were nonetheless too shallow to contain my cynicism and anger. I wanted this shit out of the house. I was originally going to just throw it all away, but I was worried that it might be discovered in the trash. I thought about burning it in the fireplace, but envisioned all sorts of aging hippies following their noses up to my doorstep, the sirens of the cops wailing in the distance. I had settled on flushing it down the toilet, when Thom, the alcoholic friend of the family who had taken refuge with Dad in return for care giving and cooking, suggested I contact the dealer who had supplied it originally.

"Can you take the plants, too? I don't want the plants," I explained as I shoved a spindly, sticky leafed cannabis plant in a terra cotta pot into his hands. "Maybe you can keep them or give them away. Whatever." We put black garbage bags over them before we walked out to Stan's car and shoved them in among the cardboard boxes in the back. Stan seemed kind of pale, doing this out in the open, and I found myself enjoying his discomfort. It was hot in the car and the sun was really on. I had not much optimism for the plants.

"So you'll be in touch with the money then." I didn't phrase it as a question, but he said that he'd probably be able to unload the stuff that week. I smiled at this because it sure seemed like a joke to me. He drove off slowly and I climbed the stairs up from the street to find Thom at the front door. He shook his head at me sadly.

"What was I supposed to do? Get a receipt?" I asked. While the money would have been nice, it just wasn't the issue. As I said before, I wanted that shit out of the house.

I smoked cigarettes for a few years myself, first guiltily at high school parties during track season, then sitting around the campfire up in the mountains, more seriously resting outside the salmon cannery where I worked my summers in college. And the best of these smokes were with my dad in the last few years of his life. He had noted a pack in my pocket one day when I was leaning over the sink, washing a dish. He was drying on my left. In a gesture at one intrusive and circumspect, he reached over with his right hand, and with the back of his thumb, tapped twice the pack, pulling my shirt pocket out. I gave him the exasperated look of which I was fond that year, now that at twenty I was taller and heavier and stronger than he. He didn't say anything. Two weeks later, just days before I had to catch my plane to Alaska, he and I worked steadily on a fence, trying to get it all finished in spite of our congenital lack of mechanical ability. He had been fighting HIV for almost seven years at that point, had given up drinking, worked out at the club all the time, and preached the gospel of endurance to his lover Joe, who was fading fast that year. He had stopped smoking tobacco over a period of three weeks, years before, joining a clinical study, hauling in a chemical mist from an inhaler and holding it like a hit three times a day, using the patch and then the gum. He could barely function for a while there, and acted like all of his nerves were outside his body, subject to fits of sensation from every passing breeze. For about a month his lungs kept sloughing off layers of brown mucus, which he'd hack up until he was light in the head. He left them floating in the toilet too, or staining wads of tissue that mounded up in the wicker trash baskets of the bathrooms. But it worked, and he didn't smoke tobacco for years.

He put a nail in his lips, leaned forward to place a board, and I saw the front of his shirt pocket swing out. More furtively than he had, I imagine, I reached out and repeated his gesture, thumping the pack with my thumb. He raised an eyebrow.

"What's this?" I asked, craning my neck to see the foil top of the Camel Straights.

"That's the silver lining," he said with a chuckle.

We laughed a long time there in the yard. It wasn't such a hard thing to understand, the desire to cut one's losses. To get what you could out of the time you had left. He made it another three years. The last time

I saw him able to speak, he mostly smoked pot to help with pain and appetite, but he also kept a pack of cigarettes in a little glass jar with an orange peel, to keep them from going stale as he meted them out, about two a day. This was among the many artifacts I cleared out of his room that summer after he died. As with everything, I sorted it into one of three piles, things without value, things with value that we didn't want, and things we would keep for now, though they likely held no value of their own, and would in time, cease to mean anything.

Both my parents smoked endlessly when I was very young. They were always lighting up and emptying ashtrays, and blowing smoke rings for our amusement at the supper table. Dad's office at the church smelled exactly like an Episcopal priest's office is supposed to smell, rank with tobacco and fusty books and leather armchairs. At any time of day, you could drop in and there he would be among the mess of books and sermon notes, talking earnestly with an aged parishioner while streams of smoke rose up from their hands. My mother smoked mostly alone in the kitchen, or else in front of the piano while she played what I remember as sad and complicated pieces.

She quit first, back in the seventies when she had some heart trouble. She did it the way my father said it couldn't be done, and this infuriated him. From a full pack a day, she cut down to nineteen the next day, eighteen the next, till in ten days she had it down to ten cigarettes a day. She did that for a week, dividing up her day into ten smokeless increments punctuated by her moments of real living. We kids had no idea such a battle was on in the house. I mean, she seemed tense, and there were a couple more arguments over chores or money or whether the eggs were done right, the kind of things my folks argued about all the time but this didn't even register seriously on the kid radar, as my parents regularly went through seasons of conflict so tempestuous that crockery would fly through the house and tremendous slaps could be heard from where we huddled on the stairs. Slamming doors, raised voices, a fist pounded on the table, these were just cues to turn the TV up, or maybe to take the dog out, or move that checkers game out to the porch.

I've got to give it to Mom; she made it through with no real bumps.

The next week she went to nine a day. After nine weeks, she got down to one little cigarette a day, which she kept up till she got bored with it, and after that, she would give Dad this look whenever he sucked away on his Camels. She would never smoke pot with Dad, and slowly encouraged him to do the bulk of his inhalation of carcinogens during his long sessions in the can. He'd take my comic books in there, especially the X-Men, and emerge forty-five minutes later in this haze of funky smoke. Or else, on our annual trips to Pender Island, he'd smoke in the outhouse, so that when my brother and I would walk out along the trail to the woods where the outhouse stood, we'd see this glowing amber light out in the darkness. It was like the guy in Dr. Seuss's eco-classic *The Lorax*, not the Lorax himself—with his eager tree-loving self-righteousness, the sadly smug prophet of doom who lifts himself into the air by his own ass—not him, but the green-armed, faceless, failed industrialist, the maker of Sneeds, who lurks by the old stump ready to seize young boys and tell them cautionary tales about environmental conservation. Dad was like that, this voice and shadowy shape who never emerged from the privy, but just asked after our sleep while we peed in the ditch in pointless embarrassment, scolded us for not wearing shoes, urged us back to bed. There were nights where we weren't really sure it was him in there.

"Why does he leave the door open?" I whispered to my brother one time as we tiptoed back down the path, my father's shouts still ringing in my ears from when I'd turned the flashlight on him. "It's so creepy."

"Shut up," my brother said. "Give me that flashlight."

After the divorce, when Dad left, and my brother went off to college, and Mom's schemes of selling Mary Kay cosmetics and winning the lottery and launching a new career of some sort all went into the tank, just like the promised child-support payments, and Mom got the letter from the bank about the house, she cried for a while and went off to the store for the groceries. After dinner, I found her there, sitting with her feet on the stool and her knees pulled up to her chest as she often sat, but from her mouth, incredibly, curled this thin stream of smoke. Outraged, as I was so often that my beleaguered mother began to give me this look of weary disdain that could outlast my latest accusations of inadequacy, I reminded her of the health dangers, of the pattern of addictive behavior the Alanon people were always warning us about, of my allergies, of our dire financial straits. There was no money for my allowance, I reminded her, nor soda.

"You have no idea," she said, her voice close to the edge. "Just one little comfort, all right? One little thing." She kept on sucking away at the cigarette, though she agreed to smoke the subsequent ones out on the porch if I would just leave her alone, a promise she mostly kept. She smoked in the garage at the new place, and on the balcony at the one after that, and then she moved into this log cabin with my sister and would sometimes smoke next to the fireplace, where the draft would pull the smoke into the chimney. Though I still scolded her, it actually was always pretty cozy there, drinking coffee and teaching her chess while we played with the puppies her dog had whelped. She was so deferential to me on those visits, so eager to show me that I was welcome and that her life was in order, after all the hard things I'd said when I'd decided to move in with my dad, who was living in a beautiful apartment in North-west Portland at that time. And I couldn't exactly complain about the smoking, because Dad was toking away on the old pot pipe at every available opportunity and having a hell of a time quitting the cigarettes. About that time, he and I had been forced to run downtown through a snowstorm so that he could get to a Portland Gay Men's Chorus concert in which he was to sing. After the concert, which had its good moments and lots of campy, sentimental numbers ("Steam Heat," "I Sing the Body Electric") that made me uncomfortable there in the balcony among the tearful guys in turtlenecks and leather caps, we decided to get a ride home with a part-time truck-driving instructor named John Wisdom, because Dad didn't think his lungs could take the walk back through the cold air. As we shivered in John's Datsun, waiting for the heat to thaw out the vinyl seats, Dad groused that someone ought to make a cigarette so powerful that one would only have to smoke one a day. "Someone does," said John. "It's called the Camel Straight and you smoke a pack a day." They had a good laugh about that and then the cigarette lighter popped out, its glowing coil bright there in the front seat as they passed it between them. Then they laughed some more.

It took Mom about five years to quit again. At the end of it she was walking her miniature schnauzer down to the corner convenience store in the morning and the evening, where they sold cigarettes for a dime apiece from a small jar they kept on the counter. Eventually, she gave up the walk, took up chewing gum, and as far as I know, resisted smoking even when she moved in with a friend who smoked compulsively, chaining five or six in a row until she got too dizzy to get off the couch right away. The year she turned sixty, Mom was pulling herself back together after a long struggle with breast cancer. For her birthday, I offered to take her hiking around Mount St. Helens, the Washington volcano whose recovering blasted landscape had become a kind of geological metaphor for hopeful ill people everywhere. To get her ready for what would be her first backpacking trip, I took her on a ten-mile hike on Mount Hood. She had some troubles: her satchel strap rubbed on her prosthesis in a way that felt strange, she said. And the chemo had really weakened her heart. "And, you know, I smoked for something like twenty years."

I've never been very careful about what I say to my mother. I sort of free-associate and hope she'll follow along. And so I didn't hesitate to ask her if she'd noticed, on the copy of Dad's death certificate I'd forwarded her in case she needed it to claim social security or anything, that there was a little box where it asked if tobacco was a factor in the individual's death, and the doctor (or the secretary preparing it for his signature anyway) had typed yes. Didn't she think that was weird? And interesting that someone was keeping track?

"Well," she sighed, "they'll put that on mine I'm sure too. Even though I only smoked for fifteen or twenty years, not like your father who smoked a pack a day since he was fifteen. Not to mention the marijuana." We set off up the trail again, slowly inching our way along. She'd pick a tree and we'd hike to it. She'd rest against it for a few seconds then pick a new one up the hill.

When I smoked, the best cigarettes, and the hardest ones to turn down, always belonged to someone else. Covered in goo in the cannery break room, ten hours into an eighteen-hour shift, the smoke that your buddy shook out to you was not some ethical dilemma or painful decision, it was sheer, zap-drag, anti-jonesing, blood to your head, itch-the-scratchy-lungs goodness. With fifteen minutes for break, less three at the front for the cursory scrub and jostling into the break room for coffee and a snack, less three at the end to get your gloves on and your earplugs in and get your spot on the line, you had nine minutes of smoke time there. Some guys could smoke three, but I never had more than one, and sometimes didn't finish it. I'd puff and exhale, and pull the smoke back into my nostrils, squint against the way it got in my tired eyes, enjoy the mindless activity of watching the ash grow and fall into the black plastic tray. The whole set of rituals, or clichés, each in its sequence, made me feel like I belonged to some larger tradition. When I became a supervisor, I didn't get the regular breaks, but often got to step out on the dock and light one up when my boss, whose fiancé always caught him when he carried his own, had me carry his pack. He'd show up outside the cannery door with two cups of coffee and I'd go out to meet him. This did not endear us to the men on the line. His boss, a pudgy fellow who was about as implacably tough as anyone I've ever met, sometimes joined us. Between yelling over machinery and chain smoking, his voice had faded to a soft rasp. In the back corner of his office stood an old, round-topped refrigerator stocked with creamsicles, which he used for his throat while he told us who we had to fire, or what production numbers we had to get.

The worst of it was the fall after Dad died, when Mary and I were working weird jobs trying to scrape together the house payment and figure out what it meant to be married and still, there was more to sort out in every closet, every cupboard. I was teaching ESL to a group of naval cadets from the United Arab Emirates. The deal was that UAE had bought a high-tech warship from the UK. It was being built that year. All computer systems and operations manuals for this ship were in English, and I gathered it was to be deployed in international waters. So the UAE Navy sent three thousand cadets to America for English instruction, from which, after two years, the five-hundred-man crew would be drawn. My students estimated their chances as low. Each of them made more money a day than I did, and bought new cars and stereos, luxury condominiums, projection TVs, CD players, video game consoles, and new guitars, playing when they should have been studying. They felt bad for me, I think, and would, between classes, if I walked down the halls, make a big show of competing to offer me a cigarette. "Meester Crees! Meester Crees!" they would chant. And then, the snapping of lighters, the actual heat from all those friendly flames that would light up. And the comradely warmth of huddling together under the eaves, out of the rain, where they probably learned more English trying to tell me about their lives and make polite conversation than they ever did in my class-room with its chalkboard filled with count and non-count nouns ("Yes, the animal comes in numbers, like one chicken, two chickens, but the food only comes in quantities, like more chicken, less chicken, some chicken. Why? Because English is stupid," I'd explain). These were guilty, guilty cigarettes, because Mary had asked me point-blank if I was smok-ing, and I, now four months married, had looked her right in the eye and told her no. It was my students who smoked, and their smoke got in my clothes and hair. Guilty, guilty cigarettes and Arabic in the rain.

Somehow less guilty, but not for any good reason when you think about it, were the smokes my father would shake out of his pack to me while we sat on the front porch in the summer. I stopped going to Alaska after three summers, in part to get more experience in education by working locally with kids, and in part to spend more time with my dad. So that first summer home, Joe's last summer, when I helped build the patio in the front yard, there were a number of hot afternoons that gave way to cooler evenings when we'd sit out there looking at what we'd done and what we had to do the next day. Joe would wander out with a plate of sandwiches, or chips and salsa, and a few bottles of cold beer, and we three would sit there, and Dad would, in this infinitely slow way, lean over and shake a cigarette out of his pack, just so one or two stuck out an inch or so from the others, and he'd grin under his mustache while he extended the pack to me. And we'd smoke together, he stopping to cough up something from time to time. In those moments I sometimes knew I should refuse, I should scold him, I should lay down the law and let him know that I wanted him around as long as possible and that I would not stand idly by while he did yet more damage to his lungs. But at the same time, we were together in a kind of father-son way that hap-pened rarely for us, and I counted those little coffin nails on the porch as perfect moments in time that was limited, was running away.

I never saw Stan the dealer again, nor any of the money he promised. I did speak to him several times on the phone. A couple of weeks after he drove away with the steaming plants under plastic in the back of his car, I was going through a box of stuff from the basement. The easy stuff was gone now. The pipes and the leather harness and the box of sex toys and the beefcake posters and gazillion dry-cleaning bags, the broken dishwasher, the bamboo from the backyard, the technical reports from his job as an environmental scientist—all that stuff had posed problems of disposal, but hadn't been hard to part with. Then I found a box, an old apple crate, full of charts from the long-lost sailboat. There was an orange bag containing the mainsail, which unfurled bright red across the basement floor, draping over all the piles I meant to discard. Dots of black mildew peppered the sail, and in one corner the mold was a black stain two feet across. And worst of all, the tiller, its varnish still shining smooth over the grain. I held it a long time in my hand, thinking of Dad in the sun at the stern, beaming as he steered us on.

I found photos of relatives no one could identify, records that might or might not prove evocative of childhood memory if we could get the turntable working and took the time to listen to them. There were coats just a little too small that I'd seen him wear a thousand times, clericals and vestments and stoles, framed ordination certificates, boxes of letters, tax files, ten years of check registers, addresses and phone numbers of old family friends I didn't really know, broken but familiar tools, slippers I'd given him for Christmas, and all of Joe's leavings, unclaimed by any relative, unsorted by his grieving lover preoccupied with his own dying. I spent a lot of time holding things—all kinds of things—and trying to feel something about them. That's where I was, sitting on the stairs, looking at what was mostly junk, when I thought about Stan and the money he owed me. I got his number and called him, left a message in a firm tone of voice. I called back fifteen minutes later. I got him on the third try. He'd had some troubles he said, a little cash flow issue, he explained. He'd had to use the proceeds of my sale to supplement a larger purchase, but that would surely produce some cash here in the next few days.

"Well, I'm expecting that money, and I'm expecting to hear from you," I told him, and hung up. These were, in fact, lies. We had two months rent free, I was making money at a summer camp teaching writing and telling stories, and the life insurance policies kept appearing as we went through files, generating huge checks that kept coming in the mail. We were fine for money, and I didn't expect to hear from Stan. But when you are in a bad place, and there is no one to blame, you relish the opportunity for rightful anger, I swear. Some would argue the guy was a saint who delivered needed balm to those who were suffering, and there's some truth to that viewpoint. But I kept thinking about how stupid my Dad was when he was stoned, how bland and deadened he'd been most of the last year, how tired one grew of hearing him exclaim how happy he was, how wonderful things were. Plus, the audacity of Stan the drug dealer walking into his room and not coming through with what he'd said he would do. The more this guy wronged me, the more I became eager for confrontation. The more boxes I sorted, the more I thought about Stan. He did finally call me, one last time. He was near tears. He didn't have the money. He felt terrible. I rolled my eyes at this. He'd sold my dope and spent the money. He felt terrible.

"Maybe I could pay you back over a few months or something. I really feel terrible."

"No, Stan. You won't pay me back. I know that. But I want you to understand something," I hissed into the phone. I was warming up to this. "You're going to have to live with yourself, Stan, and the knowledge that you stole a son's inheritance. You took what my father left me." Silence on the other end. I didn't let me know if I had Stan shaking in his drug dealer shoes or laughing, but I pressed on. I would never ever have to see this guy again. Why not let him have it? "And you better pray I don't come across you in some dark alley somewhere, friend. Cause if I do, I'll kick your fuckin' ass." And then I hung up. I'd worked up a pretty good fume there, but now I just felt like laughing, like my part was over and I could walk backstage to yuck it up with my fellow actors. I could go back to folding clothes, pausing to smell the sweaters I placed in bags for the Salvation Army, sniffing for any memory there before deciding to part with it.

In the End

When it was over, we both stayed kneeling on the bed next to him. I held his left hand, my brother his right. His face, so ravaged and thinned out by the disease, immediately took on the waxen look of a thing. His eyes were half open; one hadn't been focusing on anything for several days now. Thom, fresh from phone calls to Aunt Shan and Grandmother, so recently returned to Shan's house down the street, came up to find us there.

"Ah, Renne," Thom said. "It's over." He reached out a trembly hand and deftly, with a few strokes, closed Dad's eyes, whispering, "shh" to him. Soon, Shan and Grandma came in, faces gone shaky with weeping, and I relinquished my spot there by the bed. It was a little after one in the morning. Thom made the phone call to the mortuary, where everything had been prearranged, but something went wrong, and it took him multiple angry calls, where he blustered icily through answering service employees and finally got a van dispatched, interactions on which he perseverated for the next month. This fuss all happened in the background while the rest of us sat in chairs in Dad's bedroom under the much-neglected ficus tree. We had the lights on bright and Thom brought us cups of coffee he'd made. A strange inertia set in.

When the white van with the two big guys in suits with latex gloves sticking out of their pockets showed up, it was after three, I think, and we weren't really there. We viewed them in a dream light, from somewhere way back of exhaustion and crying. Both had mustaches, and one a knit tie. I thought they looked like bouncers, or seedy private eyes, except for the gloves. I remember their strange mix of care and work-manlike routine. They struggled into their gloves athletically, snapping them to their wrists. They quietly asked permission to wrap him in the sheet where he lay, and tucked the bag and the catheter line right in there with him. When they had trouble making the turn on the stairs, they solved the problem like movers, and even indulged in a little shop-talk about a gentleman whose obesity had forced them to take him out through his bedroom windows with a cherry picker. If I report this with detachment, it's because I was detached in the moment, floating really, far away from the strange circumstances I found myself in, both exactly like what I'd been expecting and totally different. When they put his body into the van, my grandmother began to sob again, and we crowded around her while they drove him away down the quiet street. After the taillights passed from view, we turned back to the steps and climbed them. In the end, we went back inside, and we took turns making our phone calls and making more coffee. I fell asleep in the tub.

At some point over the next few days, my brother had to buy a suit. He had his dress uniform with him, but he felt out of place, he said. I had a suit that I'd purchased the summer before, when Mary and I drove out to tell Dad of our engagement. The night we announced our plans to wed, we were having chili, and Dad had a standing auto-eroticism ap-pointment, it turned out, just after dinner. The appointment came about through his association with a group called The Body Electric, one of the many organizations—like The Right to Privacy PAC, that gave an annual award named for the early Oregonian transgender doctor Alan Hart—with whom Dad felt solidarity, like the Radical Faeries and Nomenus and the Gay Men's Chorus. This new group, The Body Electric, we came to understand, practiced an updated tantrism where participants, on a schedule, all over the world, simultaneously engaged in non-ejaculatory sex or non-ejaculatory masturbation, which helped them enhance sex-ual and spiritual energies. There was a dating scene associated with the organization too, which held conferences in major urban markets, San Francisco, New York, Chicago. In any case, after I announced that Mary had agreed to marry me, Thom stood partway up and shook my hand, reached over to hug Mary, said, "Wonderful! Wonderful!" over and over while my Dad gazed beatifically across the table. When Thom's congratulations ebbed, Dad spoke up to ask for more chili. There was a lull in the dialogue as I passed the bowl. "Wonderful. Just wonderful!" Thom said into the silence. Later, Dad had to excuse himself and Thom seemed embarrassed to explain the circumstances while Dad shuffled off to the stairs and his bedroom.

The next day, Dad apologized for his apparent lack of enthusiasm, complaining of exhaustion and distraction. We said we understood. In the afternoon, Mary and I left the napping house to go look at suits. I explained to the salesman that I needed a suit I could wear to two weddings in the next year, and probably a funeral. Standing by a rack of what appeared to be identical suit coats in faintly differing shades that ran a whole muted spectrum, in the dim light and brass fixtures of Nordstrom's men's department, an older gentleman put the temple of his glasses in his mouth to look me over. After a moment's pause, he suggested charcoal gray. Not quite a year later, I'd worn it to Mary's sister's wedding, was ready to wear it at my own inside a month, and had packed it when I flew out from Iowa City to be there when Dad died.

In the end, the funeral was partly planned and partly a last-minute compilation of things we thought he would want. A piper piped him in and out of Saints Peter and Paul, where the parish that forced him out of active service brought him home. They did it with grace and custom, allowing him to be borne from the sacristy in his plain box, the privilege of a priest. There were tall candles set up around the casket, which occupied the aisle just a few pews down from the front, right about where he used to stop his acolytes and read out the gospel. I'd been the tough one up to the moment when we stepped into the church, a place I'd thought I'd left behind me at thirteen. Tears kept choking me during the ceremony, which surprised me. What sticks with me about that funeral most strongly is two details, two awkward specifics. First, with every hymn, I had a terrible twinge of guilt. I'd had quick and easy suggestions about the hymns while we were planning the funeral with the celebrant, sitting around the living room with a to-do list—hymns, readings, caterer for the reception, obituary to write, people to contact, chores to accomplish before all the mourners arrived at the house. I had the hymns ready to suggest in part because I'd been doing a lot of hymnal perusing in the last weeks, as Mary and I planned our wedding, which was just a few weeks away. "St. Patrick's Breastplate," for instance, was a favorite hymn of my dad's, but given that it would be a hymn in our wedding, and our young music-student wedding organist had arranged a kind of fantasy on it for the recessional music, and the text of one verse was a sort of epigraph on the bulletins we'd already had printed, I probably shouldn't have suggested it. "Love Divine, All Loves Excelling" was popular with everyone in the room, and fit, but when we were trying to sing it through tears at the funeral, I was imagining standing at the altar three weeks later singing it, again, with the same group of people in the family pew, probably in the same formal attire. My brother and I, for instance, would both be wearing these suits, I remember thinking, and then felt bad for not paying attention.

Second, my brother's kids were driving me nuts.

I can't easily explain why I felt such anger, such prominent shame at my nieces' antics. They wouldn't shut up, wouldn't sit still, kept trying to escape the family pew. The youngest even knocked into the candles around the casket during the sermon. An outrage! I was channeling my father in his most aggrieved rage, his vexation, what he called his high dudgeon. I could see him shaking his fist inside the box. I don't remember if I hissed at their mother to take the baby out of the building or just wanted to so badly that I fantasized it from the roaring in my ears.

In the end, the church was packed, the eulogy more homiletic than sappy, the pipers beautiful, and I seemed to be the only one to notice the deceased man's grandchildren screaming when the pallbearers loaded him into the hearse and drove him away for the last time.

At the reception I held it together pretty well. Though many of us could have used an Irish wake, we served no alcohol. Dad had issued one of his edicts, that as long as Thom lived in the house, there would be no booze, and no one knew whether he was serious or not. (Later in the summer, while Mary and I lived there and Thom stayed on for a couple of months, we honored this request by having the occasional bottle of wine on the deck when Thom was out for the evening.) The caterers set up a coffee and tea service in the living room, and relatives I didn't know I had wandered the weedy garden with cups in their hands. I met a great aunt under the purple blooms of the rhododendrons in the side yard and explained to my crying grandmother that I had omitted the children of her second marriage from the "survived by" list in the obituary entirely by accident. They were hurt, and I felt stupid, the kind of stupid that kept coming to me over the next weeks when old family friends asked me why no one called them, or when I had to make decisions about finances and papers and junk in the basement. I discovered that the caterer's silver sugar bowl was filled with salt, and while I exchanged its contents in the kitchen, I wondered how that came to be for a long time, and why I felt so angry about it.

In the end, everyone behaved except Glen, my brother's high-school buddy and one-time housemate, who had gained a lot of weight and lost his natural human sensitivity to a conversation's ending. He was still muttering something to Joseph in the full dark when Sara and I loaded the sleepy nieces into the car and she started the ignition and gently said his name twenty or thirty times, as in "Joe. Joe. Joe, it's time. Joe," and pulled the car out of its parking place and waited under the streetlight. In my memory, the day ends there, in the street, Glen's voice growing faint, the shadows deepening around us standing, asleep on our feet, on our good manners, on our postures of grief.

Dad lived on the mantle in his little brassy box until the fall, and sometimes, late of an evening, when I had finished the dishes and poured myself yet another glass of wine and was padding through the dark rooms of the house, I found myself whispering to him there, putting my head in close. The box itself was tasteful; the funeral home guy was very helpful and honest and respectful of Dad's wish to not waste a lot of money on the damn thing. Where the box would ultimately go was a larger problem, as Dad had never made up his mind. He was tempted, sorely tempted, by Saints Peter and Paul's offer to let him rest in perpetuity inside the altar columbarium. An honor, a reconciliation, a fitting conclusion to the prejudice that lost him that altar and his pension and so much pride. But what about the windswept cemetery in Heppner, high on the hill above town, looking across the valley to a succession of sagebrush hills, one topped by a solitary white cross? What about the idea of homecoming, going back to the beginning of things, return to the same ground of your father, uncles, and grandparents? Propped up in bed, wearing his little house hat and a ratty blue robe, the IV delivering a milky drip of drugs, he wrestled with these concerns but left no clue as to what he wanted. It came down to a question of who he was, for us. Best to understand him as the aggrieved priest, the character of the parish's drama? We counted years and figured his time in the church was a small portion of who he was, in the end. His time at that particular church, for all its reversals, was a tiny sliver of life. We made our decision, ordered a stone, and then life went on while he waited in my living room.

On a fine fall day, we drove the twisty-windy road to Heppner and met up with the family at the Saling house. There had been a sharp frost, and Grandma was out back spraying her flowers and tomatoes with her hose before the sun hit them. Her husband, Mike Saling, whom we never called Grandpa, was up on his feet again, having barely survived a bad stroke earlier that year. He'd lost the paunch that defined his middle, and now his western shirt billowed above his pants in the breeze. We leaned against my brother's new Land Cruiser, which he'd bought with a chunk of the life insurance money. He had just finished showing us the leather interior and redundant belts inside the engine compartment. Mike told us about getting his elk that year.

"Shot him from the cab, goddammit. Couldn't walk much that day, but my buddy flushed him for me. Spooked him out of the woods, and I had the barrel out the window already." He tapped his temple with two fingers of his right hand. "A good shot."

"Wow," I said, wondering if that was legal.

"That's great, Mike. Glad you got to go out this year," said my brother. There was a pause in the conversation as Mike looked over the yard, where the nieces cavorted and other family members were talking by the ground stumps of the old elms. Mike's pickup was parked for good in the garage, among lawn mowers and an old recliner.

"Yep," he said, and spat a stream of tobacco juice between his boots, "everything I got is paid for."

"That's great, Mike," said my brother.

Up on the hill, we put the urn on the little concrete wall that marked the family plot. There was no actual stone, as the guy had messed it up or lost the check or something. I had envisioned some professionals on scene, some representative of that helpful class of men who had steered us through everything involving my father's death with such practiced ease, but no one was on hand. It was just the family, standing around and chatting in the sun, noting how, over the box, back beyond the stones, past the sweep of grass and markers, someone was waterskiing out on the reservoir that the new dam had created above the town. Twenty minutes went by, and then I spoke up. I was nervous asking for anything, even for a circle and a minute of silence, and it took a little volume to get everyone's attention, but no one complained. They even joined hands around the circle, except for the little space we left open at the top, next to the box. Great Uncle Darrell, who cried great silent tears, was there, and my cousins, and the aunts I'd left out of the obituary, and many others, all of us holding hands in the cemetery, disparate folk from all walks of life, including my cousin's Korean wife the pole dancer and the WWII vets and bible-thumping racists and my Latina sister-in-law and all the aged ranchers and loggers and schoolteachers brought together around Heppner's first AIDS victim, the prodigal son come home. All the adults, that is, leaving no one to hold the hands of my nieces, the younger of whom was crying loudly and trying to get to the urn. I like to think that everyone was using their latent psychic energy to will the children back, but my niece, she doesn't will easily. She wanted to pick that thing up, and she was yelling for it. I could feel my blood rushing to my face, but now, looking back all these years later, I smile when I think of those girls, who laughed out loud and cried out loud and didn't "get" the solemnity of the occasion. In the end, I like to think my Dad would have approved, but probably he'd have been barking some sharp commands, and that makes me smile as well.

In the end, Dad stopped coming to my dreams, and I stopped waking with tears on the pillow, though sometimes if I have been telling stories about him or those days, he makes an appearance, sometimes to chide me for things that I've forgotten to do in the dream, like bury him, or come get him from where they have been holding him in this terrible mistake we all made. The other night we were laughing about something, rocking back in the old captain's chairs and laughing, and he put his hand on mine and I woke up to stare at my palm in the moonlight coming through the window.

In the end, I plant a lot of trees in my yard here in northeast Ohio. In the blissful calm of summers when I'm not teaching, I spend a lot of time walking around with a cup of coffee or a beer in my hand, checking on how they are growing. Pines have topped twenty feet. The tulip trees shoot up and reach for some sky. And everywhere, crabapples, oaks, maples, locusts, Russian olives, catalpas, dogwoods are volunteering, creating the ground floor for a little woods. One year, wild iris bloomed in an unmown patch with larches planted in it. Walking with the dew on my shoes, the dog up ahead spooking a rabbit or groundhog, noting with satisfaction new growth, he is with me still, I think. Though it is easy, I rarely recall the moments when he left me, or the moment when we drove away from the cemetery, leaving the little brassy box still on the concrete wall, hoping that sooner or later, someone would come around and bury that thing. In the end, perhaps, we never leave each other after all.

Afterword

When you write about your family, you face some obligations. Some stories are easy to narrate, some involve creating vulnerabilities, some are not yours to tell. It is my hope that the people I have written about here recognize these times and events and characterizations as true, even though they are necessarily subjective and incomplete. And because this is a book about me and my relationship with my father, it ends with the immediate aftermath of his death, instead of keeping up with his survivors. In the larger story, we all faced trauma in our relationship with the Rev. Renne L. Harris, we all have our scars, and we all found our ways to a measure of healing and peace. For me, that involved learning to forgive what I could and owning my anger for what I could not. It has, so far, taken several decades, but I live daily with a mixture of acceptance and regret for the early part of my life, and find meaning in that tension.

My siblings went on to create their own lives, careers, and families, which are in fact much larger than the glimpses of their younger selves in this book. My brother Joseph stayed in the military, and at this writing, Brigadier General Harris commands the Hawaii Air National Guard, is a loving presence in the lives of his wife, three daughters, and his growing cadre of grandchildren. Carolyn pursued degrees in art and design, and then found her passion in nursing, particularly in home-health. She, her husband, and her spooky smart daughter live in Sacramento, are very active in their church and community, and don't miss the rain of the Pacific Northwest too much.

Our mother, Margaret Harris, long suffering, always a day late and a dollar short, chronically tragic, has in fact proved to be the strongest of us. She's survived many medical challenges, including breast cancer, a brutal fall that crushed four cervical vertebrae, and now progressive dementia. Nevertheless, as they say, the lady persisted. Though down to ninety pounds, she's outlived several rounds of hospice, still reads five mystery novels a week, captures flowers in pastel drawings, is active in her prayer groups, and loves watching the hummingbirds come to her feeder. Her quality of life is largely due to my sister's full-time care; Mom is her only patient these days and lives a peaceful, beautiful life in her home because of that sacrifice. While my sister and I were never close in childhood, caring for our mother has brought us together, all of us, here in the second halves of our lives.

Recently, I reconnected with my Darrell, my father's first lover, who forgave me my characterization of him in my essay and confirmed the details of his attempted bank robbery. He has, by his count, lost four hundred friends to HIV since 1986, and lives on despite major health challenges of his own. During the COVID-19 pandemic, he has been living at Our House in Portland, where he is at work on a memoir of his own.

I owe many thanks to those who have supported my efforts to tell this story. My family, of course, who have been patient and encouraging as I gleefully open up old wounds. The Ohio Arts Council, whose Individual Excellence Award gave me much needed encouragement. Friends and family like Sean McEnroe, Alan Ambrisco, and my sister and brother-in-law Heather and John Ostergren, who read or listened to early drafts and were generous with their feedback. Kim Hogeland, Micki Reaman, Marty Brown, and Tom Booth at Oregon State University Press shepherded me through a very thoughtful editing process on the way to publication, including soliciting very helpful commentary from Denice Turner at Black Hills State University, whose insights helped me focus several essays on their essentials.

And of course, there is no way to adequately acknowledge my partner, soulmate, and wife of a quarter century for all she has done. Mary Quade provided encouragement when I needed it, tough editing when I could handle it, and never gave up on me or this project. To her I owe so much love and thanks.